Plausible worlds is an original study of the place of counterfactual judgements in explanation in history and the social sciences. All explanations suggest counterfactuals; but unlike many recent theorists of history and the social sciences, Geoffrey Hawthorn argues that there can be no theoretical answer to the question of precisely which counterfactuals to admit. We must use our judgement, and in particular our practical judgement. Such judgements, however, are inherently particular, and the argument must be made through examples. Accordingly Hawthorn takes three: mortality from plague in early modern Europe and rural fertility in France and England in the seventeenth and eighteenth centuries; the United States' occupation of southern Korea between 1945 and 1948; and Duccio's painting in Florence and Siena. Each one illustrates a different use of counterfactual speculation. The argument that emerges from all three casts doubt on existing assumptions about the nature and place of theory, and indeed of the possibility of knowledge itself, in the human sciences.

PLAUSIBLE WORLDS

PLAUSIBLE WORLDS

Possibility and understanding in
history and the social sciences

GEOFFREY HAWTHORN

Reader in sociology and politics
University of Cambridge

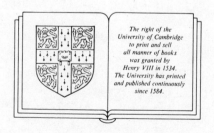

The right of the
University of Cambridge
to print and sell
all manner of books
was granted by
Henry VIII in 1534.
The University has printed
and published continuously
since 1584.

CAMBRIDGE UNIVERSITY PRESS
Cambridge
New York   Port Chester
Melbourne   Sydney

Published by the Press Syndicate of the University of Cambridge
The Pitt Building, Trumpington Street, Cambridge CB2 1RP
40 West 20th Street, New York, NY 10011–4211, USA
10 Stamford Road, Oakleigh, Melbourne 3166, Australia

First published 1991

Printed in Great Britain at the University Press, Cambridge

British Library cataloguing in publication data
Hawthorn. Geoffrey 1941–
Plausible worlds: possibility and understanding in
history and the social sciences.
1. Possibility
I. Title
121.2

Library of Congress cataloguing in publication data
Hawthorn, Geoffrey.
Plausible worlds: possibility and understanding in history and
the social sciences / Geoffrey Hawthorn.
p.   cm.
Includes index.
ISBN 0 521 40359 6 (hard)
1. History – Philosophy.   2. History – Methodology.   3. Social
sciences – Philosophy.   4. Social sciences – Methodology.   I. Title.
D16.9.H39   1991
901 – dc20   90-21801 CIP

ISBN 0521 403596 hardback

To Tom, Dan, Eugenio and Carlos

Contents

ix

Preface and acknowledgements

Possibilities haunt the human sciences. In empirical enquiry, they are suggested by the explanations we offer, and might even be said to support those explanations. (The *Armada Invencible*, the Spanish thought, was beaten by the weather. 'I sent it to fight the English', complained Philip II, 'not God.' If, therefore, the weather had been good . . .) In practical reflection, possibility is itself the point. If we think clearly, can summon the will, and have the right conditions, we can do what it is that we want to do; if not, not. In each kind of case, however, the possibilities remain uncertain. In the first, we cannot usually experiment. In the second, where we sometimes can, the experiment can prove a costly failure. This, it will be said, is why we have theories. They support our explanations and guide our practice. But theories have themselves to be supported. Counterfactuals and other kinds of subjunctive conditional will not go away.

In this book, I consider them. In chapter 1, I briefly consider the ways in which others have done so, and introduce my own argument. This starts from the claim that in History, sociology, and the study of politics, understanding possibility is at the heart of understanding itself. Although this is in a sense a theoretical issue, no theory, I suggest, can resolve it. Answers to questions about humanly plausible worlds are not given by the social scientists' generalisations, or the philosophers' possible worlds, or by any other method or model. They are given by judgement, in particular, by practical judgement. And the resources that we need to make such judgements, I argue, are given in the details of particular cases. Hence the examples in chapters 2, 3 and 4. These are not merely illustrations of an argument which could be put without them. They carry that argument. (Hence their length, offset, I hope, by my having managed to convey something of the fascination that each has for me.) If the argument they carry has force, however, it invites reflection on some general questions about explanation, understanding and the place of theory in History and the social sciences. The relations between theoretical and practical reasoning, the argument suggests, are close. But if the procedures and conclusions of each turn on considerations of possibility, and possibilities cannot be known, what knowledge can each kind of reasoning provide? And if human possibilities are largely particular, as the argument also suggests, and turn on judgement, what then can theory do? I suggest some answers in chapter 5.

I began to think about counterfactuals at the Institute for Advanced Study in Princeton in 1979–80. I read myself into some of the philosophical literature there and started to explore the subject which is now chapter 4. I am grateful for that time, for the invitation itself and the marvellous company. (A French fellow visitor who in my talk on counterfactuals heard me talking about 'counterfeits' – he made an interesting point about Duchamps' *Fountain* – may have heard more than he knew.) It has taken me a long time since then to see what I wanted to say and how. In coming to do so, I have incurred many debts.

Examples, as I have said, are intrinsic to the argument. My widest debt for these is to the authors whose work I discuss. (I only hope that in standing on their shoulders, I have observed the Chinese instruction, and not also spat on their heads.) Chapter 3 began in a paper to the Korean Association for International Relations on South Korea's strategic situation in the 1980s. It reached its present form in a paper in Cambridge on the political division of the peninsula in the 1940s. I am grateful to Kim Ho-jin for the invitation to Seoul and to John Thompson for his advice on what appears here. Gloria Carnevali opened my eyes, under Orinoco skies, to the modernists' view of the Renaissance. And looking at Duccio's 'Crucifixion with St Nicholas and St Gregory' with her in the Museum of Fine Arts in Boston crystallised my thoughts for chapter 4.

Stefan Collini, Anthony Pagden, John Thompson and two readers for the Cambridge University Press commented on one or another of three early drafts. Bernard Williams commented on all three and then a fourth. My greatest debt is to him. John Dunn, Richard Rorty and Mary-Kay Wilmers each made remarks which showed me how to go on. Talking to Roberto Unger has enabled me to see what a social theory can be. At the crucial last moment, I also gained much from conversations (separately and together in a discussion at Peter Hall's seminar at Harvard) with Charles Maier, Mike Miller, Judith Shklar and Peter Hall himself. Stefan Collini gave me my title. Jeremy Mynott has been a model of editorial tact and support.

None of these people is responsible for what I say. Without them, however, I would not have been able to say what I do. A term in the sociology department at Harvard (for which I especially thank Daniel Bell), the Boston area's radio stations, Nota Bene, and a Compaq laptop and Carlos's frequent occupation of its assigned place all made my final attempt to say it more of a pleasure than I had dared to hope.

Cambridge

— 1 —

Counterfactuals, explanation
and understanding

I

It can be tempting to play what E. H. Carr called 'parlour-games with might-have-beens'.[1]

Granada was defeated in 1492. But suppose it had not been: suppose with Philip Guedalla that Boabdil had himself defeated Ferdinand and Isabella at Lanjarón a year before. In hindsight, 'it was simply inconceivable', as Grisley remarked in his *Modern Europe*, 'that the rash adventure of the Catholic kings should have had any other ending' than the one it did beneath the Sierra Nevada in 1491. Intelligent, resourceful, and organised, the Moors were bound to beat the still uneasily allied and overstretched forces of Aragon and Castile. The consequences, moreover, have been immense. (Others, including Edward Gibbon, have thought that if Charles Martel had not stopped the Moors near Poitiers in 732, they were consequences which might have been evident much earlier.) Grisley agreed with Sir William Creasy: Lanjarón had been one of the more decisive battles of the modern world.

The *Cambridge History of Islam* – actually a collection of essays prepared in the faculties at Granada and published under licence in Cambridge – deals at length with the alliances between Granada and the powers which in the sixteenth, seventeenth and eighteenth centuries, it played off against one another. Napier's *History of the War in the Peninsula* records the invaluable assistance that the king gave the British after Napoleon had rashly decreed in 1808 that the house of Boabdil had ceased to reign and that Pierre François Joseph Lefebvre, Duke of Dantzick, was henceforth to rule as Yussuf I.

---

[1] E. H. Carr, *What is History?*, Harmondsworth: Penguin, 1964, p. 97.

1

Granada's alliance with Britain throughout the nineteenth century
(in spite of the difficulty caused by Swinburne's mysterious disappearance near the royal seraglio in 1865) assured the kingdom's
strength and independence. And the kings continued to be careful.

This became very clear after 1914. When the Bolsheviks effected
their coup in 1917 and Germany was defeated a year later, Boabdil
VII sensed Britain's new weakness and America's new strength. In
combination with what was left of the Ottoman empire and with
Islamic states to the east – who saw that they could be caught
between the revolutionary regime in Moscow and the other European empires – he cleverly effected alliances both with the United
States and with the new and now beleaguered Soviet Union.
Meanwhile, the Moors' command of the resources of southern
Europe, their advances in science and technology, the advantages
they had gained from Protestant refugees, their control of Gibraltar,
and their connections beyond the continent, together with their
energy everywhere in trade, had already made Spain the commercial
and industrial centre of the world. For these reasons, and notwithstanding the reservations of its isolationist and anti-imperialist ally
across the Atlantic, Granada became the pre-eminent empire of the
twentieth century. It was the territorially most connected since
Rome, and the most enlightened of them all.

Ernest Gellner explains why. 'By various obvious criteria', he
reminds us, 'universalism, scripturalism, spiritual egalitarianism, the
extension of full participation in the sacred community not to one,
or some, but to all, and the rational systematisation of social life,
Islam is of the three great monotheisms, the one closest to modernity.' Medieval Christianity, as Ibn Weber had so persuasively
put it in *The Kharejite Ethic and the Spirit of Capitalism*, with its
'baroque, manipulative, patronage-ridden, quasi-animistic and disorderly vision of the world', its belief that justice could be bought
by donations and pious works, 'could never have taught its ad-
herents to rely on faith alone and to produce and accumulate in
an impersonal, orderly, systematic manner'. And by the time of the
Reformation in parts of northern Europe, which had itself been
impelled by admiration for the intellectual openness and adventure
of Islam, Granada had secured its advantage.[2]

[2] Philip Guedalla, 'If the Moors in Spain had won', in J. C. Squire ed., *If it
had Happened Otherwise: Lapses into Imaginary History*, London: Longmans,

It is not difficult to explain how after 1491, this more Moorish southern Europe came to be what it did. But the explanation, if entertaining, is surely idle. This Europe did not exist. And it is not immediately clear how thinking about how it might have done illuminates the one that did. So what, we might ask, if the Moors had managed to defeat Charles Martel or the Castilian kings? Or as Roy Strong has wondered, if the eldest son of James I had not died so young in 1612, and by his evident connoisseurship and enthusiasm for the arts, used his influence as king to inspire that renaissance in England which, on our understanding of what such a renaissance is, never was? Or as Robert Fogel has asked, if the Confederacy had been allowed to secede from the United States, presented a powerful challenge to democracy, and with its political example and econ-omic power, changed what we might now take to have been the 'natural' course of modern politics? Or as Hugh Trevor-Roper has fancied, if in the early 1940s there had not been a leader able to hold

1932, pp. 1–19. I adjust and embellish his speculations. (The defeat of a mar-auding band of Moors near Poitiers in 732 by Charles Martel's Frankish cavalry, with help from Lombards, may not have been as decisive for the Moors them-selves as Gibbon and others have suggested. The Moorish forces were weak in the west; although they had sacked Autun in 725, they had already been defeated near Toulouse in 721. More decisive were their success against Chinese forces in Turkestan in 751 and their two defeats at the centre of the Byzantine world in 739 and 747. None the less, Charles Martel's victory at Poitiers did give the Carolingian kings what proved to be a consequential impetus against Rome. As I explain in chapter 5, the defeat of the Moors in Spain in the fifteenth century was not sudden. The Arabs' own memory of Muslim Spain lapsed until the early nineteenth century when, at a moment when they needed a vindication of a more glorious past, it was revived for them by some European romantics (Bernard Lewis, *History: Remembered, Recovered, Invented*, New York: Simon and Schuster, 1975, pp. 71–8). Spain was not Islam's last chance in Europe; Jan Sobieski stopped a Turkish advance at Vienna in 1683.) Squire's collection also includes essays on the possibility that Don John of Austria had married Mary, Queen of Scots; that Louis XVI had an atom of firmness; that Napoleon had escaped from St Helena to found the United States of South America; that Lee had won the battle at Gettysburg; and that the general strike in Britain in 1926 had been successful. There is also Daniel Snowman ed. and intro., *If I had Been . . . : Ten Historical Fantasies*, London: Robson, 1979, in which historians imagine what they would have done at critical moments if they had been the Earl of Sherburne, Franklin, Juárez, Thiers, Gladstone, Kerensky, Tojo, Adenauer, Dubcek or Allende. I am grateful to Dorothy Emmet for tell-ing me of Squire's collection and to Karl Sabbagh for telling me of Snowman's. Ernest Gellner, *Muslim Society*, Cambridge: Cambridge University Press, 1981, p. 7, whose fancy I also embellish.

Britain together; if German signals had not been decoded; if Mussolini had not diverted Germany with his unforeseen attack on Greece; and if Franco had not refused Hitler permission to march down to take Gibraltar?[3]

It may 'be a gesture of despair', as Trevor-Roper himself believed, 'to dismiss as ephemeral a movement which, by a slight variation of fortune, might have dominated the history of a whole age'. 'If there is such a thing as a sense of reality', Robert Musil had agreed in *The Man Without Qualities*, – and no-one will doubt that it has its *raison d'être* – then there must also be something that one can call a sense of possibility.' But in History and the social sciences, it has not usually been clear what there is to be gained in developing it. On the contrary. Most historians and social scientists, if they have considered counterfactuals at all, have done so only nervously, in asides. (Fogel and Charles Maier are unusual in taking the view, as Maier puts it, that history provides the insight that it does 'primarily by virtue of the historian's laying bare its counterfactual implications'.)[4] Most have resisted Musil's irony and given every sign of

[3] Roy Strong, *Henry, Prince of Wales, and England's Lost Renaissance*, London: Thames and Hudson, 1986. Strong explains that the English court in the sixteenth century, unlike many elsewhere in Europe, had not previously shown any interest in the arts. 'Prince Henry takes his place as the final figure in a series of still-born renaissances. Sidney was killed at thirty-two, Essex was executed at thirty-five, and Prince Henry died at eighteen.' The artistically lively court at St James was dissolved on his death (pp. 224, 136). Robert W. Fogel, *Without Consent or Contract: The Rise and Fall of American Slavery*, New York: Norton, 1989, pp. 413–17. These are a powerful five pages and I am grateful to Judith Shklar for drawing my attention to them. Hugh Trevor-Roper, 'History and imagination', in Hugh Lloyd-Jones, Blair Worden, and Valerie Pearl eds., *History and Imagination: Essays in Honour of Hugh Trevor-Roper*, London: Duckworth, 1981, pp. 360–1.

[4] Charles Maier, 'Wargames: 1914–1919', in Robert I. Rotberg and Theodore K. Rabb eds., *The Origins and Prevention of Major Wars*, Cambridge: Cambridge University Press, 1988, p. 251 (and Joseph Nye's final remark in his introduction to this collection, p. 12). Also Fogel, *Without Consent*, p. 413: 'Every historian who has set out to deal with the causes of the Civil War (certainly all those who have debated its necessity or avoidability) has implicitly or explicitly presumed what would have happened to slavery if some events had unfolded in a way that was different from the actual course. Indeed, much of the voluminous literature on the causes of the Civil War is nothing more or less than the marshalling of evidence on the events leading up to the Civil War that is dictated by different visions of this counterfactual world.' Although they do not

agreeing that a sense of the possible 'might be defined outright as the capacity to think how everything could "just as easily" be, and to attach no more importance to what is than to what is not'. They might of course concede to Musil that 'the consequences of such a creative disposition may be remarkable'. There is, after all, fiction. But most might insist that these are the sorts of consequence which 'not infrequently make the things that other people admire appear wrong and the things that other people prohibit permissible, or even make both a matter of indifference'. 'Such possibilitarians', they might conclude, 'live within a finer web, a web of haze, imaginings, fantasy and the subjunctive mood.' After all, if children show signs of succumbing, it is resisted, 'vigorously driven out of them', or so Musil thought; 'in their presence such people are referred to as crackbrains, dreamers, weaklings, know-alls, and carpers and cavillers'.[5]

II

There can also be more principled objections. One could come from the claim that all there is in any world is just 'a vast mosaic of local matters of particular fact', as David Lewis puts it, 'just one little thing and then another'. ('In honour of the great denier of necessary connections', Lewis calls this the doctrine of 'Humean supervenience'. All else supervenes on particular facts.) We may discern regularities in and between the particular things. We may sort them and the relations between them into a schedule of importance. We may imagine a total set of such particulars and of the relations between them. We may even suggest their pre-determination. But the last word is with the particulars of the world, which supervene.

use the language of counterfactuals, David Blackbourn and Geoff Eley make much the same point about the disposition of many historians to dwell on the 'peculiarity' of modern Germany (*The Peculiarities of German History: Bourgeois Society and Politics in Nineteenth-century Germany*, Oxford and New York: Oxford University Press, 1984). For an example of the contrary view, chapter 3, note 14.

[5] Robert Musil, Eithne Wilkins and Ernst Kaiser trans., *The Man Without Qualities*, London: Pan, 1979, p. 12. I am grateful to Bianca Fontana for drawing my attention to this passage.

And since these particulars are as they are, and do supervene, they override the thought that this world might have been other than it is. Other possibilities, if they exist at all, obtain at other worlds.[6]

A second objection could come from the opposite point. The world is as it is necessarily. Leibniz for instance, from whom the modern philosophical talk of 'possible worlds' derives, believed that this and all the possible worlds which at the start of all the worlds, God had in mind, are inhabited by individuals or singular things. Each individual is defined by its concept. This is a set of attributes which constitute it and which it alone satisfies. These attributes are simple and complex. Simple attributes are primitive and 'positive', those that an individual has intrinsically. Complex attributes are negative or conjunctive, those that it has in virtue of its relations with all other individuals at all points, past, present and future, in the world to which it belongs. Individual concepts are 'compossible' if they are capable of being realised together. Compossibility is at once a logical matter and an empirical one, a matter of consistency and compatibility. Any world consists in a set of compossible individuals peculiar to it. In virtue of the connections that each individual has with all the others in its world, therefore, to change any one is to change the world itself. With Leibniz, we cannot think counterfactually about anything less than whole worlds.[7]

    [6] David Lewis, *Philosophical Papers*. vol. 2, New York: Oxford University Press, 1986, pp. ix ff. Lewis admits that he finds it difficult to account for chance, which *as* chance, is not a property of the world (pp. xiv–xvi, 111–12). On Lewis on other worlds, see IV below. Hume's actual view was more complicated: he agreed that there might be real necessities, and insisted only that we had no reliable way of knowing whether there were or what they were. This sceptical realism is explained by Galen Strawson, *The Secret Connection: Causation, Realism and David Hume*, Oxford: Clarendon Press, 1989; also again section IV below.
    [7] *Theodicy*, paras. 1–2, 7–10, 34, 37, 42, 52, 58, 174, 225, 291, 310–11, 349, 360 and 367; *Discourse on Metaphysics*, paras. 8, 9 and 13; *Monadology*, paras. 33, 37, and 38; Leibniz's letter of 12 April 1686 to von Hessen-Rheinfels, and his remarks on a letter from Arnauld written in May 1686. There is a useful review in Benson Mates, 'Leibniz on possible worlds', in B. van Rootselaar and J. F. Staal eds., *Logic, Methodology and Philosophy of Science III*, Amsterdam: North-Holland, 1968, pp. 507–29; also Hide Ishiguro, *Leibniz's Philosophy of Logic and Language*, London: Duckworth, 1972. Despite Fabrizio Mondadori, 'Reference, essentialism and modality in Leibniz's metaphysics', *Studia Leibnitiana* 5 (1973), 96, 101, it might be wise to regard Leibniz's concession to

So also with Hegel and Marx. For Leibniz, a complete understanding of singular things requires us to understand their necessary
relation to all other such things. For Hegel, it requires us rationally
to grasp their necessary relation to the one single thing which even
as it preserves their singularity, will come to encompass them all.
The one world there is, it is true, is not yet manifestly rational. But
the task of reason is to make it so, not to think about how it might
have been, or how to make it other than it is. That would be contrary to reason, and mistaken. Of course, there may be diversions.
In 1875, for instance, there was what Marx described as the 'democratic clang' of the proposal at Gotha to combine the two socialist movements in Germany into one Social-Democratic Workers'
Party, a proposal, he thought, 'thoroughly infested with the Las-
sallean sect's servile belief in the state, or, what is no better, by a
democratic faith in miracles'. But no such diversion can be sustained. There are no miracles. The move to freedom is preordained.
It is a move to a possible world of rational reconciliation which is
also a necessary world; a world given in the premises of a theory
which are themselves given in the nature of being. It is a world into
which we are invited imaginatively and practically to transfer ourselves but which, whether we accept the invitation or not, we are
bound rationally to accept. On this argument also, might-have-
beens and might-yet-bes have no place in understanding what is.[8]

(what Lewis believes to be) 'counterparts' in other worlds in *Theodicy* para. 414,
as a lapse; but interpreting Leibniz is a skill I do not pretend to. Louis Dumont is
a rare example of a latter-day Leibnizian sociologist: e.g. 'La communauté
anthropologique et l'idéologie', *L'Homme* 18 (1978), 83–110, especially 90–1,
and *Homo Hierarchicus: le Système de Caste et ses implications*, 2ème ed., Paris:
Gallimard, 1979, pp. i–xl (and my brief remarks on that in 'Caste and politics in
India since 1947', in Dennis B. McGilvray ed., *Caste Ideology and Interaction*,
Cambridge: Cambridge University Press, 1982, pp. 233–4).
[8] On Hegel on necessity Charles Taylor, *Hegel*, Cambridge: Cambridge
University Press, 1975, especially pp. 345–9. Marx's theory as a theory of internal relations is explained by Bertell Ollman, *Alienation: Marx's Conception
of Man in a Capitalist Society*, Cambridge: Cambridge University Press, 1971.
Some characteristic remarks of Marx's on freedom and necessity in Frederick
Engels ed., *Capital*, vol. 3, London: Lawrence and Wishart, 1972, p. 820; the
remarks on the Gotha programme in David Fernbach ed., *The First International
and After: Political Writings Vol. 3*, Harmondsworth: Penguin, 1974, pp. 356,
357.

A third objection can also come from a holism, but a holism, as it has been put, of form rather than content.[9] (A holism, that's to say, which accepts the kind of view that Hegel took of the knowing subject, but not the view he took of being.) Carr himself, who was hostile to parlour-games with might-have-beens, put it in a once familiar way. He conceded that it was 'futile to attempt to spirit chances away, or to pretend that in some way or another they had no effect'. Had Antony not been bemused by Cleopatra's nose, he might not have lost his nerve at Actium. Trotsky, in the middle of his manoeuverings with Kamenev, Zinoviev, Bukharin and Stalin, might not (as he did) have caught a cold, gone to bed, and (as he thought) missed a crucial move in the fight to succeed Lenin. ('One can foresee a revolution or a war', he claimed later, 'but it is impossible to foresee the consequences of an autumn shooting trip for ducks.') Boabdil might have beaten the Catholic kings. But 'in so far as chances are accidental', Carr insisted, 'they do not enter into any rational interpretation of history, or into the historian's hierarchy of significant causes'. 'If a particular cause, like the accidental result of a battle', he invokes Montesquieu in support, 'has ruined a state, there was a general cause which made the downfall of this state issue from a single battle.' 'Just as from the infinite ocean of facts', Carr continued, the historian 'selects those which are significant for his purpose, so from the multiplicity of sequences of cause and effect he extracts those which are historically significant; and the standard of historical significance is his ability to fit them into his pattern of rational explanation and interpretation.' (Life, to paraphrase Kierkegaard, may have to be lived forwards, but the historian is privileged to understand it backwards.) 'Everything the devotees of chance and contingency say', Carr rather desperately concluded, 'is perfectly true and perfectly logical. It has the kind of remorseless logic which we find in *Alice in Wonderland* and *Through the Looking Glass*.' But 'the Dodgsonian mode is not the mode of history'.[10]

[9] The distinction between the two holisms, one about what the world is like, the other about how we understand it, is well set out by Susan James, *The Content of Social Explanation*, Cambridge: Cambridge University Press, 1984, pp. 1–9. I return to it in chapter 5, sections IV and V.

[10] Carr, *History*, p. 105; Trotsky quoted at p. 98, Montesquieu at p. 101.

Chance only matters when it can be shown not to be chance. If it does, but cannot be, it does not. The argument is itself a little Dodgsonian. But the objection can be more persuasively put. It is the claim – the claim which Carr mixed up, as others have done, with what he took to be the properties of the world itself – that however the world may appear to be or really is, to understand it is to make it coherent. The coherence is ours and in it, the loose ends of mere possibles have no place. Michael Oakeshott made a case more than fifty years ago. 'If the historian finds himself considering by a kind of ideal experiment what might have happened, as well as what the evidence obliges him to believe did happen, he would find himself becalmed outside the current of historical thought.' And there is no such place to be. 'In so far as history is a world of facts', Oakeshott explained, ' (which will scarcely be denied), it is a world of ideas, and a world which is true or false according to the degree of its coherence.' Indeed, Oakeshott went so far as to say that in the construction which is History, 'it is impossible', because senseless, 'to distinguish between the importance of necessities'. There is nothing that is more or less necessary, more or less contingent, more or less extraordinary. Anthony's hesitation, Trotsky's chill, Churchill's will, Boabdil's capacities, are no more or less crucial than are the condition and context of the forces they commanded or any other fact. 'Historical thought' is 'the attempt to find a world of experience satisfactory in itself.' In this internal, holist sense of what it is to explain, the past, insists Oakeshott, 'explains itself'. 'The relation between events is always other events, and is established in history by a full relation of the events.'[11]

[11] Michael Oakeshott, *Experience and its Modes*, Cambridge: Cambridge University Press, 1933, reprinted 1985, pp. 93, 128–9, 143–5. His remarks (like Carr's) should be read against what was between the 1920s and the 1950s in Britain a lively and not very covertly ideological debate about chance and necessity in history. But Oakeshott's last two sentences suggest some unsteadiness in his argument. At p. 139, he claims, consistently with his commitment to total history, but oddly in relation to his view that history is a world of ideas assessed by its coherence, that 'the question . . . is never what must, or what might have taken place, but solely what the evidence obliges us to conclude did take place'. Marx is an obvious instance of a theorist of internal relations (a holist of form and of content) who by contrast distanced himself from what appearance might oblige us to accept (Ollman, *Alienation*, pp. 27 ff., 249 ff.). I return briefly to internal explanations in chapter 5, sections IV and V.

III

The objection from a Leibniz or a Hegel insists that actuality is a whole and is so necessarily. The objection from what is taken to be a Hume denies this. Even those who are sceptical of metaphysics may believe that coherence is the criterion for understanding what there is. But whatever their views about the nature of the world and its contents, and about how we can have access to these, those who press one or other of these objections to considering the merely possible converge on the conviction that what we wish to do is to explain the actual. And they agree that to do so is to locate it in a scheme of other actuals, to show 'its actual connections with other actual things'.[12] It would be odd to dispute this aim, and I do not want to. But I do want to press the claims of the possible: to argue that to entertain it is to do more than just play parlour-games with might-have-beens.

This is not because I want to press another metaphysics. I do start from a few assumptions. I am inclined to the view that the human world consists of contingent particulars. I am accordingly at odds with necessitarians and holists of form. But I am not setting out to argue on their ground. I start rather from a paradox which is inherent in explaining the one world there is: a paradox, I believe, which has implications for understanding in History and the social sciences more generally, and for the knowledge that we can reasonably aspire to of human affairs. This is that in explanation, possibilities at once decrease and increase.

An example will make this clear. Suppose that we wish to explain why the Labour Party received such a small proportion of the votes cast – just twenty-eight per cent – in the British general election in 1983. We would adduce some general facts. We might point out that the party's membership and its share of the vote had been in continuous decline since 1951; that its largest single national constituency, the industrial working class, was contracting (some estimate Labour's supposed 'natural constituency' to have fallen to about thirty-five per cent of the electorate by the early 1980s); that a

[12] Robert Nozick, *Philosophical Explanations*, Cambridge MA: Harvard University Press, 1981, p. 12.

smaller proportion of the industrial working class (and actually a minority of those who were officially classed as skilled) was now voting Labour; that the absence of proportional representation ruled out the possibility of coalitions with parts of other parties; and that the party's decline coincided with low rates of economic growth, repeated balance of payments crises, and thus increasing difficulties in funding the social expenditure to which its policies committed it. We would also emphasise the increasing internal divisions in the party. In the later 1940s and early 1950s there had been an uneasy but workable alliance between the leadership, the parliamentary party, and the trade union leaders against intermittent eruptions in the constituency parties. (In the later 1940s and 1950s this was seriously threatened only by Aneurin Bevan, but his capacity to do so derived more from his personal power and ambition than from any section in the party.) By the 1960s, however, the alliance was under strain.

We would also recall more particular events. After the third electoral defeat in a row in 1959, and the natural exacerbation of the differences between right and left, the leader, Hugh Gaitskell, decided to make an issue of the party's constitutional commitment to nationalisation, and decided also to insist on Britain's obligation in virtue of its membership of the North Atlantic Treaty Organisation and – although he himself was sceptical of it – on keeping open the option of an independent British nuclear deterrent. This sharpened the hostility, both of the left and of some previously complaisant trade union leaders, to the parliamentary party. The parliamentary party's relations with the unions came under further strain in the course of the Wilson administration's attempts to regulate industrial disputes in 1969 and again in the deteriorating economic circumstances of the Labour administrations after 1974. These events increased the anger of unionists, both in industry and in the public services, at the cuts in expenditure which the Chancellor of the Exchequer imposed to meet the conditions of a loan from the International Monetary Fund in 1976. The tensions increased as moribund constituency parties in the larger cities were taken over by a younger generation of active left-wingers. By 1979, the party authorities and many union secretaries themselves had lost control of both the unions and the constituencies. And at a moment when he might conceivably have scraped a victory, the Labour Prime Minister, James Callaghan, had, against all expectation, hesitated to go to the country. In 1980, the party conference, determined now to take power against the parliamentarians it thought had betrayed it, agreed to revise the procedure for electing the leader, which had previously been the prerogative of the parliamentary members, in order to give more say – if they were to combine, a decisive say – to the trade unions and the constituency parties. The new procedure was formally agreed in 1981 and as a result, several Labour MPs left to form a completely new party. A new leader, we might conclude, elected in 1979 and more congenial to the more powerful left than the previous three, fought the 1983 election on a programme that was more aggressively socialist than any on which Labour had campaigned since the war; and whatever the activists may have thought, and despite the poor opinion which by the end of 1981 most voters had of the Conservative government, this programme commanded little general support.[13]

This is the merest sketch of an explanation. (It is nevertheless the sketch of an explanation, and not of something else. It asks the question 'why?' and answers it by taking a 'contrast class', social democratic parties elsewhere in Europe which did not exhibit such a decline, and then adducing facts relevant to that contrast.[14] It does so in connecting actuals by causes and reasons, the two connectives in a widely accepted model of how the human world works.) The

---

[13] There are several histories and many first-hand accounts. Selectively, on the disputes between 1955 and 1961, Philip M. Williams, *Hugh Gaitskell: A Political Biography*, London: Cape, 1979; on the 1970s, David and Maurice Kogan, *The Battle for the Labour Party*, London: Collins, 1982; on the 1970s and early and mid 1980s, Peter Jenkins, *Mrs Thatcher's Revolution*, London: Chatto and Windus, 1987; and for an interesting analysis of the reasons for Labour's decline (and an in some respects persuasive defence of the intrinsic – as distinct from more immediately political – reasonableness of the economic policies it might have adopted), Paul Whiteley, *The Labour Party in Crisis*, London: Methuen, 1983.

[14] This characterisation of explanation owes much to Bas C. van Fraassen, *The Scientific Image*, Oxford: Clarendon Press, 1980, pp. 142–3, 153–7; Hilary Putnam, *Meaning and the Moral Sciences*, London: Routledge and Kegan Paul, 1978, pp. 41–5, and Putnam, *The Many Faces of Realism*, LaSalle: Open Court, 1987, pp. 3–40, especially pp. 6–8. I come to more formal arguments about explanation in the next section; also chapter 5, section IV.

sketch of an explanation of Labour's decline to the early 1980s nevertheless serves to show the paradox I am pointing to.

On the one hand, the more causes and reasons we bring to bear on what it is that we want to explain, the more difficult it is to see how the decline could have turned out to be other than it was. The Labour Party was not in power for most of the 1950s and could do nothing to prevent the Conservatives' lack of attention to investment in those years. In any event, the economy was weakening and the industrial working class decreasing in size for reasons that were in part beyond the control of any government. Even in hindsight, it is difficult to see how this could not have divided Labour according to the difference of opinion within it about whether the economy could be controlled, and about the compatibility of (and the priority to be given to) maintaining social expenditure. It is certainly difficult to see how, once the increasing economic difficulties put the alliance between the unions and the parliamentary party (and indeed the relations between union leaders and their own members) under strain, the coalition between Labour Members of Parliament, the unions and the constituency parties, reflected in the hitherto accepted division of powers between the parliamentary party on the one hand and the unions and the constituency parties at conference on the other, could be maintained. The Labour Party's problems seem all but unavoidable. And indeed, it is quite natural, having sketched an explanation, to try to make it all but impossible to resist. We will want to make it difficult to believe in any alternative course of events that does not take us so far away from what did happen, or so far back, as to be indeterminate and uninteresting.

The second part of the paradox I am pointing to, however, is almost immediately apparent. In all but a thoroughly Leibnizian world, an explanation suggests alternatives. Possibilities increase under it. If the Labour Party had been able to maintain its membership, or its vote in the industrial working class; if it had realised that this class was going to contract; if, notwithstanding its dependence on the trade unions at its conference, the parliamentary party had maintained its previously steady political distance from them, in which the one looked after policy and the other after industrial affairs; and if it had at the same time more skilfully tried to revise its programme and thus its likely appeal to other class interests (in the way that the Swedish and German social democrats were doing in the 1950s); if it had not undercut its social programme by insisting on the priority of maintaining sterling in the 1960s; if a greater political distance from the unions had enabled it to control the high rates of inflation and increase in pay in the early and mid 1970s; if it had not tried to recover its financial (and also perhaps political) control in 1976 by going to the IMF and using the Fund's authority to cut expenditure on the public services which employed many of its nominal but now more demanding supporters; if it had paid more attention to what was happening in the constituency parties, or tried to attract more ordinary members to counter the local activists; if Callaghan had had the courage to go to the country in the autumn of 1978; in short, if the party had not got itself into a position where its own constitution forced it to concede to the left at the end of the 1970s . . . The line of explanation which I have sketched for Labour's poor performance in the election in 1983 suggests that if some such set possibilities had been actual, the party might by then have been able to do better than it did. This is because the force of an explanation turns on the counterfactual which it implies. If such-and-such a cause or combination of causes had not been present, we imply, or if such-and-such an action or series of actions had not been taken, things would have been different. If we do not believe they would have been, we should not give the causes or actions in question the importance that we do.

In History and the social sciences, possibilities in this sense increase under explanation for one or other and usually both of two reasons. The first is that in so far as our explanations impute what we call causes, the clearer it becomes how contingent most of these causes and their conditions are. The reduction in the number of people in industrial employment in Britain from the peak it had reached in the early 1950s, for instance, was not inevitable. It was caused in part by the increasing uncompetitiveness of British industry, which was itself in part caused by at least a century of domestic under-investment, and in part by independent changes in Britain's advantages in overseas trade. (These changes were later accelerated by oil, which increased the demand for domestically produced manufactured goods and paradoxically served further to reduce the incentives for investment in manufacturing.) But even if we were to take the decline in industrial investment, or the increase in the trade of non-manufactures, or whatever else may have caused the fall in the size of the industrial working class, as a given, perhaps because there would in any event have been a sectoral change away from manufacturing industry as the economy 'matured', the effect that this change actually had on the Labour Party's political fortunes might not have been as severe as it was if the party's accustomed dependence on the trade unions had not for so long been taken so much for granted.[15]

Many explanations in History and the social sciences, however, turn not on causal connections between states of affairs that are beyond human control, but on the relevant agents' own practical reasonings. Practical reasonings are not pre-determined by nature, and certainly not by human nature, which always under-determines. Nor, except in the way in which these matters are seen in the most extreme of rationalisms, or sociologies, or sociological rationalisms, are practical reasonings entirely pre-ordained by rules or reasons. They are conditional, subjunctive hypotheticals, a matter of counterfactual judgement. They turn on what agents more or less reflectively believe, in the light of their inclinations and the circumstances, to be possible. ('Single hypothetical conditionals', as Stuart Hampshire puts it, are 'the meeting point between theoretical and practical reasoning.')[16] Those on the left in the Labour Party in the

---

[15] This last is suggested by Adam Przeworski's assessment of the fortunes of social democratic parties elsewhere in western Europe – he does not discuss the British case – over the past sixty or seventy years (*Capitalism and Social Democracy*, Cambridge: Cambridge University Press, 1985). Przeworski adds several other conditions for the electoral success of these parties under capitalism: that there is only one party of the left (so that social democrats cannot be outflanked by communists), that there are no parties of a more narrowly communal or confessional kind (so that Catholic workers, for instance, are not drawn away), and that the leaders of the left do not prefer ideological purity to electoral success. (For Przeworski's pessimistic assessment of arriving at agreed counterfactual assessments in politics, chapter 3, note 1.) The reasons for the decline in British industrial employment from the 1950s are discussed by R. E. Rowthorn and John Wells, *De-Industrialisation and Foreign Trade*, Cambridge: Cambridge University Press, 1987.

[16] Stuart Hampshire, *Innocence and Experience*, Cambridge MA: Harvard University Press, 1989, p. 16. One can of course formulate practical reasonings in a causally conditional way, by suggesting that such-and-such will lead agents to decide and do so-and-so 'unless they change their mind'; but because, as I mention at the end of this chapter and say again at the end of chapter 5, it is an important – even constitutive – feature of practical reasonings that they are

1950s were in many respects conservative; but however difficult they might have found it, it would not, we might suppose, have literally been impossible for them, in the light of the facts, of the case that the revisionists were making from those facts, of discussions in the Socialist International, and above all, of the future electoral interests of their own party, to change their mind. Likewise, at that point in the mid and late 1950s when the relations between the parliamentary party and the unions were good, at which each accepted a political division of labour and at which both were united against the Bevanite left and its allies from the constituency parties at conference, the two might have done more than they did to reconsider their constitutional relations. And some of the cabinet decisions between 1964 and 1970 and 1974 and 1979, as some members of those cabinets have ruefully recalled, might have been different.

An explanation, in short, locates something in actuality, showing its actual connections with other actual things. Its success as an answer to the question 'why?' will turn on the plausibility of the reasoning – the model, mechanism, or what J. L. Mackie called the inductively arrived-at 'running on' – that we invoke to make the connection.[17] The plausibility of this reasoning will turn on the counterfactual it suggests. And if the counterfactual is itself not

particular, and not general, and because practical reasoning is in Aristotle's distinction dialectical rather than demonstrative, I prefer not to. A lively recent instance of a sociological rationalism is Martin Hollis's *The Cunning of Reason*, Cambridge: Cambridge University Press, 1987, e.g. at pp. 91, 172. Hollis sets out to eliminate the indeterminacy and uneasy individualism of standard rational choice theory (on which see e.g. Jon Elster, 'Introduction', in ed., *Rational Choice*, Oxford: Blackwell, 1986, pp. 12–6, and more briefly *Nuts and Bolts for the Social Sciences*, Cambridge: Cambridge University Press, 1989, pp. 22–9) by suggesting a Kantian person driven by external reasons that derive from the constitutive rules of his or her social roles. For the distinction between external and internal reasons, and the view which Hollis directly rejects, Bernard Williams, 'Internal and external reasons', in *Moral Luck: Philosophical Papers, 1973–1980*, Cambridge: Cambridge University Press, 1981, pp. 101–13.

[17] Mackie, who takes it as a 'hard fact' that we do reason inductively (*Truth, Probability and Paradox: Studies in Philosophical Logic*, Oxford: Clarendon Press, 1972, p. 118), explains his idea of inductively arrived-at 'runnings on' in *The Cement of the Universe: A Study of Causation*, Oxford: Clarendon Press, 1974, p. 51.

plausible, we should not give the explanation the credence we otherwise might. Even if we remain undecided about what in any instance would have been possible – which will usually be the case if the possibility our explanation suggests is counter to fact, and cannot be tested against further evidence – we will usually have to concede that something or other would have been.

Yet causal possibilities, if they remain merely possible, are not actualised. Practical possibilities are before the event at most actualised in someone's thoughts, as something that an agent or set of agents might have done or might yet do; after the event, in celebration or regret. Possibilities are not items at any world or in any head on which we can suppose that we or actual agents will cognitively converge, or about which, even if they do, they could be said to be certain, and thus to know. There is no fact of them, in Robert Nozick's word, to 'track'.[18]

Except to those who want to talk only about the actual, or who wish in some other way cognitively to foreclose, this is not dispiriting. On the contrary. It promises that kind of understanding, as Nozick describes it, which comes from locating an actual in a space of possibles, showing 'the connections it would have to other non-actual things': the kind of understanding we gain, for instance, when we see how possible, even probable, other lines of species evolution were at some distant point in the past, and realise how improbable our own has been; when, in considering the success of Europe since the end of the fifteenth century, we realise that a

---

[18] Nozick's subjunctive formulation of knowledge, devised to challenge the sceptic, is that 'a person knows that *p* when he does not only truly believe it, but also would truly believe it and wouldn't falsely believe it. He not only actually has a true belief, he subjunctively has one. It is true that *p* and he believes it; if it weren't true he wouldn't believe it, and if it were true he would believe it. To know that *p* is to be someone who would believe it if it were true, and who wouldn't believe it if it were false . . . To know is to have a belief that *tracks* the truth that *p*' (*Explanations*, p. 178). (There is much discussion to be had about what is for any *p* the appropriate means of tracking and about what this means produces; but this does not affect the larger argument.) Knowledge in this sense is probably not possible for the psychological contents of the world (Bernard Williams, *Descartes: The Project of Pure Enquiry*, Harmondsworth: Penguin, 1978, pp. 292–302). It is certainly stretching credulity to suggest that it's possible for what Nozick calls 'bestness', for ethical facts, although Nozick himself thinks it is: *Explanations*, p. 319 ff.

reformed Christianity might not have been essential to it, or Islam inimical; when, in seeing how powerful a Confederate nation-state would have been at a moment when the extension of democracy and lower-class rights more generally, even in the United States, was by no means assured, we realise how what we now think of as 'progress' was by no means assured; when, in considering the fate of social democracy elsewhere in northern and western Europe since the 1950s, we see more clearly what did not happen in Britain and why; when, in reflecting on our own lives, we see how else we might have lived them.[19]

IV

But in seeking this kind of understanding, which of the innumerable possibilities should we consider? And how should we decide between the ones we do? One answer to the first question has been, the possibilities which our explanations suggest; one answer to the

[19] Nozick, *Explanations*, p. 12. Stephen J. Gould, *Wonderful Life: the Burgess Shale and the Nature of History*, New York: Norton, 1989, pp. 306 ff., where he sketches seven alternative possible evolutionary worlds, and from the evidence of the Canadian fossils that he discusses earlier in the book, suggests that the eighth, the only one to include us, turned on the probably highly improbable survival of one phylum. The paradox in explanation can be avoided, and in some of the non-experimental social sciences often is, by proposing models which are closed. These are often described as theoretical, and although the explanations which they suggest themselves suggest alternatives, the fact that these explanations derive from closed models allows these alternatives to be assessed from within the model itself. Stable population theory in demography and general equilibrium theory in economics are theories of this kind. (Amartya Sen explains that the interest in this respect of Piero Sraffa's idea of the production of commodities by commodities is that it was an idea which, in Sraffa's elaboration of it, avoided the difficulty: 'Economic methodology: heterogeneity and relevance', *Social Research* 56 (1989), 299–329 at 303, 304–6.) Przeworski's thought that in the sorts of social and political conditions that have obtained in Europe since the 1920s, and other things being equal, political parties of the left lose elections if they remain politically and financially tied to trade unions is a more modest example. It deliberately restricts the issue to one of electoral strategy, and gives a decision on the alternative which it suggests. Always supposing that there is sufficient warrant for the model in the first place, this analytical strategy is, on its own terms, perfectly reasonable. And even for those who want fuller explanations, it can often do much to clear the ground. But it is not mine: see chapter 5, section III, especially note 5.

second, those which are true. The first of these seems more acceptable than the second. Explanations, as I have said, do suggest alternatives. But as I have also said, it is not at all easy to see how, if
their antecedents are counter-to-fact, they are alternatives which
can be said to be either true or false. But both answers have been
given, and have been given together, in a family of formal arguments. None of these arguments will stand, and even if they did, it
is not clear how they would bear on understanding in History and
the social sciences. To see why not, however, is more clearly to see
what might.

The arguments start from the assumption that it is theories which
explain, and that theories consist of sets of statements of law. Laws
have standardly been thought of as causal. They have also been
thought to imply counterfactuals. Hume made a case. A cause, he
argued, 'is an object followed by another . . . where all the objects,
similar to the first, are followed by objects similar to the second. *Or*',
he at once emphasised, 'where if the first object had not been, the
second had never existed.' But this suggestion – quite apart from the
fact, which is here incidental, that it overlooks the possibility that
the second object could have had another cause – is far from self-
evident. It runs together regularities and laws. In each of its two
parts, it gives a different sense to 'cause'. And in the second part,
but not the first, it hints at necessity.[20]

Regularities, laws and causes are each distinct. It is as regular as
most regularities are in the human sciences that countries in which
people are fond of dancing have in the 1980s had unmanageably
high debts. Given the taste for dancing, which, we may suppose,
preceded the taking of loans, we can expect the debt. But few would
believe that there is a causal connection between the two. Most,
indeed, would regard the connection, if they are prepared to
consider it all, as accidental. Accordingly, few would see any sense
or interest in the claim that if the citizens had not been so fond of

[20] Hume, L. A. Selby-Bigge ed., *Enquiries*, Oxford: Oxford University Press,
2nd. edition, 1902, p. 76. On Hume's conviction (against Lewis's characterisation of him as the 'great denier of necessary connections') that there were
real necessities, necessary 'powers', in the world, and his hope that he could
determine them through the 'impressions' which they made on us, Strawson,
Secret Connection and Mackie, *Cement*, pp. 10–14.

dancing, the country's debt would not now be so difficult. Accidental regularities do suggest counterfactuals, but they cannot support them. Non-accidental regularities, on the other hand, can. Those 'low-' and 'middle-income' countries, as the World Bank thinks of them, whose terms of trade in the early 1970s seemed very promising, had by the 1980s accumulated fearsome debts. Here, the counterfactual is more plausible. If their terms of trade had not seemed so promising, their debts would not now be so forbidding. But there is no more necessity than in the first example. In Poland, the terms of trade never seemed promising; yet the country received many loans and its debt is now large. In South Korea, where the terms of trade seemed very promising indeed, and large loans were taken, the debt had, by 1990, largely been paid off.

It is nevertheless clear why, in the formal arguments I am considering in this section, the issues of regularity, cause and necessity do arise together. Necessity, not mere possibility or accident, is thought to be implied in the idea of a cause. A cause, it has also been said, and certainly a necessity, implies a regularity (if not conversely). And the three issues converge in the idea of a law. Statements of law (which may refer to many actual instances, or only to one) are statements of connection which are true, universal, neither tautologous nor accidental, and which support counterfactuals. 'A satisfactory definition of scientific law', as Nelson Goodman put it more than forty years ago, 'a satisfactory theory of confirmation or disposition terms (and this includes not only predicates ending in "ible" or "able" but almost every objective predicate, such as "is red"), would solve a large part of the problem of counterfactuals'; 'conversely, a solution to the problems of counterfactuals would give an answer to critical questions about law, confirmation and the meaning of potentiality'. If we had a defensible theory of laws, so that we knew when we could project, or an independently defensible theory of counterfactuals, so that we knew when we could assert them, we could indeed decide whether a counter-to-fact could be inserted into the world and what would then follow.[21] The formal arguments consist in two kinds of attempt to enter this circle.

[21] Nelson Goodman, *Fact, Fiction and Forecast*, Cambridge MA: Harvard University Press, 4th edition, 1983, p. 3, a paper first written in 1946. There has

The first confronts the issue directly.[22] But it has repeatedly come up against two difficulties. The first, which might be called the problem of inference, arises in the statement 'if it is a law of nature that A, therefore A'. The inferential claim in this statement is not about any A, but about a law of *nature* that A. Those who make the statement have thus to be able to show how they can infer that the necessity exists in the world. They can of course simply say that necessity itself implies actuality. But that introduces the second difficulty. This, the problem of identification, lies in being able to show what sort of fact it is about the world that gives 'law', as distinct from accidental regularity, its distinctive sense. The reply could be, 'the fact of necessity'. But that restates the problem of inference.

The second entry to the circle is designed to avoid this dilemma, and is more indirect. Wilfrid Sellars suggested it in 1948, two years after Goodman's paper, and it has since been developed by David Lewis and others.[23] It approaches law through necessity, and not *vice versa*, and does so by adapting Leibniz's story of possible worlds.

been an argument about the difference between the projection of single predi-cates, in Goodman's much-discussed examples 'green' and 'grue' (green-and/or-blue) and the projection of laws: Goodman's answer to the first problem is that we project or continue to use those predicates which are 'entrenched' in our practice, but with the example 'all emeroses are gred', Donald Davidson argued that this cannot be so for laws ('Emeroses by other names', *Journal of Philosophy* 63 (1966), pp. 778–80).

[22] I draw for what follows largely on Putnam, *Many Faces of Realism*, and Bas C. van Fraassen, *Laws and Symmetry*, Oxford: Clarendon Press, 1989. Van Fraassen's account is much more refined than what I say here suggests. But since, as I go on to argue, the relation between laws and explanation is much looser than many have supposed, if indeed it exists at all (this is van Fraassen's main point), and since there are anyway few if any laws in history and the social sciences, the refinements are not relevant here. The kind of view which Putnam and van Fraassen reject is defended by D. M. Armstrong, *What is a Law of Nature?*, Cambridge: Cambridge University Press, 1983.

[23] For historical interest, Sellars, 'Concepts as involving laws and incon-ceivable without them', *Philosophy of Science* 15 (1948), 287–315. Also Bas C. van Fraassen, 'Report on conditionals', *Teorema* 5 (1976), 5–25. Robert Pargetter, 'Laws and modal realism', *Philosophical Studies* 46 (1984), 335–47. David Lewis, *Counterfactuals*, Oxford: Blackwell, 1973; *Papers* 2, 122–6; 'New work for a theory of universals', *Australasian Journal of Philosophy* 61 (1983), 343–77. Van Fraassen, *Laws and Symmetry*, pp. 65–93 and further references there.

It starts from the thought that the ancient modal subcontraries, 'it is possible that A' and 'it is possible that not-A', can illuminatingly be translated into the language of possible worlds and thereby be given truth conditions. 'It is possible that A' is true if and only if 'there are possible worlds in which there is A'. This then slides into the argument that if there is a proposition A such that both 'it is possible that A' and 'it is possible that not-A', then there are at least two possible worlds, and thus, at least one other world than this one. Lewis has extended this to give an account of laws. There are, he suggests, innumerable true theories, by which he means deductively closed sets of true sentences. But some of these are simpler than others, and some stronger or more informative. Laws are those sentences describing regularities which are common to those true theories that achieve the best combination of simplicity and strength. Laws, however, do not only have to be true. They also have to be necessary. Lewis claims that 'it is necessary that A' is true in a world if and only if A is true in every other world which is possible relative to that world. He sees that he has to address the problem of inference and define 'necessary', and does so by stipulating physical necessity. 'It is necessary that A' thus becomes 'it is physically necessary that A', and this is true in a world if and only if A is true in every other world which is physically possible relative to that world. Accordingly, 'it is physically necessary that A is true in a world if and only if A is implied by the laws of that world'.

This may solve the problem of inference. But the problem of identification remains. It arises in the criterion of simplicity, in the question, simplicity in what language? It is conceivable that what is the simplest language today will be translated tomorrow into another which is simpler still. (In the natural sciences, this happens.) It might seem possible to meet this complication by saying that we will prefer those theories which are simplest not in just one language, but in any. These theories, however, may turn out be too many, and only have tautologies in common. Lewis has therefore introduced a further condition, which is that we should prefer the language which marks out real or 'natural' distinctions. This is difficult enough in the sciences of nature. In the example in political economy that I took earlier, it does not help at all. Is the best language the one which picks out those countries in which primary products figure prominently in exports? Or the one which picks out those in which there is much dancing, or to which northern warblers migrate in the winter, or whose names have been changed since the eighteenth century? Moreover, in talking of other worlds in which laws are true, Lewis is required to say that these other worlds are real. For it is the particulars of worlds, as he believes, both the particulars of the actual world and the particulars of all other possible ones, which supervene.

In these two respects, Lewis's move, although economical, exacts a high price. Not only does it demand a canonical, indeed correct, language which, as Quine would say, 'limns' the world as it is, independently of who does the limning, and which does not therefore depend at all on the vagaries of circumstance, culture, psychology or interest. It also requires us to believe that there really are real other worlds which exist quite independently of ours, worlds which, although they stand in no causal relation to our own – such that we cannot get to them by beams from mountain tops in Hawaii or by a yet to be devised simultaneity machine – are none the less perspicuous. (Lewis is not the first to believe in such worlds. Nozick reports that the claim in the Talmud that 'God rides on his swift cherub and roams over eighteen thousand worlds' is usually interpreted by Talmudic scholars to mean 18,000 quite distinct worlds, unconnected to each other in space or time.) This is difficult enough.[24]

---

[24] Lewis, *Counterfactuals*, p. 85; a further summary in 'Counterfactuals and comparative possibility', in *Papers 2*, 3–31. Lewis has confounded Arnauld's expectation in a letter to Leibniz (13 May 1686): 'I am much mistaken if there is anyone who dares to say that he can conceive of a purely possible substance, for I am convinced in my own mind that although one talks so much of these purely possible substances, nonetheless one never conceives of them except according to the notion of those [in the one world] which God has created.' Lewis admits that when he first proposed his other worlds, he was everywhere met by 'incredulous stares'. Kripke resisted the implication that they were like foreign countries or things to be picked up through what Kaplan had called a 'Jules Verne o'scope'. Powers thought the very idea of them, 'perhaps laid out like raisins in a pudding', quite ludicrous. Putnam too declared it 'dotty'. Quine fastidiously dismissed such other worlds as 'disorderly', 'creatures of darkness', lounging idly in the doorways of the actual world. (Saul Kripke, 'Naming and necessity', in Donald Davidson, Gilbert Harman eds., *Semantics of Natural Language*, Dordrecht: Riedel, 1972, p. 271 (republished as *Naming and Necessity*, Oxford: Blackwell, 1980); Lawrence Powers, 'Comments' on Robert Stalnaker's

And since the laws that hold in the actual world may not hold in some others, we are free to believe that there is at least one possible world at which anything is true. There is always at least one world (beyond the 18,000 countenanced in the Talmud) at which the Moors beat the Catholic kings, Trotsky won, humans are marsupials and pigs have wings. Yet by the abolition of identities across worlds, we are at the same time prevented from making any counterfactual claim about any particular thing in the actual world. Boabdil, Trotsky, pouched humans and pigs in all other worlds are mere counterparts of themselves in this. In being freed to talk about one or more of a multiplicity of other worlds, we are free to say far too much about what there is not; constrained into saying nothing except about what there is about what is. At the same time, there are excessive demands on our mental capacities. (For every proposition, Lewis wants to say, there is at least one world. Yet if, as he also says, there are too few sentences in any ordinary language to express all the propositions there are, it is also the case that there are too few worlds in most other heads to back all the counterfactual propositions there are.)

Real other worlds of the same sort as ours, it seems safe to say, do not exist. But even if they did, and were to fix our modal statements in the way that Lewis suggests, they would not help us to decide

'Propositions', in Alfred M. Mackay, Daniel D. Merrill eds., *Issues in the Philosophy of Language*, New Haven: Yale University Press, 1976, p. 95; W. V. O. Quine, 'On what there is', in *From a Logical Point of View*, Cambridge MA: Harvard University Press, 1953, p. 4; Mackie, *Truth, Probability and Paradox*, p. 84.) Lewis has collected these and other criticisms and replied to them in *On the Plurality of Worlds*, Oxford: Blackwell, 1986, putting the onus on his critics to find a more economical formulation of their modal intuitions. A related argument turns not on other real possible worlds but on different combinations of possibilities in this one: D. M. Armstrong, *A Combinatorial Theory of Possibility*, Cambridge: Cambridge University Press, 1989. Stalnaker defends the primitiveness of possible worlds by suggesting that a causally or practically possible world is 'what truth is relative to, what people distinguish between in their rational activities'; that 'to believe in possible worlds is to believe only that those activities have a certain structure, the structure which possible worlds theory helps to bring out' (*Inquiry*, Cambridge MA: MIT Press, 1984, p. 57). Mackie took an analogous view: 'people can consider possibilities; but the possibilities exist only as the content of such considerings' (*Truth, Probability and Paradox*, p. 92). Also van Fraassen, *Laws and Symmetry*, p. 93. On the Talmud, Nozick, *Explanations*, p. 670 n10.

what it is that we want to decide, which are counterfactual claims for this world. We cannot sidestep the workings of the one world we are interested in by pointing to others, where the workings may or may not be different, or transpose the agents of this world into their counterparts elsewhere, and there make them reason and act in any way we will. If we do, we sidestep the problem itself. Indeed, the difficulties in each of the two attempts to enter Goodman's circle, the first and more direct, and Lewis's, serve to show that the attempt itself may be mistaken. If we say that our explanations turn on laws, we are committed to the view that they turn on statements of necessity for which the inference to necessity is itself difficult to specify and from which (once we dispense with possible worlds) the identification to the fact of necessity in the one world there is, including causal necessity, remains as obscure as it did to Hume. It seems best to forget laws altogether.

This is no loss. On the contrary. We are freed once again to concentrate on explanation itself. An explanation, as I said, is an answer to the question 'why?'. It tells a story which is guided by contrasts with what we want to explain. It succeeds, where it does, by giving descriptions which in the conventions of telling that story to that kind of audience, are relevant *as* explanations. If laws, whatever they might be, do exist, and if a successful explanation invokes them, that will at most be incidental. (Statements which are simple, strong and true may not be sufficiently informative for any explanation. Even if they are, they may not – if they refer only to what is physically possible, they certainly will not – contain the kind of information which, in History or the social sciences, we need in order to explain.) And if we cast what we offer as descriptions for explanation in terms of 'causes', we do so not because we believe that we have identified any powers – let alone any necessary powers – at work in the world, but simply because 'cause' (and 'reason' and suchlike terms) serve to say that it is an *explanation* we are offering.[25]

---

[25] This may seem excessively agnostic. But even the most casual inspection of even the most ametaphysical arguments about causality suggests that 'cause' is an irremediably metaphysical notion. To those who know the history of the argument, this will seem merely to be a restatement of Duhem's argument that 'cause' is metaphysical, science should not have anything to do with metaphy-

Explanations, this is to say, are not fixed. There is nothing in the world itself to tell us what they are. And there is no good argument from elsewhere always to rule in some kinds of account, those in terms of theories, for example, or of laws, or of causes, or in History and the social sciences, of reasons, as explanatory, and always to rule out others. We simply set out to explain the facts and we adduce information to do so. What that information is, and how it is cast, depends on what is being asked. Explanations, we can say, are dependent, *as* explanations, on context. If this is so, and if we add the assumption that the world is contingent, or at least, not known to be necessary, and the belief also (the implications of which I hint at in section VII in this chapter and elaborate on in the rest of the book) that the human world is in part constructed by practical reasoning which has to be seen as the practical reasoning of *particular* agents, then in so far as any explanation in History and the social sciences will increase possibilities as it also reduces them, we can only consider the possibilities suggested in explanation, and thereby enhance our understanding, by considering particular instances. We must discuss examples.

V

I take three. The first is the course of bubonic plague in Europe from the fourteenth century to the eighteenth and of marital fertility in rural France and England in the hundred years or so before the French Revolution; the second, of the politics of the division of the Korean peninsula in 1945; the third, of the painting that Duccio did

---

sics, and causal talk is thus alien to science. But one does not have to be too sceptical an empiricist, or too concerned with what 'science' does, to take the point. Mackie was no metaphysician, yet his view that 'a singular causal sequence instantiates some pure law of working', which as he concedes, can never be the subject of observation, a law 'which is . . . a form of partial persistence', which is 'identical with some process that has qualitative or structural continuity, and [which] incorporates the fixity relations which constitute the direction of causation', certainly seems to resort to substantial imputation (*Cement*, pp. 229–30). For an attractively agnostic argument, propelled by a wish to save physics as well as 'the phenomena', van Fraassen, *Scientific Image*, pp. 112–57.

in Florence and Siena at the end of the thirteenth century and the beginning of the fourteenth.

I take each to make a different point. The example of vital events in early modern Europe shows that taking up the alternatives suggested in the best available explanation of what some have seen as 'structural' facts can indicate that these facts are not so structural after all. The politics of the United States in south Korea between 1945 and 1950, by contrast, shows that taking up the alternatives suggested in the best available explanations of a series of practical decisions can show that alternative courses of action are not always so easily taken as we might imagine them to be. Looking at Duccio's painting in relation to that of his contemporaries, especially Cimabue and Giotto, famous 'precursors' of the Renaissance, and thinking more about that painting, shows that to pursue the possibilities suggested in an explanation can lead one to revise the initial description of what is to be explained and thus, the explanatory question itself. Together, therefore, the examples also make a general point. The belief that the world is all of piece, a 'system', as it is sometimes put, or a 'structure', a belief which is often prompted by knowing too little about its inter-connections;[26] the belief that decisions are predetermined or the effect of a conspiracy, the one prompted by a lingering conviction of a providence in events, the other of an anti-providence; and the belief in a telos, that events, for instance, were ineluctably tending to a Renaissance in painting; are each beliefs which have more or less wittingly foreclosed the explanations that have been proposed for one or other of the cases I take.

None of the examples is trivial. Indeed, counterfactuals suggest the interest of each. If plague had not killed such a high proportion of the population in the western part of Europe after the middle of the fourteenth century, social mobility there might not subsequently have been so considerable and later advances in agricultural investment and technique might not have been so great. Two of the probable causes of Europe's later economic growth might thus have been absent. If rural fertility in France in the later seven-

---

[26] In Turgenev's image, prompted by the hope that to catch the tail of truth will be to catch (or at least wag) the whole beast, not realising that truth is a lizard, and leaves its tail behind.

teenth and eighteenth centuries had not been so high, living conditions there would not have been so depressed. One of the incentives to political change by the 1780s might thus have been weaker. If the United States had not occupied the south of Korea, there would have been no war on the peninsula in 1950, the United States would not have had such a good case for rearming against both the Soviet Union and China, and the price of commodities on the world markets might not have risen so far and so fast. If Cimabue and Giotto had been more conservative, the move to a greater realism might not have been made, or at least, it might not have been made in Christian painting.

VI

In the term made famous by Fernand Braudel, both Duccio's painting in Siena and the policies of the great powers in Korea, like the failures of the British Labour Party in the later 1970s and 1980s, are each examples of the *événementielle*. They were what Braudel and some of the *Annales* historians after him regarded as instances of the most instantial sort: 'brief, rapid, nervous fluctuations, by definition ultra-sensitive', events of a kind which are 'often only momentary outbursts, surface manifestations'. They might have been manifestations 'of larger movements', but even then, they were at most *conjonctures*, items in what Braudel occasionally called the *moyenne durée*. They certainly stood in sharp contrast to the *longue durée*, to the 'permanent' or 'slow-moving', to those kinds of phenomena which Braudel at one point rashly said even 'withstand the march of time'. In early modern Europe, these were exemplified in what he called 'the old biological regime', 'a collection of restrictions, obstacles, structures, proportions and numerical relationships' which until the eighteenth century, had been 'the norm': restrictions, Braudel argued, which set 'the inflexible boundaries between the possible and the impossible' and limited 'the liberty of men and the role of chance itself'.[27]

---

[27] Braudel, quoted in James, *Content*, pp. 160–1; Miriam Kochan trans., *Capitalism and Material Life, 1400–1800*, London: Weidenfeld and Nicolson, 1973, p. 37, pp. xiv; Sîan Reynolds trans., *The Mediterranean and the Mediterranean*

Braudel had no steady conception of the connections between his different *durées*. He confused the issue further by failing often to distinguish kinds of time from kinds of fact. Nevertheless, in what Susan James nicely describes as the 'concessive holism' of the *Annales* school, holistic in its intention to capture the whole, concessive in its reluctance to explain every single thing (as more extreme structuralists have wanted to do) in terms of its relations to all the other things in the system, there was at least the hint of a theory. Features of the *longue durée* are fixed and unalterable; *conjonctures* can be taken either way; and the events of the *événementielle* are explained as more or less rational responses to the other two. The exigencies of the *longue durée* are objects of theoretical reason, the events of the *événementielle* are the outcomes of a more or less rational practical reason, and *conjonctures* stand somewhere in between. But if this is so, it is clear that the distinction is not so much a distinction in theory, a distinction between kinds of states

World in the Age of Philip II, London: Collins, 1972, II, p. 520. Also his 'Histoire et sciences sociales: la longue durée', *Annales ESC* 13 (1958), 725–53, and for a more recent characterisation, Sîan Reynolds trans., *Civilisation and Capitalism, 15th to 18th Century: The Perspective of the World*, London: Collins, 1984, pp. 17, 71, *passim*. Even more constraining, and more resistant to 'the march of time', in their duration perhaps multi-millennial rather than merely millennial, are those other kinds of supposedly 'structural' instance, semantic fields which are also fields of thought; fields which are systematic in the internal interdependence of their constituent parts, although any actual instance of which is 'only one possible combination among others'. These are the structures of Lévi-Strauss's sort of structuralism, 'règles conscientes and préméditées' as he called them, which constitute and so constrain what is thought. Such structures, material for Braudel, mental for Lévi-Strauss, are in the conceptions which these two men have had of them sometimes so enduring as scarcely to be historical instances at all; but if we do not, like Lévi-Strauss, actually contrast them (even for rhetorical effect) with events in time, and if we believe in them at all, they can be seen (as Braudel himself saw them) as items in the *très longue durée* (Claude Lévi-Strauss, Rodney Needham trans., *Totemism*, London: Merlin, 1964, pp. 16, 91 and *passim*; *La Pensée sauvage*, Paris: Plon, 1962, p. 333; Edmund Leach, *Culture and Communication: The Logic by which Symbols are Connected*, Cambridge: Cambridge University Press, 1976, pp. 3–7, and Braudel's remarks on the *trop longues durées* of Levi-Strauss's structures in Sarah Matthews trans., *On History*, London: Weidenfeld and Nicolson, 1980, p. 75). On the exaggerations and errors which can follow from in this respect taking Lévi-Strauss too strongly, G. E. R. Lloyd, *Demystifing Mentalities*, Cambridge: Cambridge University Press, 1990.

of affairs or events, different kinds of thing in the world, as a distinction in practice, between those states of affairs or events which could have been altered by agency and those, it is supposed, which could not have been.[28]

The course of the plague in late medieval and early modern Europe and of the levels of marital fertility in the French and English countryside in the seventeenth century and most of the eighteenth are on this reading each aspects of the *longue durée*, of states of affairs to which alternatives both of a causal and of a practical kind would seem to have been remote. Against the incidence and effects of plague, there appeared to be almost nothing that anyone could do until the isolation of the bacillus in the 1890s. Against the incidence and effects of high fertility, the only effective resort before the twentieth century would seem to have been not to marry, or to marry later, or to restrain or divert one's sexuality. The generalisations or theories in each case are strong; the conditions are tight; the interconnections of both are complex, and seem usually to point to one outcome. The 'structure', as the *Annales* historians would have it, was set, and set a long way back. I want to suggest however that in some respects, both for mortality from the plague and for fertility in rural France in the seventeenth and eighteenth centuries,

---

[28] Some assessments of Braudel are collected by J. H. Hexter, 'Fernand Braudel and the *Monde Braudellien*', *Journal of Modern History* 44 (1972), pp. 531–3, who offers a sparkling exposition and appraisal of his own. Also James, *Content*, 167–9. The origin of *Annales* and what lay behind it are explained in Carole Fink's illuminating *Marc Bloch: A Life in History*, Cambridge: Cambridge University Press, 1989, especially p. 128 ff. and Braudel's own 'Personal testimony' in *Journal of Modern History* 44 (1972), 448–67. The *Annales* 'school' after Braudel was less distinctive, certainly less committed to Braudel's own particular kind of structuralism (for what this was, Stuart Clark, 'The *Annales* historians', in Quentin Skinner ed., *The Return of Grand Theory in the Human Sciences*, Cambridge: Cambridge University Press, 1984, pp. 179–96). There is an interesting account of the school by François Furet, an increasingly dissident member of the third generation, in 'Beyond the *Annales*', *Journal of Modern History* 55 (1983), 389–94. Furet mentions the importance of the Communist Party to that generation; the political point of his own distance from the presumptions of the earlier *Annales* historians in this and some other respects is well brought out in Sunil Khilnani, *The Decline of the Intellectual Left in France, 1945–1985*, Ph.D dissertation, University of Cambridge, 1989, pp. 260–306.

it was not. As one pursues the demographic historians' accounts, more immediate possibilities suggest themselves. And some at least of these turn out to turn on contingent decision. Braudel's *événementielle* had a discernible impact on the *longue durée*; in certain ways, to a certain extent, at certain moments, it could have had more. This is a conclusion that casts a wider doubt on the often coarse distinction that sociologists and others have made between 'structure' and 'agency'; at the least, it casts doubt on the ways in which that distinction has often been drawn.

The example of the division of Korea, by contrast, corresponds more closely to that kind of case – Trotsky's chill, Churchill's will, Boabdil's capacities – which historians more usually have in mind when they talk of possibilities. It is, as I have said, an exemplary instance of the *événementielle*. It consists in the decisions which the United States took between 1943 and August 1945 for its post-war policy towards Korea, and of the policies that it pursued once it had occupied the area there south of the 38th parallel to receive the Japanese surrender. Historians have taken sharply different views of these moves. Some have argued that the United States' hasty decision to occupy the south in early August 1945, and the policies it pursued once it was there, were both pre-ordained. They were consistent with and followed from an already fixed policy for the post-war world. These historians disagree only about what this policy was. Yet others doubt whether the United States had any considered intention at all, and are inclined to see what happened as a series of (often unfortunate) improvisations. There is a considerable difference of opinion on what might have been possible; and yet the same historian can often be found coming to contrary conclusions in the same work. None has pressed the implications of his explanation as far as it can be pressed. As a result, the interpretations are either too extreme or muddled.

The skills of a political agent, even if they require some imagination, and even if the agent in question is the pre-eminent power among agents, like the United States in international politics after 1945, are skills which have always to be deployed in a field of forces that is partly set by others. (After all, 'politics', in John Dunn's excellent characterisation, 'is an exacting and necessarily heavily improvisatory practical skill, deployed in permanently competitive

conditions and on the basis of very limited information'.)[29] Artistic
creation, by contrast, might seem to be a field of free invention. Or
at least, that is the opinion that comes down from early fourteenth-
century Florentines through Vasari's influential *Lives* to the nineteenth-century romantics and some modern art historians. In fact,
of course, the explanatory picture is more complicated, and also
more confused. Looking more closely at Duccio's painting in the
late Duecento and early Trecento suggests, to a degree that the
other two examples do not, how considering how things might
have been different can lead us to a different view of what those
things actually were.

There are actually three opinions. The first is that artists are
indeed artists and do simply create. 'Cimabue thought to hold the
field in painting', Dante remarked in the opening section of the
Divine Comedy, at the time at which Duccio was painting his altarpiece for the cathedral in Siena; 'and now Giotto has the cry'.[30] The
second is that artistic creation is to be seen as moving to an end
which artists themselves may not know. Looking back from what
Michelangelo managed to do on the Sistine ceiling, Vasari and
many subsequent historians have tended to suggest either that
painters in the late Duecento and early Trecento grasped what
Bernard Berenson called 'the real issue' of realism or they did not,
and that is that.[31] Painters were free because they were artists; but
as artists, they would have grasped this issue; and being free, and
being artists, they would have followed it. Third, there is the distinct and more mechanical view, familiar in the work of many
modern art historians, that artists do what they do under the
influence of others.

The three opinions do not sit easily together. And as we pursue
the existing explanations for what painters in central Italy at the
end of the thirteenth century and the beginning of the fourteenth
actually did and did not do, the puzzle becomes more acute rather

---

[29] 'Conclusion', in Donal B. Cruise O'Brien, Dunn and Richard Rathbone
eds., *Contemporary West African States*, Cambridge: Cambridge University Press,
1989, pp. 190–1.

[30] Canto XI, 94–5.

[31] Bernard Berenson, *The Italian Painters of the Renaissance*, London: Fontana,
1960, p. 121.

than less, and the explanations less certain. If Cimabue and Giotto, as the second opinion has it, realised realism, why did Duccio not? Was it, as an implication of the first opinion might have it, because he could not? Or was it, as the third would suggest, that the 'advances' were being made in Florence but he was working in Siena, under the influence of earlier Sienese painters? Or did Duccio realise the 'real issue' in another way? Or did he realise something rather different, which the dazzling light from Florence and the consequent teleology have since obscured? Indeed, what exactly is it that he did and did not do, and why? To answer these questions is to begin to see what he might have done. And to see that is to see what he did do in a more complex way; to see it more, I think, as it actually was, and as he intended it to be.

VII

I use these examples to explore the paradox that the more satisfying the answers to an explanatory question appear to be, the more provisional will they be also. Compelling accounts suggest alternatives as they reduce them. There is no general method with which to assess these. But this is not to say that nothing of a general kind can be said about what makes them more and less plausible. I return to what this might be in the final chapter. I also there indicate what I think may follow for the relation between knowledge and understanding, and for the place of theoretical reasoning in History and the social sciences. But the direction in which I am pointing may already be clear.

The possibilities suggested by answers to explanatory questions in these kinds of inquiry are of two kinds. One is of those events and states of affairs which are, as we see it, or which become, independent of human agency, and which are for that reason amenable to what we call a causal explanation. The other is of those that are not. The first kind, if they fall easily under general descriptions, and if general descriptions serve our interests (something that is more likely to be true of mortality and fertility than politics or painting), are for this reason also amenable to what we can think of as a theoretical formulation. In practice, of course, there will be difficulties.

In any actual instance, several law-like generalisations or inductively known runnings-on will be at work under conditions whose nature, number, incidence and importance is usually not easy to specify. (Indeed, it will more often than not be impossible to disentangle cause and condition.) And the more formal difficulties aside, to use such theories to project (from actual antecedents just as much as from those which are counter-to-fact) is always a hazard.[32]

Theories will be even less suitable to deciding about the other kind of possibility which an explanatory answer will often suggest. 'Practical wisdom', Aristotle remarked, 'is not concerned with universals only; it must also recognise particulars, for it is practical, and practice concerns particulars.'[33] He was suggesting how to think about moral deliberation, but his point has a more general force. In so far as what people do is not guided by a hidden hand, some causal force they do not know, and is affected by what they think; and in so far as what they think is not also entirely guided by a hidden hand; what in any instance they think about what they should do is not usually something which can be sufficiently described or explained (to themselves or by others) in a general way. Practical reasoning is done by particular agents in the light of their particular experiences and the particular circumstances in which they find themselves. This is obviously so if they are reasoning from their desires or their

---

[32] Jon Elster once went so far as to argue that 'for the working historian . . . the crucial point is that . . . counterfactual statements must be explained in terms of some *actual* theory . . . that the speaker, if challenged, could produce to back his assertion' (*Logic and Society: Contradictions and Possible Worlds*, Chichester: Wiley, 1978, p. 182). Brian Barry agreed that the point of counterfactuals is to check our theories, and that 'any counterfactual is [itself] a creature of theory', but argued that if this is all that they are for, then Elster did not need to insist that we be able to insert their counter-to-fact antecedents at some point in the real world ('Superfox' [review of Elster *Logic and Society*], *Political Studies* 28 (1980), 136–43 at p. 142). I return to this argument of Elster's at the end of the next chapter, and to the wider question of theory in the last. But the argument, though worth taking seriously, is not one that Elster himself would now wish to press. In his more recent work (which he summarises in *Nuts and Bolts*), he rejects the ambition to general theories of social affairs and insists that we can only hope to discover more particular if still widely-prevalent 'mechanisms'.

[33] *Nichomachean Ethics*, 1141b4–16.

conceptions of themselves. But it is also so if they are reasoning from generalities, from the rules which they take to govern a role or an office, for instance, or from some more abstract precept. Possible reasonings for them are reasonings for them as them, there and then, reasonings that they can or could have made as those agents *from* where they are; not alternatives only *for* or *to* them, or for some category of agents, or for any agent at all.

We can of course abstract agents, categorise them, generalise their experience and judgement, and draw inferences about what it would have been or would be reasonable for them, as agents of that kind, in that kind of situation, to do or to have done. Social and political theories, both explanatory and exhortatory, like the moral theories from which many of them derive, have made a habit of this; one might even say that as the theories they have attempted to be, this has been their constitutive characteristic. But the more that they do so, and the more powerful in this sense they may claim to be, also the more indeterminate, or inappropriate, or at the limit simply the more empty, they tend to become. It is impossible to give a general account of what it is reasonable to do in advance of the act which is also a sufficient account. And to recover a piece of practical reasoning as rational after the event, and to generalise from that, does not itself warrant a generalisation about the circumstances and deliberation that gave rise to it.

These considerations together suggest two reservations about what we think of as theories in History and the social sciences. The first is about their generality. We might say that if the point of any theory of anything is to be general and also realistic (or at least rich) and precise; that if none can be all three; and that if social and political theories, for the purposes of explanation or practice, are intended to be theories of intelligible and appropriate practical action under constraints of what we think of as a causal kind; then they are torn in opposite directions.[34] Causal constraints – including, if we like to see them in this way, the rules under which people might be thinking and acting – can in principle be generalised, but practicality itself, even where there are such rules, cannot. For this

---

[34] On the purposes of theory in general, Richard Levins, *Evolution in Changing Environments*, Princeton: Princeton University Press, 1968, pp. 6–9.

reason, what I am arguing in this book leads me to acknowledge the importance of a wider understanding, in Nozick's sense, but to resist the common assumption in the social sciences that this understanding is sufficiently met by general accounts.

In insisting on understanding rather than explanation, I also resist the conventional supposition that accounts of human affairs, more and less theoretical, add to knowledge. This is not a new thought. One or another kind of sceptic has been voicing it for more than two hundred years. If all theories, as Quine has put it, are under-determined by all possible observations; if a realist theory of meaning is thereby ruled out; and if no sentence has a determinate meaning and no action a determinate intentional description; then explanations of anything, and not just explanations of human affairs, must themselves be indeterminate. As Quine himself has said, the argument may have only a philosophical interest. Its implication may only – although for some pre-existing convictions, also dramatically – be that we should not suppose that reality can do the justificatory work. It may explain how we come to have the beliefs that we do; but it cannot by itself support those beliefs. (Hence Donald Davidson's suggestion that we might do well to dispense with 'the very idea of a conceptual scheme', of a distinction between scheme and reality.)[35]

If we nevertheless accept Quine's conclusion; if we add to it the argument for a distinct and further indeterminacy in any characterisation of desires, beliefs, imagined alternatives, intentions and so on, the stuff of practical reason; if we also add the argument that there is no incontestable fact of the matter about such things, and no privileged access to them of a cognitive kind – no privileged access, if we take Quine's argument to its limit, even for speakers

[35] Christopher Hookway discusses the implications of Quine's thinking for the human sciences in 'Indeterminacy and interpretation', in Hookway and Philip Pettit eds., *Action and Interpretation*, Cambridge: Cambridge University Press, 1978, pp. 17–41. Quine himself has not been interested in these subjects; but it is not difficult to infer what his own approach to them, on the assumption that they *are* sciences, that's to say interested in prediction and not other sorts of 'game', like fiction or poetry, would be (e.g. *Pursuit of Truth*, Cambridge MA: Harvard University Press, 1990, 20, pp. 37–49). Donald Davidson, 'On the very idea of a conceptual scheme', *Proceedings and Addresses of the Aristotelian Society* 67 (1974), 5–20. I return to the pragmatists in chapter 5.

with a shared understanding of the same language; then it is clear that cumulative and convergent certainty, not just about the workings of the world, but also about its particular contents, which we take to mark knowledge, will always elude the social sciences.[36]

My own argument strengthens this conviction. My first paradox of explanation, which is that in explaining we increase alternatives as we also reduce them, accordingly leads to a second. In explaining, we gather facts and make the best sense of them that we can in answer to the question we are asking. In this respect, we do indeed come to know more. But if the point of inquiring into human affairs is, in the sense in which I am using the word, also to understand; if to understand is to consider what might have been possible; if what might causally or practically have been possible is not true of something at some other possible world but is at best only plausible at this; and if what was possible can at best be assessed but, since it did not occur, not be known: then the dialectic of inquiry and reflection by which we come to understand is one which reduces our certainty and in that sense our knowledge as it adds to it. In this way and to this extent, success in History and the social sciences, as perhaps in life itself, consists in understanding more and knowing less.

[36] This is crisply put by Williams, *Descartes*, 1978, pp. 301–3.

— 2 —

Plague and fertility in
early modern Europe

I

Braudel has not been alone in supposing that 'the biological regime' in pre-modern Europe was pre-ordained and unalterable, and marked the limit between the possible and the impossible. Mortality, Michael Flinn agrees, was 'in God's sector'. Fertility also, in Jean Bourgeois-Pichat's view, was throughout this period 'determined by a network of sociological and biological factors and when the network is known, the result can be predicted . . . Couples [had] the number of children that biology or society decided to give them.'[1] Demographers tend now to suggest that this was not so for fertility, at least in the sense that Bourgeois-Pichat appears to intend. But nor was it so, more recent accounts suggest, for morbidity and mortality. As the explanations for each have been refined, so our sense of why what happened did, and thus, of what else might have done, has extended.

II

Arguably the most important single factor in what Braudel thought of as the biological regime in Europe between the sixth century and the seventeenth, in the numbers that it caused to die, and in what most historians agree to have been the economic, social and political consequences of that fact, is plague. The first of the two pandemics of this disease in the continent between the early Christian

[1] Michael W. Flinn, *The European Demographic System, 1500–1820*, Brighton: Harvester, 1981, p. 18. Jean Bourgeois-Pichat, *Proceedings of the Amercian Philosophical Society* 3 (1967), 163.

period and the present appears to have come from Ethiopia into Egypt and thence to the Middle East, Constantinople, north Africa, Spain and France. It appeared in Saragossa in 542 and reached at least as far to the north and west as Trèves, in central France, by 543. In its first outbreaks, however, to 544, and in what appear to have its eight main succeeding ones, to 767, it was largely restricted to the Mediterranean littoral. But little is known about its magnitude and effects.

The second pandemic reached the relatively dense populations of the Kipchak Khanate in the Crimea in 1346, most probably along the Don valley from the shores of the Caspian in Kurdistan and Iraq. By the end of 1352, it had spread to most of Europe except Iceland, the northern part of what is now Scandinavia and some parts of the east. This pandemic, whose first and most virulent years in the second half of the 1340s are in a seventeenth-century English phrase now often called the 'Black Death', continued to re-appear in western Europe until the 1670s. There were outbreaks in the Baltic ports in the second decade of the eighteenth century and one last, severe but not widespread incidence in Provence between 1720 and 1722. The last outbreak in Moscow occurred in the early 1770s, in the Balkans, in the 1840s.

The effects of this pandemic in Europe were considerable. The likely extent of cultivated land in parts of the continent at the start of the 1340s may not have been recovered for another four or five hundred years. And in the initial outbreak at the end of the 1340s, perhaps a third of the population may have died. To many of those in the fourteenth century whose views on it survive, it was an act of God. But as others then and before saw, it did have causes. One can get a preliminary grip on how to think about what they were in Elisabeth Carpentier's question: 'was the plague', she asks, 'an evil made necessary by an ineluctable evolution? Or was it a tragic accident at variance with the normal course of events?'[2]

----

[2] It is more accurate to say that the largest single killer in Europe is unknown. In their first epidemics in the continent, measles, smallpox and one or two other diseases were devastating, as indeed was the strain of influenza which arrived in the continent just after the First World War. But in earlier periods, many diseases, including plague itself, were imperfectly described, and their demographic consequences remain uncertain. It is a reasonable judgement, if

Carpentier's question is addressed to those who have argued that Europe was over-populated in the early fourteenth century, and that the plague was a corrective, Malthusian, check to this state of affairs. This is not a claim that need detain us. In the beginnings of its spread from the areas in western Asia in which it was (and remains) enzoötic, the plague attacked some very sparse populations. Also, the recoveries from it were delayed and variable and appear to stand in no consistent and plausible relation to the carrying capacity of the land. Most decisively, outbreaks of plague, although frequently associated with famines, or at least with crises of subsistence, were as often in advance of such crises as after them, as much perhaps one of their causes as one of their effects. Although the plague does, like other contagious and infectious diseases, tend disproportionately to affect the less well-nourished, there is no physiological reason to suppose that it does so for any other reason than

not a sure one, that between 542 and 1722 plague killed more people on the continent than did any other one disease (Jean-Nöel Biraben, *Les hommes et la peste en France et les pays européennes et méditerranéans*, I, Paris: Mouton, 1975, pp. 22–48, 88–9; Philip Ziegler, *The Black Death*, Harmondsworth: Penguin, 1970, pp. 30–5; Elisabeth Carpentier, 'Autour de la Peste Noire: famines et épidémies dans l'histoire du XIVe siècle', *Annales ESC* 17 (1962), 1062–92 at 1092). Although the most recent general review that I know of (Robert S. Gottfried, *The Black Death: Natural and Human Disaster in Medieval Europe*, New York: Free Press, 1983) takes account of much new work, it is not in my view sound in all its reasoning; Ziegler remains the best (and certainly the best-written) full-length account. Carpentier's summaries of the questions historians have asked of the plague in 'Autour de la peste noire' and *Une ville devant la peste: Orvieto et la Peste Noire de 1348*, Ecole Practique des Hautes Etudes VIe séction, Demographie et Sociétés VII, Paris: SEVPEN, 1962, 8–14 still stand. Her extraordinary *Une ville*, conceived in the *Annales* manner as a total history, is the outstanding account of the plague in one place in the second great outbreak. There are helpful bibliographies of research on plague in Europe in Biraben, Flinn and most recently, Ann G. Carmichael, *Plague and the Poor in Renaissance Florence*, Cambridge: Cambridge University Press, 1986, pp. 172–5. The route by which the plague arrived in Europe in the late 1340s is discussed by Michael Wols, *The Black Death in the Middle East*, Princeton: Princeton University Press, 1977, pp. 35–67, who accepts the older view that it came from western China, and John Norris, 'East or West? The geographic origin of the Black Death', *Bulletin of the History of Medicine* 51 (1977), 1–24, who argues – to me more convincingly – for its origins around the Caspian. Its arrival in Italy was described among others by the chronicler Agnolo di Tura who also described the procession of the *Maestà* in Siena from Duccio's workshop to the cathedral in June 1311 (chapter 4 below and Carpentier, *Une ville*, p. 99).

because lack of nourishment is related to poverty, and poverty, at least in towns and cities, to density of settlement and the associated density of its carriers. Any lingering Malthusianism of this kind can only be an echo of older notions of a divine retribution. Plague is initially exogenous, not endogenous, a function of the relations between its bacillus, its insect vectors, which are fleas, the carriers of the fleas, and man. In its inception, if not its spread and effects on humans, it was and indeed seems to remain 'a tragic accident at variance with the normal course of events'.[3]

Its incidence in human populations is a function of the relations between the bacillus, the fleas, the rodents which usually carry the fleas, and man. These relations are complex and still not fully understood. For an outbreak to occur, the bacillus must be present at the right density in all the relevant populations, and the members of these populations must be at the right level of infectivity. This in turn means that the bacillus must be abundant, the fleas and the fleas' hosts infected, and the hosts susceptible. The permutations of relation within this system, however, are many, and the probabilities of their producing the disease in the hosts are accordingly very variable and in advance of the fact, unknown.

The epidemiologically most consequential of the disputes is between what Emmanuel Le Roy Ladurie has nicely described as the 'English rat flea' and the 'French human flea' schools. Following Yersin's isolation of the bacillus *Yersina pestus* in Hong Kong in 1894, in the course of the third and most recent of the Eurasian pandemics, the pandemic which did not on any scale at all reach Europe, it has more recently been established that in other mammals, plague is primarily a disease of rodents, and that it is transmitted by what Ladurie has in mind as the 'rat fleas' *Xenopsylla cheopsis* and *Cortophylus fasciatus*. The transmission is effected when the flea's stomach becomes blocked with bacilli and it cannot feed

---

[3] On the association between famines and crises of subsistence, Biraben, *Les hommes et la peste*, I, pp. 147–54, also the discussions in François Lebrun, 'Les crises demographiques en France au XVIIè et XVIIIè siècles', *Annales ESC* 35 (1980), 205–34, and Paul Slack, 'Mortality crises and epidemic diseases in England, 1485–1610', in Charles Webster ed., *Health, Medicine and Mortality in the Sixteenth Century*, Cambridge: Cambridge University Press, 1979, especially p. 56.

without disgorging some of these bacilli into its host. This itself is said to be relatively unusual, and so also is the movement of fleas from one species to another. Hence the relative rarity still of infection outside the enzoötic rodents and also, of epizoötics amongst even them. *X. cheopsis*, perhaps the more consequential of the two species of 'rat flea', feeds also and importantly – for the understanding of the disease's transmission to humans – on grain. But both species of flea can and do bite man, who has much the same body temperature as their more usual rodent hosts. *Pulex irritans*, on the other hand, the human flea, seems to be a much less efficient carrier of the bacillus than the *Xenopsylla* or *Cortophylus*. And because the bacillus does not normally cause the degree of septicemia in man that it does in rodents, it has been thought that *P. irritans* ingests too little of this bacillus in its meals of human blood to enable the bacillus to colonise its stomach and so allow the flea to transmit the bacillus from person to person. But more recent work has shown that *P. irritans* can indeed transmit the disease from man to man.

The story, however, is even more complicated than this. *Y. pestis* can itself vary greatly in virulence and infectivity, and does so independently either of the condition of the rodents on which the *Xenopsylla* and *Cortophylus* depend or of the condition of the humans on which the *Pulex* does. The original inception of the plague in human populations, whatever its subsequent incidence in the *Pulex*, is entirely to do with its levels and severity in the two 'rat fleas' and thus in those rodents – tarbagons, marmots, susliks, prairie dogs, squirrels, gerbils, voles and some mice – in which it is enzoötic. It is not, however, enzoötic in rats, who are only infected when the disease reaches epizoötic proportions in the other rodents. Its spread then depends upon its carriers, which in the case of the bubonic form do include rats; in the case of what was in Europe – except in the 1340s – the rarer pneumonic form, droplets in the air. But in wetter and cooler (although not cold) climates, which also favour pneumonic transmission, and where hygiene is also poor, the human flea can transmit the bacillus directly. For some reason, perhaps to do with climate, perhaps to do with the fact that rats, who were its main carriers in the fourteenth century, may not have been present in Europe before the eleventh, and perhaps therefore to do with the fact that *X. cheopsis*, although it feeds most successfully on grain debris, did not have a host which was close to man, the first pandemic, from the middle of the sixth century, seems to have been largely restricted to people who were bitten by fleas that had survived in cargoes of grain which came by sea from the east and were thence transferred into riverine boats. The second pandemic, from the middle of the fourteenth century, certainly started in the same way, with the arrival at Messina at the end of September 1347 of some Genoese ships from the Crimea. But perhaps because black rats were by then widespread in Europe, especially where there was human settlement, and also because settlements, after the long secular increase in population, were more dense, it spread almost everywhere.[4]

III

The account we can give even now of the incidence of the plague in human populations in Europe in the fourteenth century is in-

---

[4] E. Le Roy Ladurie, 'Un concept: l'unification microbienne du monde (XIVe – XVIIe siècles)', *Revue suisse d'histoire* 23 (1973), 627–96 at 632. Leonard Hirst, *The Conquest of Plague: A Study of the Evolution of Epidemiology*, Oxford: Clarendon Press, 1953, especially pp. 236–46. Biraben, *Les hommes et la peste*, I, pp. 7–21, 53–4, 335–7. Hirst and Biraben explain the distinctions between the bubonic, pneumonic and septicemic forms of the disease; at p. 30 Hirst also describes what appear to have been the much rarer cellulocutaneous, tonsillar and vesicular forms. (Also R. Pollitzer, *Plague*, Geneva: World Health Organisation, 1954; Jack D. Poland, 'Plague', in Paul Hoeprich ed., *Infectious Diseases*, 2nd edition, New York: Harper and Row, 1977, pp. 1050–60; M. Baltazard, 'Epidemiology of plague', *WHO Chronicle* 14 (1960), 419–26.) M. I. Finley (*The Ancient Economy*, London: Chatto and Windus, 1973, pp. 107, 126) explains the economics of moving grain in late ancient Europe; *X. cheopsis* can survive in grain debris for about fifty days. It is by no means agreed that the incidence of plague in the fourteenth century was even correlated with, let alone causally connected to, density of population: the incidence was higher in the Dutch countryside, for instance, than in the towns, high in sparsely settled Norway, and in respect of population density, almost random in Cornwall (for Britain, John Hatcher, *Plague, Population and the English Economy, 1348–1530*, London: Macmillan, 1977, p. 24); nevertheless mortality in the towns and cities of France and Italy seems generally to have been about fifty per cent, in the countryside, about thirty per cent. For an argument that the incidence of pneumonic plague in Europe in the summer of 1348, an incidence which is

sufficiently exact to suggest interestingly debatable possibilities. None the less, what we do know about the initial incidence and spread of the disease, as Flinn remarks, is sufficient to make it 'harder to understand how the repetition of epidemics was ever halted'.[5] For plague did begin to fade in western and southern Europe – with the exception of its re-appearance in Provence in 1720 – after the outbreaks of the 1660s. It is the possibilities suggested by the explanations of this decline that I want to explore.

Four explanations have been canvassed. None, however, sufficiently fits the facts. The first, an argument for an increasing natural immunity in humans, has to be set against the fact that the disease continued to affect people in the Balkans, Anatolia and western Asia. And contacts with these places did not cease. Seaborne trade between Europe and the Levant did for a while decline, but it did not disappear; indeed with the extension of empire and the arrival of steam, it increased again in the nineteenth century and in 1906 brought what was then the third Eurasian pandemic, hitherto restricted to east Asia, through the port of Ipswich to the county of Suffolk. The second explanation, an argument for an increasing immunity in rats, is put into doubt by evidence to suggest that the immunity which rats can acquire lasts only for eight or ten years and is not heritable. And if *Y. pseudotuberculosis*, a close relative of the plague bacillus which does give rats a high degree of immunity to plague, did, as some suppose, spread in the early modern period, there is no evidence to support that fact. The third explanation, that the Black Rat, *Rattus rattus*, host to *X. cheopsis* and *C. fasciatus*, was in the early modern period in Europe gradually replaced by the large, stronger and more widely-roaming Brown, *R. norvegicus*, is put into doubt by the fact that the Brown, if possibly less susceptible to the bacillus, is also affected by it. Moreover, the plague contracted from west to east, whereas the Brown Rat invaded from east to west.

The fourth of the longer-standing explanations, the suggestion that there was an internal change in the virulence of the bacillus

suggested by contemporary accounts of many sufferers' symptoms, may have been exacerbated by unusually humid weather, E. Le Roy Ladurie, 'Histoire et climat', *Annales ESC* 14 (1959), 14.

[5] Flinn, *Demographic System*, pp. 57–8.

itself – consistent with the general dictum that less virulent strains of a disease tend in time to replace the more virulent – comes up against the fact that the second great pandemic from the 1340s was at least as devastating as the first, the so-called Justinian plague, the fact that the disease – always supposing that it was the same disease – continued to kill people in eastern and south-eastern Europe into the second half of the nineteenth century, and the fact that it continues to kill – during the war in Vietnam in the late 1960s and early 1970s – still in its third pandemic. (Although plague remains even now enzoötic in desert rodents in the south-western United States and Central and northern South America, it has only rarely moved to man in those places.) For these various reasons, because its gradual disappearance in Europe was so patchy, and because it was itself so poorly correlated to any of the correlates of these factors, it seems increasingly possible that a fifth explanation, that plague was in part reduced and eventually eliminated in Europe by human action, may have force. If the origins of the pandemic, in Carpentier's phrase, were an accident 'at variance with the normal course of [human] events', its diminution and disappearance may not have been.[6]

---

[6] On the relations with trade and the quarantine of ships, Paul Slack, 'The disappearance of plague: an alternative view', *Economic History Review* 34 (1981), 469–76. On the outbreak in Suffolk, D. van Zwanenberg, 'The last epidemic of plague in England? Suffolk 1906–18', *Medical History* 14 (1970), 63–74. On the rats, Biraben, *Les hommes et la peste*, I, pp. 17–18. The Black Rat, a lazy beast, rarely moves more than two hundred metres from where it is born, usually in a house or similar place; the Brown Rat is more adventurous and less dependent on human settlement; but Black Rats do travel on ships: hence the arrival of the plague by sea. On rats' immunity, Pollitzer, *Plague*, pp. 28, 273–4, 303–4, 493–4 and Stephen R. Ell, 'Immunity as a factor in the epidemiology of medieval plague', *Reviews of Infectious Diseases* 6 (1984), 866–79. In Bombay fifty years ago, it was noticed that the proportion of non-susceptible rats was falling in 1936, but rising again in 1939, and the first human cases since 1934 were reported in 1940. A counter-argument for the importance of natural immunity is Andrew Appleby, 'The disappearance of plague: a continuing puzzle', *Economic History Review* 33 (1980), 161–73 (to which Slack, above, is a reply). On variations in strains of the bacillus, Norris, 'East or West?' On *Y. pseudotuberculosis*, Colin McEvedy, 'The bubonic plague', *Scientific American* 258 (2), February 1988, 79. Those who have pressed the claims of the importance of human action in the disappearance of the disease include Biraben (*Les hommes et la peste*, II, summarised at pp. 182–5), Flinn,

IV

It is still difficult to discern what exactly 'plague' refers to in many contemporary accounts. Contemporary identifications of the disease, let alone contemporary explanations of it, were not unnaturally diverse and where not quite wrong, inexact. But primitive induction had suggested to those not altogether content with explanations in terms of God's wrath (or in the Muslim world, His choice of martyrs in a species of holy war), that in what were not at the time but are now distinguished as its bubonic and septicemic forms, it was contagious, and in its pneumonic form, infectious. Florentines, for example, when they knew that Messina had been ravaged in October 1347 – the first appearance of the second pandemic in Europe – and Pisa stricken a month or two later, immediately feared for themselves. With several other communities in Italy, the city authorities attempted to take preventive measures.

Florence's *Statuti sanitari*, the first of their kind of which any record remains, had first been promulgated in 1321, and as soon as the plague reached the city on 3 April 1348, the Captain of the People reasserted them (which in a then conventional conception of sanitation extended to barring prostitutes and sodomites from the city) and also forbade Florentines to associate with Genoese or Pisans. (Travellers from Genoa and also Catalonia had already been proscribed, although ineffectually, in Lucca in the January.) But the disease was already within the walls of Florence, and on 11 April, a full committee of public health was appointed to fight it. The details of the actions that this body took have not survived. But its instructions have. These were to remove 'all putrid matter and infected persons, from which might arise or be induced a corruption of the air'; and it in turn appointed a body the more strictly to enforce the sanitary regulations through the summer. Nevertheless, by the June it confessed itself beaten. Even allowing for the vagueness of the diagnoses, the effects in Florence of the plague, famously

Slack, Steven J. Kunitz ('Speculations on the European mortality decline', *Economic History Review* (1983), 349–64), and – implicitly supposing that the grain-eating X. *cheopis* was largely responsible – Morris Silver ('Controlling grain prices and de-controlling bubonic plague', *Journal of Social and Biological Structures* 5 (1982), 107–20).

described by Boccaccio in the introduction to his *Decameron*, and clear from other accounts, were as severe as they were, for example, in Pistoia, where the commune issued a series of even more comprehensive decrees in the early summer, and also in Orvieto, where the commune was for political reasons in such disarray that it failed to take any steps at all.[7]

Of the cities in northern Italy, only in Milan was the effect of the first outbreak in 1347–48 evidently less severe. But although the authorities there also took steps, which included at once walling up all the inhabitants of houses in which the disease had struck, there is no reason to believe that these had more effect than their presence or absence did elsewhere. None would have done anything to contain the contagion caused by 'rat fleas', because none of them would have done anything to contain the movements of rats; few could imaginably have had a very marked effect on the infection of the pneumonic form; and since isolation was not immediately (and then no doubt unevenly) enforced, the measures would also have done

[7] Details here and in the following paragraphs from Biraben, *Les hommes et la peste*, II; Carpentier, *Une ville*, pp. 131–4 and *passim*; Carmichael, *Plague and the Poor*; and Carlo Cipolla, *Public Health and the Medical Profession in the Renaissance*, Cambridge: Cambridge University Press, 1976; *Faith, Reason and the Plague: a Tuscan Story of the Seventeenth Century*, Brighton: Harvester, 1979, and especially *Fighting the Plague in Seventeenth-Century Italy*, Madison: University of Wisconsin Press, 1981. Islamic conceptions of the disease and of how the afflicted should face it are described by Wols, *Black Death in the Middle East*, pp 84–121; the Prophet himself had denied a pre-Islamic theory of contagion and Wols speculates (pp. 92–3) that one of the reasons for the subsequent persecution of the Andalusian commentator, Ibn al-Khatib, for heresy may have been his rash declaration that 'the existence of contagion is well-established through experience, research, sense perception, autopsy, and authenticated information'. On Rouen, in which, however, there is no evidence that the measures had much effect, Guy Bois, *The Crisis of Feudalism: Economy and Society in Eastern Normandy, c1300–1550*, Cambridge: Cambridge University Press, 1984, pp. 373–4. On Nuremberg, R. Hoeniger, *Der Schwartze Tod in Deutschland*, Berlin: Grosser, 1882, pp. 28–30; on the city at the end of the Middle Ages, Gerald Strauss, *Nuremberg in the Sixteenth Century*, New York: Wiley, 1966, pp. 190–3; and for the contestable conclusion that the preventive measures adopted there could only have served to reduce the incidence of pneumonic plague, Gottfried, *Black Death*, pp. 68–9. One of the minor moves later made against the plague in England was the order issued at Eton College in 1665 that any boy found not smoking, and not thereby keeping the disease at bay, was to be flogged (Biraben, *Les hommes et la peste*, II, p. 181).

little to stop the movement of human fleas. Moreover, from the middle of the fourteenth century at least until the middle of the seventeenth, attempts of this kind were frequently frustrated by the ecclesiastical authorities, who insisted on their right of assembly and procession to pray for the disease to go; by the prejudice of merchants and others who – then as now in areas of the world in which epidemics strike – regarded the physicians' warnings as irritating interferences with the circulation of commerce; by the power of the rich, who were usually granted exemption from orders against elaborate funerals and travel; and by lack of resources.

There is therefore no reason to believe that the low morbidity and mortality in the first outbreak of the disease at the end of the 1340s, not only in Milan but also in other places in which mortality was low – Liège, Tarascon, Munich and Nuremberg, in the Low Countries more generally, southern Poland, the central Ukraine and the central Balkans – was the result of effective prevention. These low rates must have had other causes of which, however, there is no direct evidence and nothing that I can find from which even to attempt an inference. Although it was evident, as it had been in the first pandemic eight hundred years before, that the disease was contagious or infectious, and also perhaps evident that the contagion might be connected with the movement of grain and cloth, no record has come to light of anyone associating it with fleas or, more surprisingly – in view of the fact that they may not have appeared in Europe until about the tenth or eleventh century, and yet were presumably teeming by the middle of the fourteenth – with Black Rats. In so far as there was a common opinion on how it might naturally be transmitted, this opinion expressed itself in references to miasmas and malevolent vapours.

Moreover, most civil authorities in the middle of the fourteenth century, if not in quite so disordered a state as the authorities in Orvieto, were politically, administratively and financially weak; the rural areas, if not the towns and cities, were largely out of their direct control and too densely populated; the disease itself may have been more virulent than later, although not, perhaps, in its bubonic form any more virulent than it was in the last widespread outbreaks in Italy in the middle of the seventeeth century; and in the first outbreak, in the late 1340s, no one was prepared for it. Carpentier, indeed, is understandably surprised at the length of time that it seems to have taken people in Orvieto – although this was not, as I have said, true elsewhere in northern central Italy – even to have realised what was happening. The slowness of response cannot all plausibly be attributed to the inhabitants' other pre-occupations in that particular city, pressing though these seem to have been, or to the selective survival of documents. There is indeed no reason to believe, not just of the politically extreme case of Orvieto, but of anywhere else either, that there is figuratively speaking a possible world which is a mid-fourteenth-century world – a possible world, one could say, which might have branched from the actual world just before the plague arrived in Europe in the autumn of 1347 – in which the plague was effectively contained. Even in the second extensive outbreak, in the early 1360s, most communities seem to have been taken by surprise, perhaps in part because this outbreak was not preceded by any noticeable economic difficulty or climatic abnormality. And some communities, including Milan, were more seriously affected than they had been in the 1340s.

Nevertheless, new measures did begin to be taken a little later. Quarantine, which was not widely adopted on the mainland in Italy until the fifteenth century, was introduced on Venice's small island colony of Ragusa (now Dubrovnik) in 1377. But even before that, there were fierce interventions once again in Milan and also in Mantua. Both cities were ruled by tyrants, and against all the more immediate local interests, the successive Viscontis and Gonzagas tried to stop all traffic into and out of infected areas in their territories. Their penalties were absolute and enforced. They became even more severe at the end of the century, and even though, once the considerable epidemic in 1400 was raging, the authorities could do little more than try to limit the damage, they were doubly remarkable. They revealed exceptional civil powers, and in resting on the rulers' belief that plague was directly contagious, they also went against existing medical opinion. They also had the effect of increasing the amount and accuracy of information about the disease in other regions.[8]

---

[8] Carmichael, *Plague and the Poor*, pp. 110–16.

Through the fifteenth century, into the sixteenth, even into the first half of the nineteenth, the prevailing view among medical men was still that plague arrived on 'venomous atoms' in the air. These were thought to adhere to persons and their artifacts, especially to cloth, and to animals. It accordingly followed not only that circulation had to be stopped, but also that corpses and animals – including rats, although only as one more species, but excluding horses, which did not seem to be affected – had to be destroyed, and that materials, if possible, had to be burnt. The theory was of course mistaken. But if seen simply in its implications for a practical epidemiology, it would not have been wholly inappropriate to effective action. In so far as the disease was being transmitted by 'rat fleas' to man, and given that Black Rats did not ever move very far or very fast, the 'natural' rate of contagion – as among the rodents in which it is enzoötic – might have been slow. Had there been provisions against the movement of grain, it might have been even slower. But food shortages were seen to increase the disaffection of the poor, and for this reason alone importations of grain, for instance from Sicily to Venice in the 1450s, tended to increase. In so far as the disease was being transmitted also by the human flea, restricting circulation and enforcing a degree of isolation could also have slowed it down. And by the middle of the fifteenth century, such restrictions – inevitably less complete than on the island of Ragusa – were in force in much of mainland Italy. (The Venetians connected the fact that they, unusually, had 'pestilence' every year to the large number of refugees from Ottoman expansion to the east who were constantly arriving in the city in the middle of the fifteenth century, and accordingly imposed regulations against them, in desperation even offering them a quarter of a ducat to leave the city.) Unfortunately, however, the possible effects of such restrictions were almost certainly countered by the corollary decision in many places to isolate the poor into special plague hospitals. The sense of contemporaries was that the disease disproportionately affected the poor, and since the rich were usually the first to flee, this had some basis in fact; for this reason, and also because, with the increasing difficulties of maintaining authority during outbreaks, the poor were themselves displaying a disposition to riot (although nowhere so dramatically as they had in Florence in July 1383), *lazaretti* were established in several Italian cities in the 1450s and '60s.[9]

By this time, several European cities, most of them in Italy, but also elsewhere, cities like Rouen and more especially Nuremberg and Augsburg, had established authoritative boards of health. And all these boards took action which was altogether more decisive and perhaps also more effective than any taken by anyone earlier. It was certainly more draconian. It is nevertheless not easy from the evidence to decide how successful it was. Communities which did not experience the plague may, as in the first outbreaks, not have done so for some other reason. But the evidence is at the very least not inconsistent with the view that had such action not been taken, outbreaks, certainly by the early seventeenth century, if not also in the fifteenth and sixteenth, would have been much worse. To support this, there are the known facts of two later attempts.

The first of these was that made against the outbreak in Provence in 1720–22. By then, the idea of a *cordon sanitaire* had taken root, civil authorities had the power to enforce it, and they had the means with which to do so. (It is part of Steven Kunitz's argument that this is one indication of how the European absolutisms did much for public health.) Indeed, the disease might not have spread at all from the ship on which it arrived at Marseille on 25 May to the city and thence to the province if, against the orders of the magistrates in Marseille, some of the cloth that the ship had been carrying had not been sold on the quay. But it did spread. The number of dead in the city, including the ship's crew and the six dockworkers who had unloaded the cloth, had by 23 July exceeded thirty. On 1 August, it was decided to blockade the city, but the necessary number of troops – in what was to be the later blockade of the whole of Provence, one quarter of all France's cavalry was deployed, and one third of its

---

[9] Carmichael, *Plague and the Poor*. She argues that the decision to build *lazaretti* was indeed prompted not by plague itself but by the desire to 'control' the poor. In his treatise *On the Nature and Use of Lots* in 1619, Thomas Gataker reported that doctors in Geneva drew straws to decide who should visit the hospitals (quoted in Jon Elster, *Solomonic Judgements: Studies in the Limitations of Rationality*, Cambridge and Paris: Cambridge University Press and Editions de la Maison des sciences de l'Homme, 1989, p. 64).

infantry – were not in place until 20 August. But by that time, 10,000 people had fled from Marseille and the disease was out. Half of the population of Marseille died, sixty per cent in Toulon, forty-four per cent in Arles and thirty per cent in Aix and Avignon. Nevertheless, blockades were established further afield in France, and also in Piedmont, Switzerland and Spain, and the plague was eventually contained. There were still nearly 100,000 cases in Provence at the end of August 1722, but by the end of that year, the disease had gone. It has not returned again to western Europe in any but extremely small and isolated and immediately contained amounts.[10]

But it continued to affect the east. And by the eighteenth century, Europeans were in no doubt at all that it was from the Ottoman east that the disease always came. The second episode that makes the point that had something not been done against it, the plague might have continued to affect Europe even into the nineteenth century; and that if what was done against it earlier had been done at the same time elsewhere, its incidence and effects might have been reduced before; is the Habsburg authorities' decision after the Peace of Passarowitz in 1719. In a series of decrees, the *Pestpatente*, between 1728 and 1770, these authorities turned the 1,900-kilometre frontier between the Habsburg and Ottoman empires into what may remain the most extensive *cordon sanitaire* that any authority has ever imposed. Movement across this frontier was controlled by an army of peasants who, in return for a five-month service on the frontier each year, had been granted land in the newly conquered territories. In normal times, this frontier was also manned by a force of 4,000 full-time soldiers. When a newly established intelligence service brought news of plague in any part of the Ottoman empire, this frontier force was at once increased to

[10] The outbreak in Provence in 1720–2 is summarised by Biraben, *Les hommes et la peste* I, pp. 230–2, who provides a more detailed account in 'Certain demographic characteristics of the plague epidemic in France, 1720–22', in D. V. Glass and Roger Revelle eds., *Population and Social Change*, London: Arnold, 1972, pp. 233–41. There is a vivid description of some apparently effective measures taken in one community at the foot of the Luberon, then half a day's ride from Marseille to the north, by Thomas F. Sheppard, *Lourmarin in the Eighteenth Century: A Study of a French Town*, Baltimore: Johns Hopkins University Press, 1971, pp. 116–27.

7,000. When the intelligence brought news of plague in any part of the southern Balkans, on the Moldau, in Wallachia, Serbia, or Bosnia, it was increased to 11,000. At this point, each post was in sight of the next by day and within shouting distance of the next by night. The quarantine for any man or animal crossing the frontier was twenty-one days in normal times, forty-two when there was news of plague far to the east, eighty-four when there was news of it in the Balkans. All travellers were disinfected and any traveller who disobeyed any of these rules was shot.

This organisation was maintained until 1873. It was, even so, not entirely successful, but incidents of plague in the Habsburg territories were few and easily contained. The Turkish authorities were still refusing to co-operate in the *cordon* in 1824; but ten years later, after a serious outbreak of plague on the Anatolian plateau, they agreed to do so, and in 1840 they at last took comparable steps in their own territory. With the what were by then entirely effective quarantine arrangements at all the Mediterranean ports, the disease was finally pushed back into Asia, where – apart from minor outbreaks in the enzoötic area around the Caspian, the third pandemic in eastern Asia which broke at the end of the nineteenth century, the disruptions and devastations of the war in South-east Asia in the late 1960s and early 1970s, and outside Africa and southern America, that's to say, the southern states of the United States, Central America, and South America – it has since remained.[11]

V

It therefore seems clear that the effective containment of the plague in Europe in the two great pandemics, the first from the sixth century, the second from the fourteenth, did not depend, as Carlo Cipolla can be taken to imply, on knowing anything very accurate and precise about its aetiology. It depended rather on effective

[11] E. Lesky, 'Die österreichische Pestfront an der K. K. Militärgrenze', *Speculum* 8 (1957), 82–106, summarised by Flinn, *Demographic System*, pp. 60–1. G. Rothenburg, 'The Austrian sanitary cordon and the control of bubonic plague, 1710–1871', *Journal of the History of Medicine and Allied Sciences* 28 (1973), 15–23. Biraben, *Les hommes et la peste*, II, p. 175.

containment itself, on limiting the circulation of men and goods, and also on hygiene. Even in the middle of what may most simply be described as the superstitions about the disease in the first of the two European pandemics, a few, like the Bishop of Clermont in the early 650s, saw that this was so. But neither he nor anyone else in the Justinian plague had the means with which to effect their convictions. Indeed, the effects of this first pandemic no doubt did much to reduce what organisation there was and to reduce the means to pay for it. They almost certainly put paid to Justinian's own attempts to strengthen the empire by weakening the territory he held, and thereby making it more accessible to populations from the north which had been less affected by the disease. Agreement about what had to be done, the administrative means with which to do it, and the money with which to pay for it, were then, as for the next thousand years, at a premium. The possibility that attempts to contain it could have had some success is only plausible later. The interesting question, therefore, is whether what had been attempted in most of the northern Italian cities (and in one or two other places, like Augsburg and Nuremberg) by the beginning of the seventeenth century, and attempted more effectively in the Mediterranean and in the south-eastern part of the Habsburg empire by the eighteenth, could have successfully been attempted much earlier and more widely.

At first sight it seems that it could. The French and the British were already remarking on the Italian arrangements in the seventeenth century. The Dutch and many others were remarking on them by the beginning of the eighteenth. There certainly seems to have been no lack of knowledge of what to do and of what, in Italy, was actually being done. Nor, can one presume, was it merely a matter of money, although it is true that in Milan in 1576, not then a poor city, the disinfecting of nearly 9,000 rooms and the feeding of those who had been moved out of them into quarantine emptied the city's coffers in four days. But the health boards were well aware that the measures they imposed often had disastrous consequences for commerce and manufacture, for employment, and thus for the revenues on which they themselves and their measures for public health depended. It was a question of priorities, as contemporary Italians themselves said of Germany and Flanders. If

a few cities elsewhere, like Nuremberg in the first half of the sixteenth century and Rheims a hundred years later, could institute
measures every bit as wide in their scope and as meticulous in their
provisions as those in the cities in northern Italy, it is in principle
possible that others, if not all, could have done so too. Why then
did they not?

One part of the answer certainly does seem to be that they did
not consider it the first priority. But one has still to ask, even if they
had, could they have acted to any effect? The political complexion
of several of the Italian city governments of the time, a complexion
evident also in Nuremberg, was unusual. These governments were
directed by noble families – in Nuremberg by a less obviously noble
but nevertheless rich, secure and authoritative if not indeed authoritarian oligarchy – and by senates generally responsible, often
simply beholden, to these families. They were able to be ruthless
and when they wished to be, were. Bernabò Visconti in Milan and
Ludovico Gonzaga in Mantua had taken drastic action as early as
the late fourteenth century. In the later measures, taxes were imposed upon merchants to pay for the new measures, and commerce
was at times interrupted. In Venice, the health officers had powers
of arrest and torture over those who disobeyed them; in Milan and
Mantua they had the power of death itself. 'The insatiable merchants', as a Milanese chronicler reported in 1628, did no doubt
attempt to undermine 'all health measures contrary to their interest'. But in so doing, they ran a risk. (The Church was even
more impotent. The Pope's excommunication of all of Florence's
health officers in 1630 appears to have done nothing to reduce their
efforts.) As a Florentine put it in the same year, the magistrate of
public health 'is a supreme magistrate with the authority of absolute
rule granted to him by his Most Serene Grand Duke in cases
of contagion'.[12]

Such capacities were absent elsewhere. In what is now North
Rhine Westphalia in the seventeenth century, for example, town
councils did take some fitful measures, but not, it seems, with any

[12] For a sense of the care with which the Florentine authorities enforced their
measures in the plague of 1630–3, Guilia Calvi, Dario Bocca and Bryant T.
Ragan trans., *Histories of a Plague Year: The Social and the Imaginary in Baroque
Florence*, Berkeley: University of California Press, 1989.

great determination. In the outbreak there in 1626, they were criticised for not doing more, and doing it more decisively, by their
prince and the bishop of Münster. All the prince himself was politically able to do, however, was to suspend some of the few privi-
leges that remained in his gift, including that of holding markets.
Such capacities were even less evident in the Low Countries, northern France and England; as an English visitor to Venice wrote home
in 1600, they would have been inimical to the overriding interest
in his own country in 'free traffique'. The point is a political one.
The English authorities did not have the priorities or perhaps the
directive capacities of the Italian and south German cities. Plague,
an early seventeenth-century Englishman observed, 'flourished in
narrow lanes, alleys and other pestered and noisome corners where
families of poor people are thronged together as men used to pile
wool sacks one upon another'. But Paul Slack's work on the English
west country makes it plain that although these English authorities
could have done more than they did, they chose on the whole, and
certainly by comparison with those in Italy and southern Germany,
not to attempt to.[13]

It nevertheless remains the case that although for these political
reasons one can see why fierce controls were not imposed in many
other places in Europe, one cannot so immediately see why they
were not imposed more widely where they were, in Italy and
southern Germany, at an earlier time. Cipolla suggests that the
origin of the effective health boards in early sixteenth-century Italy
lies in the conjunction there by that time of extensive medical
schools in the universities and of relatively well-established medical
guilds. The example of Nuremberg, however, with no university

---

[13] Most of the facts in this paragraph, but not the argument, largely from
Cipolla, *Public Health*, 1976, pp. 11–66. On Milan and Mantua in the late
fourteenth and fifteenth centuries, Carmichael, *Plague and the Poor*, pp. 111–
16. On Rheims, Dr Langlet, *Un bureau de santé au XVIIe siècle: la peste de 1635*,
Reims: Michaud, 1893. On North Rhine Westphalia, I draw on as yet
unpublished work by Neithard Bulst. On the west of England, Slack, 'Mortality
crises', 48. A self-interested exception in England had earlier been the queen
herself, who in 1563 ordered a gallows to be erected in Windsor on which to
hang anyone running from the plague in London and thereby threatening the
health of the court in her castle (Charles Creighton, *History of Epidemics in
Britain*, I, Cambridge: Cambridge University Press, 1891, p. 317).

and more unusually – so wary were the oligarchs of possible counters to their power – no guilds either, makes one doubt that Cipolla's pre-conditions were essential. There was also no medical school in late medieval Florence. And the Viscontis in Milan and the Gonzagas in Mantua deliberately went against the medical advice they were given. What was decisive, these examples suggest, but what Cipolla only emphasises when he comes to explain the eventual collapse of the Italian health boards in the eighteenth century, at just the time at which effective boards were being established elsewhere, was the authority of the city administrations. There were of course more and more informed medical men in the seventeenth century than in the fourteenth. (In poor and politically disordered Orvieto at the end of the 1340s, the commune was only able to afford one doctor, and he was a student just half-way through his studies.) But in the seventeenth century, the doctors' understanding of the aetiology and epidemiology of the plague was no more advanced than it had been a thousand years before. The crucial fact is that by the sixteenth century, in Italy and in one or two other places, like Nuremberg, the health boards were given full and overriding authority by those who appointed them. The governments in these cities were exceptionally independent in the matter of raising taxes and exercising other forms of control over owners of property and also and perhaps crucially over commercial life. And at least some of these governments, like those of Milan and Mantua and to a lesser extent Venice, already had such powers in the last quarter of the fourteenth century. Some did even then take decisive action, although as I have already said, it was action that was at that time unlikely to have more than a marginal effect.

The answer must in the end be open. Even though the possibility that deliberate containment was important in reducing the incidence of the disease, the aetiology and epidemiology, as I have said, together contain too many conditional probabilities to enable one to decide. But the general direction of the answer does seem to be clear. Effectively controlling the spread and effects of the plague appears to have been a function of the will to do so, of the political ability to impose the will, and of the organisational capacity to carry that imposition through. There is little doubt that by the early sixteenth century, these conditions were more effectively met in the northern Italian cities than they were almost anywhere else. There is rather more doubt about whether they were met anywhere at all much earlier. The first outbreak of the disease in 1347 and 1348 took everyone by surprise, and although it disproportionately affected the poor, it did also affect the rich. But by the time that the authorities collected themselves to act it was, in every case, too late. The subsequent outbreaks of the disease in the later fourteenth century appear to have been equally unexpected. By the end of that century, however, there are the first signs of preparation. The most reasonable conclusion would seem to be that it took a very long time, as much as a hundred and fifty years, for it to be realised just how comprehensive the measures had to be. When it was, it was only also realised in a very few places that if the measures were to be effective, they had to take priority over every other interest. And that in turn required an authoritarian politics, not beholden to commercial pressures, and formidable resources.

More exactly, there are three possibilities. The first is one in which thinking Europeans took the view much earlier than they did that action could be taken against events like the plague. The second is one in which, in taking this view, they put such action as their highest priority. The third is one in which in putting it as their highest priority, they also had the means with which to effect it. The first possibility is too far away from actuality to be readily entertainable. Too much else would have had to be different. More exactly, there would have had to be a lively memory in the mid-fourteenth century, when the plague first struck, of the nature of the epidemic in southern Europe eight centuries before, and of the opinions of those like the Bishop of Clermont on what to do against it. But the means with which to carry such a memory and revive it did not exist, and were not to do so until the widespread use of printing more than a century later.

The second and third possibilities, however, are ones which were actual even as early as the 1370s. Less, one therefore supposes, would have had to be different for either of them to be actual elsewhere. So it would seem that although it is implausible to suppose that the measures which were eventually taken against plague could, in any world that is recognisable as the late medieval world, have been taken more than a hundred years or so before they were, once they actually were taken, as they were in Italy, and once they were known, as they were by visitors to Italy, they could have been attempted elsewhere. England, Holland, northern France and northern Germany in the sixteenth century were in this respect less distant from contemporary Italy than contemporary Italy was from the Italy of a hundred and fifty years before. Yet it seems less, and not more, reasonable to suppose that had the measures been attempted in the north, they could in the political circumstances there at the time have had an equal effect. Of the three possibilities, the first and the third are more distant from the places in which the plague was not controlled in the sixteenth and early seventeenth centuries than is the second. This enables one to dispense with, or at least to distance oneself from, explanations for the disappearance of the disease which are as exogenous as those which one accepts for its first appearance (unless one implausibly supposes that having reached the Crimea overland from Asia, it would then have stopped but for the Genoese boats leaving the Crimea for Sicily); it enables one more precisely to define the force of Jean-Nöel Biraben's judgement that 'the role of *bureaux de santé* with dictatorial powers was crucial'; and it leaves intact the epidemiologically obvious corollary that once these powers were exercised by the port authorities everywhere in the Mediterranean, and by the Habsburg authorities on land to the east, the continent was clear.[14]

VI

Pursuing the possibilities suggested by the existing explanations of the decline of the plague in Europe between the fourteenth century and the eighteenth delivers an answer, which even if provisional, casts doubt on the view that the course of the disease, as distinct from its inception, was immutable, and that its eventual elimination was a complete accident 'at variance', in Carpentier's phrase, 'with the normal advance of [human] events'. It also delivers an answer

---

[14] Biraben, *Les hommes et la peste*, II, pp. 143. Cipolla has no taste for counterfactual speculation and refuses to be drawn on Biraben's judgement (*Public Health*, p. 64).

which at first sight fails in any clear and simple way to privilege 'laws' over circumstance. The laws at issue are biological, more strictly so than Braudel would mean, but, as laws of the aetiology of the disease, conditional, in ways that even now biologists do not entirely understand. It is circumstances, the ecological circumstances of the rodents in which, in western Asia, the disease is enzoötic, of the Black Rat, the rat fleas and the human flea, and of the bacillus itself, together with the environmental, cognitive, emotional, technical, economic, political, and social circumstances of human Europe over four hundred years, which predominate. If therefore it is a 'theory', as Jon Elster once had it, which enables us to decide how warrantable a counterfactual is, it is in this instance a theory only in the sense of a more or less plausible picture of an extremely complex – and here, very imperfectly known and intrinsically indeterminate – combination of circumstances, and of the likelihood of this combination occurring at other times and places, with similar consequences to those that the actual combination had where it did occur.[15]

More exactly, if it is a theory, or a set of theories, about the causal connections between various kinds of preventive measure and the incidence and effects of the disease, and in turn, about the cognitive, emotional, economic, social and political causes of these kinds of measure, a theory or set of theories which is itself so hedged in by conditions, many of which are themselves more or less clearly connected; then to insist that it is a theory or set of theories which warrants the counterfactuals is to say something that may in principle be correct but is in practice idle. And yet, if we collapse instead to the conclusion that it is 'chance' that governs events, it is in this example chance in the extended and uninteresting sense of an intelligible and explicable even if complicated and unreplicable, and certainly not pre-determined, combination of circumstances. To think simply in terms of theory or chance is to fail to see how our interpretation of why what happened did turns not only on states of affairs that were beyond human control but also on an assessment of practical reasoning and public powers.

[15] Jon Elster, *Logic and Society: Contradictions and Possible Worlds*, Chichester: Wiley, 1978, pp. 184, 191; see also chapter 1, note 32.

VII

Nevertheless, assessing the alternative possible courses of the plague that are suggested by the available explanations of it is in one respect at least straightforward: we can assume that people had an interest in reducing its effects. This may not always, as I have said, have been their overriding interest; but in Christian Europe, provided, in some places, that too much else was not disturbed, no one actually wanted an epidemic to take its course. If thinking people did not at first grasp that the course and consequences of plague could be alleviated, that is because they did not know facts that we now do. Contemporary Muslims, unlike Christians, did have a complicating conviction that it would be against the teaching of the Prophet if they acted on what facts they had; but they also had few. Even then, if this countervailing complication, which led to Ibn al-Khatib's prosecution in Andalusia for heresy for suggesting that there were natural causes of the contagion and practical measures to be taken against it, had been overriding, then one might infer that the later Ottoman authorities and others to the east would never have agreed to take any steps. But, albeit belatedly, they did. There is no good reason not usually to assume an interest, if not always an overriding interest, in reducing morbidity and mortality.

No such assumption, though, can be made for that part of the 'biological regime' of early modern Europe which depended on levels of fertility. Yet the view once again from France might lead one to believe that the question of different possible interests in reproduction is beside the point. Fertility, so the conventional wisdom used to have it, was like morbidity and mortality, beyond deliberate control. 'Couples', as Bourgeois-Pichat had said, 'had the number of children that society or biology decided to give them', and that was that. There may, figuratively speaking, have been possible worlds in which they wanted more or fewer, but these are worlds that are too far away from the actual, and if not just implausible, then once again idle to consider. But there was already a suspicion by the time that Bourgeois-Pichat put his view in the late 1960s, that the later age at marriage and indeed its lower incidence in western Europe since at least 1500 may not – as uninformed common sense might also suggest – have been entirely unchosen; and more recent research on the fertility of these early modern European

Table 1 *Age at marriage and celibacy*

Year in which cohort reached age 25	Female age at marriage		Celibacy*	
	France	England	France	England
1675–99	24.7	26.6	59	230
1700–24	25.0	26.8	69	128
1725–49	25.6	25.8	78	107
1750–74	25.9	25.6	99	36
1775–99	26.3	24.7	113	72
1800–24	26.0	24.1	136	75
1825–49	25.7		128	119
1850–74	24.6		115	

* Surviving never-married women per thousand surviving women at age 50 (France) and 40–4 (England)

France (years of marriage)	TMFR*	England (period)	TMFR
1690–1719	8.36	1600–49	7.03
1720–39	8.46	1650–99	6.92
1740–69	8.35	1700–49	6.77
1770–89	7.88	1750–99	6.92
1790–1819	6.94		

* Total marital fertility rate: age-specific fertility in marriage for each five-year period 15–49 summed to give total fertility in marriage for a hypothetical cohort of women surviving to the end of the fecund period.

populations has suggested that levels of age-specific marital fertility (which discount the age at marriage itself) were frequently lower than we would expect them to have been if there was no deliberate control of births. Assessing the mutability of reproduction, in the most literal sense, in early modern Europe is necessarily to assess not only the fixity of its conditions but also the interests that couples had in it. And because of the research that has recently been done, and because of the similarities and differences which in this respect it shows, the most illuminating assessment of this mutability lies in comparisons and contrasts between Britain and France.

The contrasts in rates of nuptiality and fertility are shown in table 1.

The similarities and differences are clear. In both societies, the age at marriage was high. In France, it rose slightly in the eighteenth century and the first half of the nineteenth, to fall back again to the level it had been at the end of the seventeenth. In England, it fell slowly throughout the period. The two rates converged in the nineteenth century. In England, however, the incidence of marriage was initially much lower, and rose, whereas in France, it was initially much higher, and fell. In each country, marital fertility converged at the end of the eighteenth century, but in France, from a level that had been much higher at the end of the seventeenth. Nevertheless, there was no parallel in England to the evident brake applied by the French on both marriage and marital fertility from the years immediately before the Revolution.[16]

But these aggregate rates disguise what were in France, but to a much lesser extent in England, considerable regional variations in total marital fertility:

Table 2 *TMFR by age at marriage*

France 1670–1769	15–19	20–24	25–29
NE	8.79	6.90	4.94
NW	7.54	6.03	4.29
SE	7.25	6.33	4.55
SW	6.49	5.75	4.20
England 1600–1799	6.19	5.02	3.56

Fertility in marriage in England was always lower than it was in France. But the differences within France were nevertheless greater than the difference between the mean for the country as a whole and the mean for England.[17]

[16] D. R. Weir, 'Life under pressure: France and England, 1670–1870', *Journal of Economic History* 44 (1984), 27–47, at 33–4. It should be said that Weir is concerned to show against Wrigley and Schofield that there was no marked difference between the demographic regimes of early modern France and England.

[17] E. A. Wrigley and R. S. Schofield, 'English population history from family reconstitution: summary results 1600–1799', *Population Studies* 37 (1983), 157–84, at 173. The French data are pooled from various reconstitutions,

Malthus's *First Essay*, which he wrote in 1798, would lead one to believe that in all pre-industrial societies there was a pressure of population on resources. Rates of population growth always threatened to outrun rates of growth in the production of food. Such pressure undoubtedly existed. D. F. Weir has calculated that a twofold rise in the price of grain in France in any year between 1670 and 1732 might have increased the death rate in that year by about 150 per cent; in England, he believes, it would have done so by 120 per cent. Similarly, a twofold rise in the price of grain in any one year between 1740 and 1789 would have produced by the end of the next five years a shortfall of marriages in France of sixty-one per cent, in England of eleven per cent. Weir infers from this that there was, at least in respect of what Malthus called the 'positive checks' of resources on population, little difference between the two countries. If he is right, we do not seem to be able so confidently to say, as E. A. Wrigley and R. S. Schofield do, that one society was at a 'high-pressure' and the other at a 'low-pressure' 'equilibrium'; that the French, living always near the limit of their available resources, were markedly more susceptible to shortfalls in those resources than the English, who instead displayed what Wrigley has described as a 'dilatory homeostasis, winning the war of adjustment, but doing so

referred to in the notes to Wrigley and Schofield's original table. The data for S. W. France are for the periods 1720–39 and 1740–69 only. The English data are pooled from the reconstitutions of thirteen parishes, six in the north and north Midlands, five in the south Midlands, and two in Devon. An instance of the extremes to be found in France is the contrast between Sainghin-en-Melantois (Nord) and Thezels and Saint-Sernin (Lot): in the first, the TMFR for women married at twenty and surviving until forty-nine would have been 10.6, which approaches the highest levels recorded anywhere outside French Canada at the end of the seventeenth century; in the second, it would have been 6.6 (E. A. Wrigley, *Population and History*, London: Weidenfeld and Nicolson, 1969, p. 122). There are more general summary comparisons in Louis Henry and Didier Blanchet, 'La population de l'Angleterre de 1541 à 1871' (a summary and review of E. A. Wrigley and R. S. Schofield, *The Population History of England 1541–1871*, London: Arnold, 1981), *Population* 38 (1983), 792. Also Wrigley and Schofield, *Population History*, 1981, pp. 247–8, 478–80, where there is a comparison between England, France and Sweden from the 1750s to the 1850s; and for France, the special issue of *Population* 30 (1975), and the brief but clear discussion by Jacques Dupâquier, *La population française aux XVIIe et XVIIIe siècles*, Paris: Presses Universitaires de France, 1979, especially pp. 52–3, 108–9.

by employing a strategy appropriate to yesterday's circumstances'. The truth appears to lie between.

It would nevertheless be a mistake, as the figures show, to suppose that all the checks on population in France were 'positive'. The French responded even more markedly than the English with the 'preventive' means of marriage. But the positive checks they experienced and the preventive checks they imposed on themselves were both more extreme, or so Weir's calculations suggest, than were those in England. As Wrigley and Schofield say, they did appear always to be living nearer the limit. The explanatory question is why? Would they not have had an interest in not living so near the limit, and having had such an interest, have been able to realise it? It seems on the face of it unlikely that people would knowingly wish to put themselves so repeatedly at risk.[18]

VIII

Two answers to the simplest explanatory question can be eliminated at once. Both societies had long exhibited what has come to be called the 'European marriage pattern', a pattern of marriage in the late twenties, even occasionally, in England, into the early thirties; this indeed appears to have characterised almost all parts of all societies west of a line from what is now Leningrad to Trieste from at least the beginning of the sixteenth century. Neither society, therefore, can be presumed to have had to extricate itself, like so many economically comparable ones elsewhere in the world in the later twentieth century, from a pattern of very early marriage. Similarly, there is no suggestion that methods of controlling births within marriage were unknown in either society until the eighteenth century. Wrigley's reconstruction of the revealingly long intervals

---

[18] Weir, 'Life under pressure', 39. Schofield summarises his and Wrigley's view in 'The impact of scarcity and plenty on population change in England, 1541–1871', *Journal of Interdisciplinary History* 16 (1983), 265–91. Lebrun ('Les crises démographiques') briefly summarises the nature and extent of crises in France in the century or so before the Revolution; also, on regional differences and on the exact nature of the crisis immediately before the Revolution in particular, Olwen Hufton, 'Social conflict and the grain supply in eighteenth-century France', *Journal of Interdisciplinary History* 14 (1983), 303–31.

between the penultimate birth and the last in the Devon parish of Colyton in the later seventeenth century, and Pierre Goubert's report of comparably long intervals in south-western France before 1750, make one suspicious of remarks (like Goubert's own about the Bretons, who had unusually high rates of fertility even for their region) that there were populations 'ignorant of all birth control'. For as long as people have known how to have children, they have also known how – if not always effectively or very pleasantly – not to do so.[19]

[19] John Hajnal, 'European marriage patterns in perspective', in D. V. Glass and D. E. C. Eversley eds., *Population in History*, pp. 101–43. This pattern may have existed in north-western Europe since at least 1200 (Richard M. Smith, 'Some reflections on the evidence for the origins of the "European marriage pattern" in England', in Christopher Harris ed., *The Sociology of the Family*, Keele (England): Sociological Review, 1979, and Hajnal 'Two kinds of pre-industrial household formation system', *Population and Development Review* 8 (1982), 449–94 at 477). Alan Macfarlane's implication (*The Origins of English Individualism: The Family, Property and Social Transition*, Oxford: Blackwell, 1978, pp. 156–61) that the 'north-west European' pattern of household formation and marriage was restricted to England seems thus to be mistaken. His, however, is a full account – Hajnal's is the most systematic – of how the pattern seems to have worked. Also Smith (1981), note 20. E. A. Wrigley, 'Family limitation in pre-industrial England', *Economic History Review* 19 (1966), 82–109; this is challenged by R. B. Morrow, 'Family limitation in pre-industrial England: a reappraisal', 31 (1978), 419–28 and answered by Wrigley, 31 (1978), 429–36; Pierre Goubert, 'Legitimate fertility and infant mortality in France during the eighteenth century: a comparison', in Glass and Revelle eds., *Population and Social Change*, pp. 321–30. One sense to be given to the unavoidably indeterminate notion of 'natural fertility', the fertility rate a married population would have if none of its members was deliberately trying to control births or conceptions, is Coale's: fertility for any population as a proportion of the marital fertility of Hutterites in the 1920s. In France, marital fertility was by this measure 0.465 by 1870, whereas in England and Wales it was still 0.693. No other country in Europe, with the exception by 1880 of Hungary, had fallen below 0.639. The mean for the continent was 0.688. Coale has suggested that 0.7 may be taken to mark the point at which some control of fertility within marriage is taking place (Ansley J. Coale, 'The decline of fertility in Europe from the French Revolution to World War II', in S. J. Behrman, Leslie Corsa and Ronald Freedman eds., *Fertility and Family Planning: A World View*, Ann Arbor: University of Michigan Press, 1969, pp. 3–24; with Roy Treadway, 'A summary of changing fertility in the provinces of Europe', Paper given at the Summary Conference on European Fertility, Office of Population Research, Princeton University, July 1979). Etienne van de Walle, 'Alone in Europe: the French fertility decline until 1850', in Charles Tilly ed., *Historical*

The answer to the explanatory question appears to lie in two distinct and themselves quite separate states of affairs. The first is revealed in the correlates of the incidence of marriage. In England until the middle of the eighteenth century, marriage was not only much less widespread than in most of France. It was also, as Weir and Ronald Lee have shown, less immediately responsive to the price of grain and yet more responsive, although often with a delay of several decades, to the wage rate. These are each crucial. Richard Smith, John Hajnal and Richard Wall have argued for England and for north-western Europe more generally that there was a high and fluctuating proportion, somewhere between ten and twenty per cent, of living-in servants, who may be thought of as wage-labourers. These were usually young, between the ages of fifteen and thirty, and of both sexes. This produced a distinctive pattern of entry into marriage. As Smith describes it, when real incomes fell 'it was likely that service fell away in importance . . . Conversely, when real wages rose and when it might be supposed that young men and women would have the resources to set up new households and marry, farmers in their demand for permanent living-in labour retained servants longer in the household. Both influences would slow down the speed with which nuptiality declined in periods of real wage falls ([in England in the] late sixteenth or late eighteenth century) while inhibiting the pace of nuptiality revival in phases of real wage rise (mid-seventeenth to mid-eighteenth centuries).' Thus was marriage restrained, and thus fertility too. The check to growth was 'preventive'. The contrary pattern, clear in much of France, was one of economically and socially self-contained peasant families, existing in some form or another of joint arrangement, who were dependent upon family labour and thus upon a high rate of fertility,

Studies of Changing Fertility, Princeton: Princeton University Press, 1978, pp. 257–88 at p. 288. Van de Walle discusses the decline in France and not the pre-decline patterns either there or in England. For an alternative account of the decline in France, more consistent with my discussion here except in its recourse to a model of homeostasis, Wrigley, 'The fall of marital fertility in nineteenth-century France', in *People, Cities and Wealth: The Transformation of Traditional Society*, Oxford: Clarendon Press, 1987, pp. 270–321. Braudel, looking at Europe, Asia and America, in all of which fertility was in general on something of a downward course in the eighteenth century, did not see France as exceptional (*Capitalism and Material Life*, pp. 1–5).

which – even where marriage was late, as it was in Brittany itself
and in other parts of western Europe – had the consequence both of
inducing a high level of infant mortality and of producing a general
level of population which was more dangerously near the limit of
resources, and accordingly more likely to respond more immediately
to a sudden shortfall in those resources.[20]

English agriculture in the seventeenth and eighteenth centuries
was in general more productive than most agriculture in Europe to
the south and east. And its productivity and the amount of food
available per head were rising. (As Malthus explained, this is why
he took rates of agricultural production in England as the basis for
his estimate of the maximum possible rate of increase in resources.)
But once again, comparison suggests that this does not explain the
distinctiveness of the English agricultural labour market, or its consequences for household formation and fertility. For the English
pattern of household formation was a north-west European pattern,
and appears to have prevailed in at least one other society, Iceland,
in which agricultural production was as much for mere subsistence as
it was anywhere in Europe, north, west, east or south. Moreover,
the origins of the pattern may go back well beyond the beginning
of the seventeenth, sixteenth, even fourteenth centuries, at which
time the economic distinctiveness of north-west European agriculture becomes much less easy to see. There does not therefore appear

[20] Richard M. Smith, 'Fertility, economy and household formation in
England over three centuries', *Population and Development Review* 7 (1981),
595–622, the quotation at 604; Hajnal, 'Two kinds'; Richard Wall, 'The
household: demographic and economic change in England, 1650–1970', in
Richard Wall ed., *Family Forms in Historic Europe*, Cambridge: Cambridge
University Press, 1983, pp. 493–512. On France, Jean-Louis Flandrin, Richard
Southern trans., *Families in Former Times: Kinship, Household and Sexuality*,
Cambridge: Cambridge University Press, 1979, especially pp. 72–3. On the
relation with wage rates, Ronald Lee, 'Population homeostasis and English
demographic history', in R. S. Schofield and E. A. Wrigley eds., *Population and
Economy: From the Traditional to the Modern World*, Cambridge: Cambridge
University Press, 1986, pp. 75–100. There is a vivid account of the situation of
household servants in Norway (including their ingenious dealings with the
demands of sexual desire) in Michael Drake, *Population and Society in Norway,
1735–1865*, Cambridge: Cambridge University Press, 1969, pp. 133–49.
Wrigley and Schofield, *Population History*, pp. 402–53. On France, Goubert's
classic account, *Cent milles provinciaux au XVIIe siècle: Beauvais et les Beauvasis
1600–1730*, Paris: SEVPEN, I, 45–59.

to be any more purely economic reason to believe that the late fis-
sion of subsequently independent households, and so also later ages
at marriage and lower rates of marital fertility, could not have obtained in Brittany or southern France or anywhere else outside the
'north-western' area. The explanation for their absence would seem
to lie elsewhere. And it may well lie further back; for if Jack Goody
is right, 'once established as a trend, a particular age of marriage
may be difficult to vary; a late or early age may have to continue as
a norm in situations very different from those in which it had its
functional origins, not as a survival, but because people are locked
into a particular system'.[21]

Nevertheless, and not just for those for whom such a conclusion is
dissatisfying, a puzzle still remains. If marriage was late in France,
and can be explained by the prevalence there – on farms which did
not just use family labour – of the kind of labour market that has
been described by Wall and Smith and others for England and by
Michael Drake for a proportion of farms in Norway; then why, at
least in northern France, was fertility within marriage much higher
than in rural areas in England and Norway? The answer may lie in a
second state of affairs, one which does not so much divide north-
western Europe from the rest as divide north-western Europe itself,
and which can most simply be described as the means of insuring for
risk.

In England, there had for a very long time been poor relief. This
was initially provided by manors and guilds, later by parishes, later
still by Poor Law Unions. But through all these changes of provision
there were remarkably similar specifications of who was eligible.
Students of fertility in all sorts of poor societies have come to emphasise the importance of these communal institutions for reducing
the risks that families have themselves to bear, although there is no
agreement on the likely effect of such institutions on the demand
for children: some suggest that in reducing the family's exposure to
risk, such provisions make it more lax in its control of reproduction,
others suggest the opposite. Ron Lesthaeghe, considering the pos-

[21] On agricultural productivity in England, Wrigley in Schofield and Wrigley,
eds., *Population and Economy*, 1986, p. 142. On Iceland, Hajnal, 'Two kinds',
474, 477. Jack Goody, *The Development of the Family and Marriage in Europe*,
Cambridge: Cambridge University Press, 1983, pp. 209–10.

sible effect of these institutions on fertility in Europe at the end of the early modern period and the beginning of the modern, takes the second view, and so do I. 'The extent of risk-sharing across social class boundaries', he argues, 'is a good measure of the degree of social integration' in the society, and 'a high degree of integration corresponds with a greater preponderance of "preventive checks" over the "positive" ones that operate via mortality shocks or overall low life expectancy'. One would accordingly expect the reliance on kin and thus on children and higher fertility to be lower in these societies than in others.

England did not suffer the number of serious subsistence crises that France did in the years of what Goubert has called the *courbe tourmentée*, not so much because crops failed less often, or even because of its concentration on large farms growing grain (French agriculture was in many places in the centre and north of the country increasingly similar); but because, unlike France, it had communal institutions through which effectively to relieve hardship. In France, even in what François Lebrun calls the *conjoncture heureuse* of the years between 1748 and 1788 (a period which was nevertheless interrupted by severe outbreaks of what appears to have been dysentry in the north and west in 1779), such provisions as did exist for distributing grain to those in need were always *ad hoc* and dependent upon the whim of authorities. They did not in Olwen Hufton's judgement contribute 'in any degree whatever to increasing the grain flow or lowering prices'; they 'never stopped prices rising', could at best, from time to time, hold them steady. But since between 1769 and 1789 these prices increased in the grain-producing areas of the north and centre by about sixty-five per cent, although wages in the same areas increased only by about twenty-two per cent, it is clear that the affected population must have suffered in a way that the English had rarely done. The evidence is at the very least consistent with Lesthaeghe's view that where reliable institutions for sharing risk do not exist, people will insure by the only other means they have, which in almost all cases, and certainly in non-industrial societies, is a larger family.[22]

---

[22] Ron Lesthaeghe, 'On the social control of human reproduction', *Population and Development Review* 6 (1980), 527–48. Similar arguments are urged in the same place by Geoffrey McNicoll, 'Institutional determinants of fertility change'

What therefore seems in the early modern period, if not before, to distinguish England and northern France, together with Iceland, much of Scandinavia and other parts of northern and north-western Europe from areas to the south and east, is a pattern of entry into agricultural labour which led to a relatively late entry into marriage. And other things being equal, this served to depress fertility. Other things, however, were not equal. In the first place, there appears to have been an additional pressure to reduce marital fertility in the areas of what in France is still described as *la petite culture*. Large families, where there was (as in these parts of France) partible inheritance, would have been an increasing liability. It is certainly the case that the partition of holdings in many parts of the south and west of the country had become extreme by the eighteenth century. And there appears to have been a countervailing pressure to keep fertility high in the north and east to insure against the crises brought about from time to time by shortfalls in the harvest and rising grain prices. It is this pressure, where there was a large absolute population and no reliable support outside the family, which explains the differences in marital fertility between northern and eastern France and England. In the south and west and in the north and east, if in different ways for different reasons, France was indeed more of a 'high-pressure' demographic regime.

The final question of an explanatory kind, therefore, is why

(411–62), but challenged by J. E. Potter, 'Effects of societal and community institutions on fertility', in R. A. Bulatao and R. D. Lee eds., *Determinants of Fertility in Developing Countries*, Washington DC: National Academy Press, 1983, II, 'Fertility regulation and institutional differences', pp. 648–54, and classically, by Malthus. There is a review of the argument (including a discussion of Malthus's view) and references to other suggestive evidence in Richard M. Smith, 'Transfer incomes, risk and security: the roles of the family and the collectivity in recent theories of fertility change', in David Coleman and Roger Schofield eds., *The State of Population Theory: Forward from Malthus*, Oxford: Blackwell, 1986, pp. 188–211, and '"Modernisation" and the corporate medieval village community in England: some sceptical reflections', in A. R. H. Baker and D. Gregory eds., *Explorations in Historical Geography*, Cambridge: Cambridge University Press, 1984, pp. 140–79, especially the conclusion at 178. Lebrun, 'Les crises demographiques', 223. Goubert's phrase from *Cent milles provinciaux*, p. 69, where he contrasts this for the seventeenth century with a perhaps optimistically described *courbe sereine* for the eighteenth. Hufton, 'Social conflict', 318, 304.

fertility within marriage began to fall in France in the fourth quarter of the eighteenth century. If one concentrates on what might be described as 'demand', it is possible to imagine pressures becoming intolerable both in the areas of *la petite culture* and in the areas of commercial agriculture in the north and east: in the one, the partition of holdings had ceased to be able to provide a decent living, and selling out was at best a short-term solution; in the other, the benefits of kin for insurance had been outweighed by the costs of having to support them. But this is speculation. I do not know of evidence sufficient to determine just how far either might have been true. If, however, we concentrate on what might be described as 'supply', this final puzzle begins to unravel itself. For there was from the end of the third quarter of the eighteenth century a dramatic and as it turned out sustained fall in mortality in France and a concomitantly dramatic and sustained rise in the expectation of life. The average expectation of life at birth in France between the 1740s and the 1780s was 27.4. In England at the same time it was 36.3. But in France by the 1830s, it was 39.9, in England 40.2. In France, it had increased over the intervening period by more than twelve years, or more than forty-five per cent, in England by less than four years, or less than ten per cent. And as Wrigley makes clear, decomposing the overall tendency in France reveals that the differences in the fall in fertility (and the differences also in the rise in nuptiality) match the differences in the fall in mortality. Not only did the net reproduction rate in France as a whole remain very close to unity throughout the period of change; it also remained remarkably close to unity in almost all the French regions. Once again, the French had shown themselves to be exceptionally sensitive to changing conditions.[23]

[23] Wrigley, 'The fall of marital fertility'. France perhaps thereby ceases to 'remain the tantalising puzzle' van de Walle described it to be to students of the transition in fertility in Europe (note 19); but there is now the question of how and why mortality did decline so rapidly in so many parts of the country. An alternative response to a similar fall was that in Norway: the clearing of new lands in what had hitherto been a but partially settled country until, after two or three generations, the pressures became too great, nearly a third of the population went to the United States, and the rest reduced their fertility (Drake, *Population and Society*).

There was not a constant interest in maximising fertility in early modern societies. The fact that fertility does appear in parts of early modern France to have been, if not maximised – for in the nature of the case, it is extremely difficult to know in any population what a maximised or 'natural' fertility would be – then certainly high and near the maximum, higher and nearer than it was in England, does not mean that in this respect France exhibited a 'biological regime'. It merely means that conditions were different and generated a different interest. But in France, this was an interest bred of what often approached desperation, much like the interest now in a place like Bangladesh. It would seem on the face of it that the French might have preferred not to have had such an interest. Was it required? Could rural France have had a different fertility regime?[24]

IX

If fertility in early modern populations had been 'natural', in-dependent of all social arrangements, the answer to this question would lie in what one might, with Braudel and Bourgeois-Pichat, describe simply as 'biology'. But no fertility anywhere is or can conceivably be free of all such arrangements. Fertility always depends, among other things, upon the age at which women start a sexual life and the frequency with which they have sex through to the end of their fecund period; on breastfeeding practices; and so on.[25] Fertility in France certainly depended upon these and other

[24] Bangladesh is an extreme but for this reason illuminating case. Understanding this aspect of it is largely due to Mead Cain (e.g. 'Risk and insurance: perspectives on fertility and agrarian change in India and Bangladesh'. *Population and Development Review* 7 (1981), 435–74). For a wider comparison between what Cain describes for Bangladesh on the one hand and Tokugawa Japan, China in the 1950s, and Kwantung province (in China) and Bali since the late 1960s on the other, McNicoll, 'Institutional determinants'.

[25] An early set of estimates on the differences that can be made to fertility by varying assumptions about the age at marriage and the frequency of sex is Jean Bourgeois-Pichat, 'Les facteurs da la fécondité non dirigée', *Population* 20 (1965), 383–424; the authoritative analysis of what have come to be called the proximate determinants of fertility is J. Bongaarts and R. G. Potter, *Fertility, Biology and Behaviour: An Analysis of the Proximate Determinants*, New York:

such factors. The question, therefore, is whether any of the social arrangements in rural France which governed these 'proximate determinants' of fertility could have been different. On the face of it, of course, they could: French women could have married even later, prolonged the intervals between conception, and like their descendants, come sooner to restrict their fertility within marriage. But the rate and age of marriage themselves depended on other factors.

In much of rural France, if not indeed, and certainly by the middle of the seventeenth century, in most of it, one of the most crucial of these factors was the rate of taxation. In the decade after 1630, it actually quadrupled. 'French peasants', Goubert remarks, 'have never to my knowledge paid as much tax as they did in the seventeenth century, except perhaps in the eighteenth, but by then, they were better off'. And of all these taxes, ecclesiastical, seignurial and royal, taxes which between them may have taken a fifth of income and left most cultivators very near the margin, it was the last which was the most severe. The immediate reason for this was Richelieu's preparation for war with Spain, a war that was eventually declared in 1635. But the fiscal difficulties of the French state had been acute for at least thirty years. They were both caused and compounded by what had in the century before been a downturn in the agricultural economy, and by the sale of offices on a large scale which, although bringing in much-needed revenue to the crown, in Perry Anderson's – itself counterfactual – judgement 'side-tracked' the bourgeoisie from making money in commerce and industry and providing the crown with more revenue, which would in turn have raised the demand for food in towns and thus, agricultural prices, production and the rural standard of living. Moreover, the downturn in the agricultural economy of France in the sixteenth century was itself one more turn in what appears to have been a long cycle of expanding and contracting population, long much denser in

Academic Press, 1983. In addition to the proportion of women married at any age in the reproductive period and the frequency of sex within marriage, these determinants include postpartum abstinence, lactational amenorrhea, contraception, induced abortion, spontanous intra-uterine mortality, natural sterility and pathological sterility (on the idea of natural fertility, see note 19).

France than in England, expanding and contracting exploitation of land and expanding and contracting taxation, first from lords and then from both them and the State. By the middle of the sixteenth century, there was a rising rural population, falling productivity, and increasing inflation; people in the countryside were therefore poor and susceptible to disease. Hence their more immediate responsiveness to the supply of resources. In England, conditions were not nearly so grave.[26]

This brisk contrast between the political economies of the two countries at the start of the early modern period is not, of course, sufficient for any purpose except to suggest that the rate of reproduction in the demographic sense in each of them was a function of attempts at (and diversions from) reproduction in the economic sense. It was just as much endogenous as exogenous, just as much, if not more, a consequence of the taxing authorities' attempts to increase taxation – and indeed, in the sixteenth century, increasingly to appropriate land itself, thus producing a higher and higher proportion of agricultural labourers in the north and east of the country – as of people's disposition to extend cultivation when conditions seemed, for one reason or another, to be more propitious. And because the increases in taxation, particularly by the crown, were greater in France than in England, and because communal relief, shared risk-taking, was less in France than in England, the demographic regime in the one was more straightforwardly 'Malthusian' than in the other. The French may have had an interest in a less punishing regime, but the conditions of the regime they did have were given by the country's political economy (including its provision for destitution) which, itself to have been different, would have required a very different constellation of factors: a different

---

[26] Pierre Goubert, Ian Patterson trans., *The French Peasantry in the Seventeenth Century*, Cambridge: Cambridge University Press, 1986, pp. 179, 204; also Richard Bonney, *The King's Debts: Finance and Politics in France, 1589–1661*, Oxford: Clarendon Press, 1978. Perry Anderson, *Lineages of the Absolutist State*, London: New Left Books, 1974, p. 98. J. H. Elliott, *Richelieu and Olivares*, Cambridge: Cambridge University Press, 1984, especially pp. 113–42. On the long cycle of agriculture in France from the late medieval period to the sixteenth century, Bois, *Crisis of Feudalism*, pp. 399–403, 377–84.

constellation of factors over the *longue durée* from at least the middle
of the fourteenth century, and also, a different constellation of more
immediate and more purely political *événements* in the late sixteenth
and early seventeenth centuries themselves.

The first of these two possibilities is one which requires too much
to have been different too far back for it to have been a plausible
possibility for the world of seventeenth-century France as that world
in most other respects was; if the economic and social history of the
French countryside over this period had been different, it would by
the seventeenth century have been a very different country. The
second possibility, however, is not so implausible. On the face of it,
Richelieu could have taken the advice he was receiving not to press
his difference with Spain, and even though, in its deeper fiscal
difficulty, the taxes he raised for the war were by no means all that
the French state needed to extract from its cultivators in order to
maintain itself, they were almost certainly a causally important part.
In the later eighteenth century, after all, when the fiscal burden
began at last to lift, the rate of mortality declined, and the pattern of
marriage and fertility did at last change.

X

Pursuing the possibilities suggested by the available explanations of
what – it might now be clear – is far from being the simply
'biological' regime in the *longue durée* of early modern Europe reveals
two ironies. The first is the analytically more consequential. We
need a strong theory, Elster argued, to be able 'warrantably to assert'
a counterfactual proposition. But the stronger, that's to say the more
deterministic, this theory is, the more difficult it becomes, as he
said, to insert any antecedent that is counter-to-fact. The theory
will at the limit entirely confine the world. Elster was right about the
difficulty, but as I said earlier, not perhaps quite right in his view of
how to resolve it. The inductively-known runnings-on of the world
do set limits to what counterfactuals we can assert. The aetiology of
the plague, for instance, in all its forms, and the best generalisations
that we have about its epidemiology, set a limit to what we can

expect any imaginable measure to have been able to achieve in any particular set of conditions. What we know about the conception and gestation of children and their conditions of survival through to adulthood sets the limits to how any population can reproduce. And effective political leadership in early modern Europe tends to have been tyrannical. But the limits set by these sorts of runnings-on are extremely wide.[27] There is nothing in the first to suggest that authorities could not take steps to control the plague; nothing in the second to say that French peasants could not have produced fewer children; and nothing in the third either to explain how a tyrant will deploy his power or how a less tyrannical if nevertheless authoritative oligarchy cannot impose controls on circulation. The much narrower bounds to might-have-beens in the world of medieval and early modern Europe are set not by theories, but by the more particular circumstances of that world.

To take this point too strongly, however, can be too easily to accept the holists' argument, the claim – Leibniz's claim, in his-toriographic practice, that made by Oakeshott and Braudel – that the tight web of inter-connected states of affairs, the sheer thickness of circumstance that constitutes any past, precludes any alternative at all except a wholly different world unwinding itself from the start of all worlds. It can seem simply to exchange strong theories for thick pasts. But this is not something that can be decided in advance. It has always to be shown. I have argued that examining the alternatives suggested in the explanations of the incidence of plague and the levels of rural fertility indicates that within what would remain recognisable as late medieval and early modern Europe, the incidence of the one and also, in certain areas, the levels of the other, could have been different.

I have done so not by invoking a general theory, but by making comparisons, taking 'contrast cases', within Europe itself and ex-tending them. These comparisons consisted simply in looking at the nature, circumstances and effects of actual practical reasonings and

[27] As Elster has elsewhere, and in a different connection, since conceded (*Making Sense of Marx*, Cambridge: Cambridge University Press, 1985, pp. 200–1).

their outcomes in action in other arguably relevant circumstances at other otherwise comparable times. The plausibility – or if one wants to put it the metalinguistic mode which Elster once adopted, the 'warranted assertibility' – of what might have been depends in part upon what, somewhere, was actually tried. But it does not only depend on this. It also turns on imagining, in the light of what these comparisons suggest, what the relevant agents themselves, as those agents, might have considered and managed to effect. The imaginative extension of what the authorities in Florence or Nuremberg, for example, tried to do in the early sixteenth century; or the extension of economic and social circumstances and the interests they generated in rural England to contemporary France; do each of course depend upon an understanding the causes of what one is extending and on the likelihood that these causes and their conditions (or of substitutes for them) could have occurred and had similar effects somewhere else. In this sense, but only in this sense, which is perhaps too weak to be analytically interesting, does it turn on having a 'theory'.

For the substance of historical and social explanation, however, the second of the two ironies is the more important. In so far as they were endogenous, the mutabilities of morbidity, mortality and fertility in early modern Europe seem not to be wholly dependent upon other aspects of what the *Annales* historians and social scientists have tended to think of as the 'structure' of the societies in question. Both the control of the plague – at least in the towns – and even at crucial moments the level of fertility – at least in the countryside – turned on political factors: upon *conjonctures*, if not indeed – if one considers the consequences for rural welfare of Richelieu's determination to press France's dispute with Spain and thereby to increase the already heavy burden of taxation in the countryside – mere *événements*. For all the accumulated and imaginatively constraining force of the *longue durée*, to consider the alternatives suggested by the workings of structures can make them look decidedly less structural. Indeed a structure, we might say, is not an unchangeable state of affairs, but one that just happens not to have been much changed. And this is a truth about structures that is arrived at by considering what might have been. It is not of course incontestable. It is not, as I said in the first chapter, something about which we can expect to be certain and in that sense come to know.[28] It depends upon inherently disputable judgements of the similarly disputable practical judgements of the agents themselves.

[28] Steven Lukes rightly remarks that 'to investigate the structural constraints upon the power of agents is in part to inquire into the nature of those agents and such an investigation is of its nature an inquiry into counterfactuals'. But he offers no argument for his further view that it would 'be fallacious to conclude that there is in principle no correct answer to the question of what is within and beyond the power of agents' ('Power and structure', in *Essays in Social Theory*, London: Macmillan, 1977, pp. 3–29 at p. 29). Even for any one particular agent, and with *all* possible information, we cannot *know* in advance – know for certain or with any measurable degree of probability – what, within the interesting limits, he can do; and even if we inquire after the event, and find that he did indeed do it, that doesn't tell us for sure about his capacities: he might have had unusual help, or have been able to do even more.

— 3 —

The United States
in South Korea

I

Politics is the example *par excellence* of practical reasoning in what one can describe as a world of causes. It is, as the truism has it, the art of the possible. It invents futures and produces them; futures which are before the event open and merely possible; futures from actual presents which are themselves the consequences of actual practice in actual pasts. The ways in which its possibilities have been thought about, however, leaves something to be desired.[1]

Conditional generalisations are not sufficient. What politically has been managed in one place can provide the contrast cases for one's explanatory question. It might even give a preliminary indication of what might be managed in another. If by the 1950s, social democrats in Sweden and West Germany were able to see that economic and social trends were eroding their long-standing electoral base in the industrial working class, and to adjust their programme accordingly, the Labour Party in Britain might also have

[1] Some students of politics agree: Laurence Whitehead, Adam Przeworski and (to a lesser extent) Guillermo O'Donnell, for instance, in considering the prospects for some kind and degree of democracy – some kind and degree of openness to competition within the political classes – in Latin America in the 1980s, (O'Donnell, Philippe C. Schmitter and Whitehead eds., *Transitions from Authoritarian Rule: Tentative Conclusions about Uncertain Democracies*, Baltimore: Johns Hopkins University Press, 1986, II, p. 15, III, pp. 3–46, 47–50). Przeworski however, while accepting that counterfactual considerations are crucial, believes that 'none of the approaches to the study of historical possibilities takes us sufficiently far to make counterfactual claims intersubjectively acceptable', and does not pursue them. More generally, John Dunn, *Rethinking Modern Political Theory: Essays 1979–1983*, Cambridge: Cambridge University Press, 1985, pp. 5–12.

been able to do so. Likewise, if some authorities were able to take measures against the plague in early modern Europe, others might have been in a position to do so too. But inferences of this kind, as I have suggested in the previous two chapters, may well overestimate what could have been done. And inferences from other comparisons may equally well underestimate it. It may be relatively easy in retrospect to see how in Costa Rica in 1948 or in Colombia or Venezuela ten years later, the political classes agreed to compromise for political peace. But it was by no means clear in prospect that they would do so.[2]

Nor will it usually be sufficient to invoke theories of a different kind, theories of what it would be or would have been rational for political agents to do. Formal models of political rationality must assume that agents have fixed ends and that the circumstances in which they reason are stable; if these assumptions do not hold, the theories cease rapidly to be able to deliver determinate results. (And on those occasions on which the assumptions do hold, but the

---

[2] The general point is well brought out for the 1980s by Albert Hirschman, 'Notes on consolidating democracy in Latin America', in *Rival Views of Market Society and Other Recent Essays*, New York: Viking, 1986, pp. 176–82. On Costa Rica in comparison with other states in central America, James Dunkerley, *Power in the Isthmus*, London: Verso, 1989, on Colombia, Jonathan Hartlyn, *The Politics of Coalition Rule in Colombia*, Cambridge: Cambridge University Press, 1988, and on Venezuela, Judith Ewell, *Venezuela: A Century of Change*, London: Hurst, 1984, pp. 122 ff. Alasdair MacIntyre once advanced a strong argument not just against conditional generalisations in social science but against making any comparisons between institutions (especially political institutions) at all: 'the provision of an environment sufficiently different to make the search for counter-examples interesting will normally be the provision of an environment where we cannot hope or expect to find examples of the original phenomenon and therefore cannot hope to find counter-examples', so that 'either . . . generalisations about institutions will necessarily lack the kind of confirmation they require or they will be consequences of true generalisatioins about human rationality' ('Is a science of comparative politics possible?', in Peter Laslett, W. G. Runciman and Quentin Skinner eds., *Philosophy, Politics and Society*, 4th series, Oxford: Blackwell, 1972, pp. 14, 15). His warning – not just for comparisons in politics – is well-taken; his own example is of the difference between American and African mass parties. But he exaggerates; whether a sugggested comparison makes sense is an open question, to be answered for each case as it arises, and not, as he wants to answer it, by fiat, on the grounds that apparently similar practices in different circumstances will *always* have wholly different 'meanings' to the people involved in each.

number of agents is large, and their ends are various, the models rapidly become too complicated to use.) Some historians of politics, even if only by default, have seen the problem. But they have rarely pursued the possibilities which their own explanations suggest, or the implications that such possibilities have for the explanations which suggest them.[3]

II

The histories of the division of the Korean peninsula after 1945, of the war which resulted from that division, and of the effects of the war both in Korea and beyond, are a case in point. To Bruce Cumings, Korea was the first test of the Truman administration's policy of 'containment', and in the invasion of the south by the north in 1950, its first failure. But this policy, as Cumings sees it, was not new. It merely continued Roosevelt's intention during the Second World War to devise a policy which would 'accommodate postwar American security concerns, open the colonies to American commerce and tutelage, and corral communist and anticolonial revolution'. Truman's decision to occupy southern Korea in the autumn of 1945, and his formulation of his more general intentions in 1947 in what came to be known as the 'Truman Doctrine', was a natural consequence of this. So also was the refusal of the United States, once in Korea, to agree to Soviet conditions for a provisional government to administer the whole peninsula under a joint trusteeship until such time as the country was thought fit for independent rule. An official in the State Department in 1949 had said that it was arguable 'that without the presence of a Soviet army, and under a four power "trusteeship", where there would always have been three votes to one, the result might have been as in France or Italy'. But this, Cumings thinks, was a mistaken judgement. 'The first year after liberation ... provided a crucible ... in which a new imperium worked out the logic of its own interests.'[4] The interests were set, and so were their consequences.

[3] Charles Maier is a rare exception; see chapter 1, note 4.
[4] Bruce Cumings, *The Origins of the Korean War: Liberation and the Emergence of Separate Regimes, 1945–47*, Princeton: Princeton University Press, 1981, pp.

James Matray agrees, but for a different reason. In the first place, Matray suggests, 'only an Allied agreement' could have encouraged 'an atmosphere of stability' in Korea after the surrender of the Japanese there and their departure from the peninsula. The Koreans were not prepared for self-rule, and even if they had been, it is almost certain that a self-governing Korea would have succumbed to the competition that developed between the Soviet Union and China in north-east Asia. The American occupation of the southern part of the country was intended to prevent this. Once there, the United States accordingly committed itself to the idea that had already been agreed in principle with the Soviet Union for a joint trusteeship. But Soviet and American interests proved to be too apart, and the conditions for trusteeship could not be agreed. Truman's policy before the North Korean attack in 1950, Matray argues, was nevertheless sensible. 'It recognised the superior strength of nationalism over communism as a force in international affairs. Furthermore, it acknowledged the obvious limitations on the power of the United States to control events in Asia.' The Americans may have been clumsy in their occupation, and they may have made mistakes. But Syngman Rhee's eventual realisation of his wish for a separate republic in the south in 1948, which sealed the opposition between south and north, was in Matray's opinion 'the outgrowth of forces' (not the least of which was the persistent hostility of most Koreans to the idea of renewed foreign rule) that were 'largely beyond Truman's control'.[5]

Other historians think that the official in the State Department may have been right. Events were not preordained. The United States need not have occupied south Korea, and their occupation need not have led to two opposed states and war. Gregory Henderson was himself a State Department officer, a vice-consul, in

129–30, 443–4; Cumings offers a calmer gloss on Roosevelt's 'internationalism' at p. 438 and occasionally wavers about the consistency of US policy, e.g. at pp. 116 and 438. Similarly William Stueck, 'The march to the Yalu: the perspective from Washington', in Bruce Cumings ed., *Child of Conflict: The Korean-American Relationship, 1943–1953*, Seattle: University of Washington Press, 1983, pp. 195–237 at p. 237.

[5] James I. Matray, *The Reluctant Crusade: American Foreign Policy in Korea, 1941–1950*, Honolulu: University of Hawaii Press, 1985, pp. 26, 258, 161. The Republic of Korea in the south came into being on 15 August 1948, the Democratic People's Republic in the north on 9 September.

Seoul in the late 1940s. The Americans, he claims in the history that he wrote twenty years later, 'had no selfish aims; indeed, they did not have aims at all, lacking policy'. 'It is difficult', concludes Michael Sandusky in the most recent of the more extended accounts, 'to discern what exactly the Truman administration intended to do with southern Korea.' Or if it did have clear intentions, they conflicted. 'Political, military, and geographical factors', argued Soon Sung Cho in one of the first accounts, 'made it difficult for America to evolve a policy consistent with both her moral commitment to Korean unification and her own self-interest.' But this interest, Charles Dobbs argues, only became clear in January 1947, just three months before Truman formally announced his doctrine. Only then, faced with what it interpreted as Soviet intransigence in negotiations for a joint trusteeship, increased pressure from the War Department to withdraw American forces, and a deteriorating situation in the American zone, did the State Department concentrate its mind. It formed an interdepartmental committee which concluded a few weeks later that the policy of the United Sates should be 'psychologically to demonstrate to the communists and Koreans that [the United States] meant to stay in Korea, and practically to create a viable economy in South Korea capable of withstanding' what Washington had come to construe as 'communist subversion'. It was at this moment, as Dobbs sees it, that Korea 'now found itself raised to a symbol in the cold war. The less strategic an issue (and the less understood)', he argues, not altogether clearly, 'the greater its value as a symbol, precisely because of its unimportance. Korea was becoming a bellwether of American intentions, a sign of American determination and, in time, the symbol would grow so large that it nearly controlled its creator.' All four historians, however, agree with each other, against both Cumings and Matray, that the policy which the United States did pursue throughout the period from 1945 to 1950 was inept because it was at first inconsistent and irresolute and later too rigid. The resultant division of the country into fiercely opposed states was to the disadvantage of Koreans and in the longer run, Henderson, Sandusky and Dobb all suggest, arguably also of the United States.[6]

[6] Gregory Henderson, *Korea: The Politics of the Vortex*, Cambridge MA: Harvard University Press, 1968, p. 121. Michael C. Sandusky, *America's Parallel*, Alexandria VA: Old Dominion Press, 1983, p. 332. Soon Sung Cho,

No history can yet be complete. The post-war fate of Korea was decided by the United States and the Soviet Union. (Britain was formally consulted, at least until December 1945, China had an indirect effect, and the United Nations was asked to endorse American policies after 1947.) Koreans themselves also played a part, before September 1945 in the Korean Provisional Government in southern China and in Mao Zedong's movement in the north; in the United States and the Soviet Union, where there were exiled

Korea in World Politics, 1940–50: An Evaluation of American Responsibility, Berkeley: University of California Press, 1967, p. 284. Charles M. Dobbs, *The Unwanted Symbol: American Foreign Policy, the Cold War, and Korea, 1945–1950*, Kent: Kent State University Press, 1981, pp. 92–3, 191–3. There is an enormous literature on American foreign policy more generally after 1945. Much of what is relevant in it to Korea is discussed in these histories. There is no detailed account of Korea from 1945 to the present; the fullest (a history of the country from earliest times to 1948 and of its two parts to 1980) is Andrew C. Nahm, *Korea: Tradition and Transformation*, Elizabeth NJ and Seoul: Hollym, 1988. I take almost all my information from these. I acknowledge them separately only where I quote from them, or where one offers information or an opinion not shared by the others. The eventual division of the peninsula into opposed states was arguably against the interests of the United States because even if one accepts that the decision to occupy the south in 1945 was the first test of containment, accepts that in 1950 this test failed, and accepts also that the failure convinced the United States that it had to spend more on (what it regarded as) a military deterrent to (what it regarded as) Soviet expansion; there is still room for dispute as to whether the new policy was to America's subsequent advantage, nationally or internationally. It generated a great deal of ill-will in the Third World, which continues into the 1990s; it led to a domestically damaging adventure in south-east Asia in the 1960s; and in the ten years before the long-standing antagonism between the United States and Soviet Union began to be alleviated in the late 1980s, it committed Washington to what may prove to have been a level of defence expenditure (and thus of borrowing) as crippling for the American economy as Moscow's has by its own admission been for the Soviet Union. The obvious counter-argument is that the antagonism between the United States and the Soviet Union would not have been reduced had it not been for the further tripling of defence expenditure in Washington after 1979. One must also remember, as I mention below, that there was some distance between what was taken to be Kennan's original suggestion in the famous 'long telegram' that he sent to Washington from Moscow in 1946, while he was chargé d'affaires there, and the decision enshrined in the National Security Council's paper NSC 68 in 1950 to triple military expenditure. As Kennan recalled in his memoirs, 'what I was talking about when I mentioned the containment of Soviet power was not the containment by military means of a military threat, but the political containment of a political threat' (*Memoirs, 1925–1950*, London: Hutchinson, 1968, p. 358).

groups both in Moscow and in the Soviet Far East; and after the American occupation, in Korea itself. Most of the pertinent American state papers are now de-classified, and these, together with the large number of first-hand accounts and memoirs, have allowed historians almost to complete the picture of the part played by the different interests in Washington (in and between the Departments of State and War and Congress) and also in the United States Military Government in Korea. There is also more information now about Koreans in the south, about the more deliberately political agents in Seoul and (as a result of the hard work which Cumings has done on Korean sources) about those outside the capital who were resisting both the American military government before 1948 and the government of the new Republic that succeeded it. But the Soviet archives are still closed, fewer Soviet politicians and military men have written memoirs, and those who have have been less forthcoming. Western and Korean historians, like the protagonists at the time, have largely had to guess what the Soviet intentions were. (This is why these intentions usually appear, as they do in what I say here, as 'Stalin's'.) And there is a similar lack of information about Koreans in the Soviet Union and northern China before 1945 and in northern Korea afterwards.

The more recent historians, therefore, have not had quite all the facts; but they have had more. However, because possibilities, as I have been saying, increase under explanation as they also decrease, the historians are less steady than those who wrote before about what their explanations suggest. On the one hand, because their accounts are fuller, they find it difficult to see how events could have turned out any other way. Cumings suggests that they could have done so only if the United States had not defined Korea as essential to the security of the Pacific and its own; indeed, they could perhaps have done so only if the United States had not more generally intended to guarantee a 'free' world and establish its 'hegemony' over it. Once it had, all else followed. Matray sees American intentions in a different way, but this brings him to a similar conclusion. On the other hand, because there is now more information about who decided what, when, and how, or (as was often the case) about how they let it inadvertently be decided for them, the more the same historians have come to suspect that some outcomes could have been different. Despite himself, Cumings does wonder whether, if the Military Government had not supported the right in the south in the autumn of 1945 and the early months of 1946, events might not have taken another turn and 'liberation', in the title of his final chapter, not therefore been 'denied'. Likewise, and not unlike the author of the State Department review in 1949, Matray suspects that more immediate and decisive support for the moderates in the south 'might have contributed to the emergence of a united, democratic, and independent Korea'.[7] The historians are both more certain and less. They have themselves to be pressed further from their own accounts.

To do so is interesting in itself. The division of the Korean peninsula led to the Korean War; without that division, there would have not been a north to invade a south. And the Korean War had consequences beyond Korea itself. It strengthened the hand of those in the United States who were arguing for increases in defence expenditure; in this way and in others, it intensified the Cold War. The antagonism between the United States and the Soviet Union in Korea after 1947 also helped convince the State Department to allow the economic regeneration of Japan; in this way and in others, some of which – the rise in commodity prices, for instance – were more immediate, it had dramatic consequences for the world economy. To decide what these consequences flowed from, and whether they were unavoidable, is important.

To press the historians further is also interesting for what I want to say here about the possibilities that close explanations suggest. There are essentially two questions about the part played by the United States in the division of Korea. The first is whether it could

[7] Cumings, *Origins*, p. 122. Matray, *Reluctant Crusade*, p. 90. Also, 'if Truman had not considered that Korea was a test case, and if Hodge [the US military commander in the south after 1945] had not already sided with the collaborationist right in South Korea, there would have been a chance for the Americans and the Russians to create what Stalin would term a bourgeois-democratic government. The two great powers might then have rapidly turned over to this new regime the responsibility for elections, withdrawn their troops, and neutralised the country' (Stephen Pelz, 'US decisions on Korean policy, 1943–1950: some hypotheses', in Cumings, *Child of Conflict*, pp. 93–132 at p. 108). The contrast might be with Austria or Finland.

have decided not to occupy the southern part of the peninsula in the autumn of 1945. The second is whether, having done so, it could then have acted in such a way as to bring about a re-unified and eventually independent country. And about each of these, as there are about any counterfactual speculation, there are two further questions. Was the possibility itself possible? And what would its being actual have led to? Where the historians do ask these questions – none asks all of them – they give contrary answers. My own conclusion is that the United States could without difficulty have decided not to occupy southern Korea, but that once it was there, it could not easily and without loss have decided to do anything very different from what it did. The argument has wider implications for how one thinks about political possibility.

III

Roosevelt, most agree, had a picture of the post-war world. The economic sovereignty of all nations would be respected, but obstacles to international trade would be reduced; this was the point of the Bretton Woods agreement. The Soviet Union would be acknowledged as a great power, but it would be enmeshed in a series of mutual agreements to preserve the security of all the powers, and not antagonised; the United Nations would be important in securing that. And the European and Japanese colonies would be led to political independence. If this was not feasible at once, the United States, the Soviet Union, perhaps Britain and France and where appropriate China would hold them in trusteeship until such time as it was. In the event, this idea was softened for the European territories; Britain, France and the Netherlands resisted it, and at the end of the war, the United States needed their cooperation in Europe.[8] But it remained the plan for Korea.

Roosevelt was rarely specific about the details of his conception. He remained, as his admirers say, flexible, and he pursued his

---

[8] Robert J. McMahon, 'Toward a post-colonial order: Truman administration policies towards South and Southeast Asia', in Michael J. Lacey ed., *The Truman Presidency*, Cambridge: Cambridge University Press and Woodrow Wilson International Center for Scholars, 1989, pp. 340–8.

objectives without close attention to the usually sympathetic but always more anxious State Department. (In reply to the occasional suggestion that he was too optimistic about the willingness of the Soviet Union to co-operate after the war, he would say, at least until just before he died, that he could handle Stalin. Andrey Gromyko recalls that the Soviet leader had liked and admired him.) Roosevelt was convinced that only an international collaboration of the kind that he envisaged could sustain a just and orderly world of the kind that he wished to see. His dealings with his wartime allies, the British dragging their feet over empire, the Chinese wanting to expand, and the Soviet Union committed to its authoritarianism – at this time more irritating to most Americans, who had been fighting 'fascism' in Germany and Japan, than its communism – together of course with the fact of the war itself, did nothing to diminish his conviction.[9] There was also a more particular strategic reason for his intention for Korea itself. General MacArthur was arguing that the Soviet Union should enter the war against Japan. Having been beaten by them in the Philippines, MacArthur suggested that Japanese forces were most vulnerable from the north. A Soviet entry there, he thought, through Manchuria and Korea, would reduce American costs and casualties. The Joint Chiefs of Staff came to agree, and at a meeting of Allied foreign ministers in Moscow in October 1943, Stalin was persuaded to declare war on Japan as soon as Germany was defeated.

In 1944, the success of new long-range bombers and fast aircraft carriers made it seem less likely to some Americans that a final attack on Japan would be prolonged. Indeed, in September of that year, General Arnold, who commanded wings of B-29s from the captured Pacific islands, and Admirals King and Nimitz even suggested that Soviet entry into the war against Japan might not be necessary at all. And some officials in the State Department became increasingly worried about the longer-term consequences. But most of those with a say in the more immediate strategy continued to believe that the Soviet Union should enter, and in May 1945, the

[9] On the nature and justification of American perceptions of the Soviet Union during as well as after the war, John L. Gaddis, 'The insecurities of victory: the United States and the perception of the Soviet threat after World War II', in Lacey ed., *The Truman Presidency*, pp. 235–72.

United States agreed on an invasion of the Japanese home islands, with conventional bombing, supported by a Soviet move against the Japanese Kwantung army on the mainland. It was planned for 1 November. Even if the United States' new S-1, the atomic bomb, were to be ready by early August, as was now hoped, there was no guarantee that Japan would surrender quickly, and the United States lacked the capacity to act on the mainland or, even if it should wish to, to prevent the Soviet Union from doing so.[10]

The disadvantages for the post-war distribution of power in Asia, however, were unavoidable. Manchuria, controlled by the Japanese, would no doubt revert to China. But whatever Chiang Kai-shek might wish, this would not be a solution which Koreans would accept for Korea. The United States' best option there would accordingly be to secure agreement with the other interested powers for a joint trusteeship. For this and other reasons, not the least of which was a growing suspicion about the Soviet leader's willingness to implement what the Americans took to be previous agreements, there was a need to meet Stalin again, but not before it was certain that the atomic bomb would be ready. The timing was fortunate. Truman arrived at the Potsdam conference on the evening of 15 July. On the early morning of the 16, he was told of the successful test of S-1 in New Mexico. The meeting began on the 17.

The United States was not well-informed about Stalin's intentions. Roosevelt, it seems, had understood Russia's defensiveness. He may not have known that the country had been invaded from the west on more than a dozen occasions since 1800. But he would have sensed that Stalin was anxious that Britain, China and the United States might between them strengthen Germany and Japan after the war's end and together attack the Soviet Union. He was more sanguine than many about Stalin's moves in Poland in 1945; just before he died, he reminded Churchill that an outcome which favoured the Warsaw government over the provisional government in London was in the spirit of the agreements they had all come to at Yalta. He had been told by Owen Lattimore that the Soviet Union was wary of China, that the east Asian mainland was a

---

[10] This consideration is emphasised by Sandusky, *America's Parallel*, pp. 99 ff.; Arnold, King, and Nimitz's reservations at p. 133.

natural sphere of Soviet interest, that communism had become a
permanent, 'respectable' and 'progressive' force there, and that co-
operation with the Soviet Union was accordingly to be preferred to
the American propensity, as Lattimore described it, 'to put our
money in liberated territories on men whom we call moderate but
whom their own people, all too often, call reactionary'.[11] He had
discovered from a conversation at Yalta that Stalin disliked the idea
of foreign troops being stationed in Korea after the war, and that the
Soviet Union wanted a predominant influence there, He had also
been told that it had been preparing some Koreans in Moscow. (As
late as November 1945, Ambassador Harriman, who was no dove,
was to cable Truman from Moscow to remind him that the Soviet
Union saw Korea in the same way as it saw Poland, Finland, and
Rumania, as a possible 'springboard' for an attack on Russia.) There
had been no sign that Stalin thought that the Soviet interest would
require anything more than what the Soviet Union described as an
'independent friendly' government there: as the Soviet negotiator
said to the Americans in Seoul in 1946, a government that would be
'friendly . . . so that in the future it will not become the base for an
attack on the Soviet Union'.[12]

But by the late spring of 1945, Washington's attitude to Moscow
had changed. This was in part because of the atomic bomb, but only
in part. Unfolding events in Europe had led Roosevelt to begin to

[11] Owen Lattimore was advising Roosevelt throughout the war; the last
phrase from his *Solution in Asia*, Boston: Atlantic Little-Brown, 1945, p. 132.
[12] Sandusky, *America's Parallel*, p. 302. Also William Taubman, *Stalin's
American Policy: From Entente to Détente to Cold War*, New York: Norton, 1982.
Colonel General Shtikov, the Soviet negotiator in the Joint Commission,
quoted by Matray, *Reluctant Crusade*, p. 81. Also Dobbs, *Unwanted Symbol*, p.
79, where Dobbs argues that this 'precluded compromise', since it made it clear
that for the Soviet Union, 'Korea had fallen into the same category as Eastern
Europe'. Less than three weeks before, Kennan had sent a memorandum from
Moscow urging the State Department to abandon the idea of co-operating with
the Soviet Union and to support the Korean Provisional Government, Kim Ku
and Rhee, who '– impractical and poorly organised though they may be –
nevertheless represent a pro-American opposition to existing Soviet-sponsored
"democratic" parties and social organisations and the concept of Soviet
domination of future provisional government'. To judge from public
pronouncements, explicit parallels between the situations on the two sides of the
country seem only to have been drawn by the Soviet Union after the spring of
1948.

suspect Stalin's good faith. And Truman was less well informed than his predecessor about foreign affairs, in any event more 'nationalist' in his inclinations, as some historians have put it, less 'internationalist'. He was also politically less secure. He relied more on advisers, and on more pessimistic ones. Themselves advised by Harriman, who returned to Washington on Roosevelt's death, these men were confirmed in their suspicions by events in Europe and later, by the 'interpretive analysis' of Soviet intentions that they requested from George Kennan, then the chargé in Moscow, in February 1946. They pressed the possibility of Soviet expansion. Nevertheless, the State Department's planning papers for Potsdam had recommended that the United States should pursue the idea of a trusteeship for Korea. By then, however, being certain about the availability of the bomb for August, and despite Soviet requests, Truman did not press the matter at the conference. (He may have been grateful to the British for diverting what discussion there was of trusteeship to territories in the Mediterranean.) He and his chiefs of staff believed that they could now pre-empt Stalin's moves into the Japanese territories on the mainland.

On 24 July, George Marshall met his opposite number, Alexsey Antonov, at Potsdam, agreed with him that the United States and the Soviet Union should co-ordinate air and sea operations against Japan in the Yellow Sea, but told Antonov that the American army would probably not be landing in Japan until late October. This was less than candid. Marshall knew about the test in New Mexico, and suspected, although could not be certain, that the bomb would have caused Japan to surrender before then. Indeed, he had on the 19 or 20 July instructed MacArthur and Nimitz to include Korea in their plans for the occupation of Japan's home islands. MacArthur's reply came back to Potsdam on the 27, his final version to Washington (after he had resolved his squabbles with Nimitz about the role of the navy) on 8 August. It envisaged occupying Seoul on 8 September. Truman was not therefore correct later to recall that at Potsdam, 'it was not anticipated by our military leaders that we would carry out operations in Korea'.[13]

---

[13] By far the best account of what he calls the 'hasty assessment' during the Potsdam meeting is Sandusky, *America's Parallel*, pp. 179–97, also pp. 174–8; Truman quoted by Sandusky at p. 194.

At Yalta, Stalin had said that his forces would be ready to attack the Japanese armies three months after the defeat of Germany. In May, he told an emissary of Truman's in Moscow, who had been sent to see what the Soviet plans were now that the Americans knew that the atomic bomb might be ready, that the Soviet army would be at the Manchurian border by 8 August. In July, at Potsdam, Stalin said they would not be ready to move until the 15. His earlier estimate proved correct. The Soviet Union handed a declaration of war to the Japanese ambassador in Moscow on the 8 (to be effective at midnight in Tokyo) and entered northern Korea on the 9. The Americans were surprised and not a little alarmed. But there was no way now of stopping the Soviet army. The best that could be done was to get as many American troops as possible into as much of Korea as possible, and quickly. Preparing the general order for the surrender of Japan on the night of 10 August, the State-War-Navy Coordinating Committee therefore asked the War Department's Operations Division for a feasible objective on the peninsula. Thinking that the Soviet advance was proceeding more quickly than it was, for it was known that all twenty-four divisions of the Kwantung army had been weakened by the diversion of their more experienced troops elsewhere, and knowing MacArthur's reluctance at that time to divert forces to Korea, the Operations Division suggested the 38th parallel. This divided the peninsula just north of Seoul. It was as much as the United States could reasonably hope for, the division believed, and perhaps more. The general order was sent out on 15 August. Stalin acknowledged that he was to accept the surrender of Japanese forces in Manchuria, Karafuto (southern Sakhalin), and Korea; he queried other details; but he said nothing about the proposed division of Korea. Washington was surprised but relieved, and assumed that he accepted it.[14]

---

[14] Dobbs, *Unwanted Symbol*, p. 26 claims that it is 'certain' that the 38th parallel had already been decided at Potsdam by Marshall and the army's chief of operations on the grounds that the Americans needed to have control of the port of Inchon; but others disagree, and Dobbs offers no evidence. It is not surprising that Stalin did accept the proposal for the surrender. Perhaps he thought that the Soviet army would have a hard task fighting its way even that far; the Kwantung army, although now weakened, was reputedly fierce, and advances through northern Korea had to be made along corridors that were narrow and easy for any army to defend. Perhaps he thought that the Americans would

MacArthur's estimate had been correct. American forces arrived in Seoul on 8 September and accepted the Japanese surrender of southern Korea the next day. But MacArthur's eventual choice to command the occupation was not an altogether happy one. Lieutenant General John Hodge was a successful field commander, honest and straightforward. But he came from Golconda, Illinois, was politically innocent and had 'an acute need', as Sandusky puts it, 'to oversimplify complex problems'. A few of his officers had been trained for the invasion of Japan, but neither they nor he were prepared for Korea. He did have a political adviser, H. Merrell Benninghoff; Benninghoff had worked briefly on trusteeship in the

divert the divisions which had been intended for the invasion of Japan in November. Perhaps he or his advisers remembered, as the Americans did not, that the Czarist government had agreed to the 38th parallel as a line to divide Russian and Japanese influence on the peninsula in the 1890s, and believed that it would provide sufficient security also for him. Perhaps he accepted what the Americans proposed in order to have a say in the post-war administration of Japan; he did ask for a Soviet zone of occupation in his reply to the general order, although his request was immediately refused. Perhaps he knew that any trusteeship for Korea would eventually produce a sympathetic regime. Mark Jacobsen and John Horsfield consider it 'unhistorical' to ask whether the Soviet Union would – despite its promises to the United States – have declared war on Japan on 8 August if the United States had not dropped an atomic bomb there on the 6 (Arthur Marder, Jacobsen and Horsfield, *Old Friends, New Enemies: The Royal Navy and the Imperial Japanese Navy*, Volume II, *The Pacific War 1942–1945*, Oxford: Clarendon Press, 1990, p. 543). I naturally disagree, but in the absence of information from the Soviet side, it is not an easy question for anyone yet to answer. Moscow may have thought that it might be able to achieve what it wanted to in the Far East without having to engage there. None the less, as Japanese intelligence reported at the time, and with alarm, Soviet military detachments did set off for the east in May 1945 without any winter clothing. As the war turned against them, the Japanese came to hope that the Soviet Union would not engage with them, mediate with the Allies, and thus facilitate a more honourable outcome. To this end, they attempted conciliation with Moscow, terminating, for example, the Anti-Comintern pact they had made with Germany and Italy in 1936. But although the Japanese Supreme Council agreed in May 1945 – at its first open discussion of the possibility of defeat – that Japan would return to the territories it had held before the war with Russia in 1904, it refused to contemplate anything but neutrality for Manchuria (under what it may have envisaged as a kind of joint trusteeship with the USSR and China) and its own continued occupation of Korea. But the divisions within the government in Tokyo were such that when asked by the Soviet ambassador there to do so, it could not give further details of the terms on which the Soviet Union might negotiate with the Allies.

State Department in 1943, where he had argued that a Soviet occupation of Korea 'would create an entirely new strategic situation in the Far East' whose 'repercussions within China and Japan might be far reaching'.[15] But Benninghoff only arrived in Okinawa on 3 September, two days before Hodge set off. He did bring some background material on Korea, and Hodge was a conscientious reader. But neither Benninghoff nor anyone else could tell him what to try to achieve; the State Department was in confusion. Hodge's only instructions were not to recognise any putative government and to re-establish law and order, as MacArthur had suggested, with 'constituted Japanese officials and police'. Southern Korea got the military administration intended for Japan, and was treated more as an occupied territory than a liberated one.[16]

As soon as he arrived in Korea, Benninghoff reported to the State Department that 'the most encouraging single factor in the political situation' was 'the presence in Seoul of several hundred conservatives among the older and better-educated Koreans'.[17] The view in Washington had been that the Koreans were not ready for steady self-rule. Kim Ku's conservative Provisional Government, which had been sitting out the war in Chungking, was known to be greedy, corrupt and divided, and there was no evidence that it represented opinion either in Korea itself or among other exiles. Rhee, its self-styled Minister Plenipotentary and Envoy Extraordinary to the United States, had little support in Washington. (At the same time, when Chiang threatened to stop financing the KPG after it had protested at the idea, first floated at the Cairo conference in 1943, of

[15] Quoted by Cumings, *Child of Conflict*, p. 13. There is no record of Roosevelt having read or reacted to the State Department report in 1943, which was supervised by John Carter Vincent, the director of the Office of Far Eastern Affairs.

[16] Cumings, *Origins*, p. 128. Sandusky, *America's Parallel*, p. 291. More appropriate commanders for Korea, as it was thought at the time, would have been Joseph Stilwell, who was MacArthur's first choice, or Albert Wedemeyer. Stilwell, however, who had served in China, had fallen out with Chiang and was unacceptable to the Kuomintang for any proposed landing 'on the China coast'; Wedemeyer, who succeeded Stillwell, was thought to be more important where he was. MacArthur's instructions from Sandusky, *America's Parallel*, p. 177.

[17] On Benninghoff in the State Department and Seoul, Cumings, *Origins*, pp. 113–14, 142–50.

a three-power trusteeship between Britain, China and the United States, the State Department said that it would not tolerate China's interference in other powers' wishes to decide their own future.)

In southern Korea itself, there were two political groupings. One was Benninghoff's local conservatives. These were the continuation of a group of landlords and professional men who had attempted some moderate opposition to the Japanese occupation, but had been rejected after the late 1920s; some had since collaborated. They described themselves to the Americans as 'patriots, notables and various circles of the intellectual stratum'. In mid September, they formed themselves into a Korean Democratic Party. They did so to oppose the second group. This had been put together just before Hodge arrived. In mid August, knowing that surrender was near, the Japanese governor-general had realised that he had to find a group of Koreans who would maintain order and protect Japanese persons and property in the retreat. He first approached the conservatives, but they would not agree.[18] He then asked Yŏ Un-hyŏng, who did. Yŏ was a left-wing nationalist who had started a Korean Independence League the year before; he now formed a new Committee for the Preparation of Korean Independence. This immediately expanded to include a large number of freed prisoners and demobilised soldiers and policemen, and as it spread beyond Seoul, of peasants in the provinces; some 145 branches seem to have been formed by the end of the month. Having heard that the Americans were coming, this Committee announced on 28 August that it would form a government with 'a people's committee elected by a national conference of people's representatives'; it convened the conference on 6 September and declared a Korean People's Republic. Many of those who aligned themselves with this new body had been more or less actively resisting the Japanese in the name of 'communism'. But the KPR was broadly based; Yŏ himself had not been a member of any Korean communist party. In deference to the known hostility of the Americans to the left, its first 'cabinet' included Rhee as its chairman, Kim Ku as its minister for the

[18] They told the governor that a post-liberation government was a matter for the Allies and the KPG; but they may have sensed that they would be seen by other Koreans as collaborators, and lose authority (Cumings, *Origins*, p. 70; Cumings gives the most detailed account of these early moves, pp. 71–99).

interior and another member of the KPG still in China, Kim Kyu-
sik, as its minister for foreign affairs. But Rhee was not to return
until the middle of October, the members of the KPG until late
November and early December. And by then, the Republic's organisation was already effective. When the KPR reconvened in
November to decide what to do if the Americans recognised the
KPG as the government for the south, it was itself surprised to
discover that its people's committees administered nearly half the
area beneath the 38th parallel. The military government confirmed
the fact. The KPR's 'communists', Benninghoff reported, were the
only effective organisation in the countryside. ('Without foreign
intervention', Cumings suggests, 'the KPR and the organisations it
sponsored would have triumphed throughout the peninsula in a
matter of months.')[19] In Seoul, however, the political situation
remained confused. Benninghoff described it to the State Department as a 'powder-keg', 'ripe for agitators'. Another American
complained that every time two Koreans sat down to dinner, they
formed a new party. All these parties agreed only that the Japanese
should go, that their property should be seized, and that Korea
should be independent at once. But only Rhee was to argue that a
separate independence for the south was better than no independence at all.

Independence, however, was the one thing the Americans would
not concede. The State Department reiterated its interest in
trusteeship in late October; but it still had no plans. Indeed, it was a
Soviet draft which, with minor modifications, was eventually to be
agreed at a foreign ministers' meeting in December. Meanwhile,
Hodge had to govern. As MacArthur had suggested he should, he
used members of the existing police force, which had been detested
by Koreans, for a new constabulary. He at first employed Japanese
administrators, although he was soon told not to by Washington.
He formed a youth group which was led and largely manned by those
opposed to the left. He contemplated a national defence force. He
established an 'advisory council' in which he tactlessly included a

[19] *Origins*, p. 91. The people's committees were also active in the north,
where the Soviet administration was pleased to let them continue, although
after February 1946 it came increasingly to direct policy through sympathetic
Koreans in Pyongyang.

known collaborator and eight members of the KDP; Yŏ was the only member from the left, and he refused to serve. He carelessly gave Rhee a platform as soon as Rhee returned from Washington – via Tokyo, on one of MacArthur's private planes – at a meeting intended to 'Welcome Our Allies', although he was annoyed when Rhee announced on this platform that the Americans had invited him back. And he appointed a shady Office of Strategic Services officer, one of the few Americans to have backed Rhee in Washington, to advise him.[20]

The KPG began to arrive from China in late November. It had had to agree that it would not claim to be a government. The Korean People's Republic, when it met to discuss the implications of the KPG's return, would not agree to the same condition; the very name of the KPG, after all, suggested a government; and as its members had now discovered, the KPR already controlled a large part of the south. Having first persuaded Yŏ to form a separate People's Party, Hodge therefore banned the KPR in early December. (He had told MacArthur in late November that he was in any case convinced that the KPR was 'the most powerful Communist backed group in Korea and has some Soviet connections'. To ban it, he saw, would be 'a "declaration of war" upon the Communistic elements, and may result in temporary disorders. It will also bring charges of political discrimination in a "free" country, both by local pinko and by pinko press.' What did Tokyo advise? MacArthur told him to use his best judgement.)

Hodge had obeyed orders.[21] He refused to acknowledge any Korean claims to be a government. He favoured the right, but made

---

[20] This man, Preston Goodfellow, followed Rhee to Seoul, but was sent back to the United States early in 1946 when it was discovered that Rhee had offered him (no doubt imaginary) 'concessions' in an independent Korea.

[21] Cumings simplifies when he says that in the matter of Rhee's return to Korea, Hodge, MacArthur and others 'conspired against established State Department policy' (*Origins*, p. 189). The State Department did not at this time have any very clear policy, except not to recognise any party of Koreans as a prospective government and somehow pursue trusteeship; and whatever his own political preferences, Hodge did respect the first, if not, at least willingly, the second. Cumings (like Dobbs) also repeats a story of Henderson's about how Rhee got a passport out of the United States against State Department wishes, which seems not to be true (see Sandusky, *America's Parallel*, pp. 34–5).

it clear that the occupation was an occupation. This antagonised all the parties, even when – as did both the left-wing KPR and the conservative KDP, although not Rhee – they accepted the temporary authority of the United States. The military government was making no progress. It was also having to cope with low morale among its troops, who wanted to go home. On 16 December, Hodge despaired. He sent a telegram to Tokyo to say that the situation was impossible, that 'every Korean knows full well that under the dual occupation any talk of real freedom and independence is purely academic', that in so far as there was any clear political inclination among the 'masses' it lay in 'an increasing tendency to look to Russia for the future', that 'every day of drifting under this situation' made the American position in Korea 'more untenable'. He proposed that United States and Soviet forces should accordingly withdraw and leave Korea 'to its own devices and an inevitable internal upheaval for its self-purification'.[22]

Two weeks before, Washington had received a report from William Langdon, temporarily replacing Benninghoff as political adviser in Seoul, who in response to the State Department's announcement in late October, said that 'I am unable to fit trusteeship to actual conditions here . . . and believe we should drop it'. The Koreans, he said, were literate and sophisticated and wanted independence; trusteeship, were it to be imposed, could only be maintained by force. The War Department, wanting to withdraw its troops, agreed. 'The major US interest in facilitating Korean independence', it noted, 'is that Korea shall become truly free, democratic, friendly to the US and not unduly dependent on any of its three major neighbours.' But the State Department persisted. It succeeded in persuading the SWNCC to argue that 'the United States occupies an exposed and untenable position in Korea from both a military and political standpoint. A prolonged occupation of Korea on our part cannot but create suspicion by the USSR that we have advanced our military strength in East Asia to points beyond those which are necessary and requisite for the security of the

---

[22] Hodge's November telegram in Cumings, *Origins*, p. 197; his December telegram in Sandusky, *America's Parallel*, pp. 304–6, Cumings, *Origins*, pp. 209–11.

United States.' This meant persisting with trusteeship. Langdon again contested the judgement, but the State Department ignored him.[23]

The Americans decided to try to get an agreement at the meeting of foreign ministers that had been arranged in Moscow for December. They appeared to succeed. Once one or two 'urgent' matters of co-operation had been settled, the United States and the Soviet Union would together establish a provisional government for the whole of Korea. Under their joint supervision, this would remove existing barriers between the two zones and prepare for a properly independent rule. The details were to be worked out in a Joint Commission. Truman was not pleased with the results of this meeting. He thought that Secretary of State Byrnes, wanting to arrive at statesmanlike agreements with the Russians on a wide variety of issues, had 'lost his nerve'; on Korea and on other, to Washington more important, matters, with which the meeting had been mainly concerned, had conceded too much to the Soviet Union; the president was tired, he wrote, of 'babying the Soviets'.[24] The United States did not observe the agreement on Korea. In the subsequent negotiations in the Joint Commission, it would not agree to establish a provisional government before the barriers were removed. And when the provisional government was discussed, the Soviet Union would not agree to its including parties from the south who were opposed to the Moscow agreement and the idea of trusteeship. The Commission arranged little, and in July 1947, it was permanently adjourned.

Meanwhile, Hodge and his advisers at once resisted the Moscow agreement. As soon as it was announced in Seoul, to predictable pandemonium, Hodge asked for time to create a broader coalition of

[23] Details of the report from Seoul in Cumings, *Origins*, pp. 184–7; of the SWNCC opinion in Matray, *Reluctant Crusade*, pp. 63–4; of Langdon's reaction to the SWNCC, Dobbs, *Unwanted Symbol*, pp. 61–2, Cumings, looking for evidence of the United States itself looking for an opportunity to renege on its initial, 'internationalist', stance, regards the report from Seoul (which as it happened, accurately predicted what would eventually happen) as 'the most important document to appear during the first year of the Occupation' (p. 186).

[24] Robert L. Messer, *The End of an Alliance: James F. Byrnes, Roosevelt, Truman, and the Origins of the Cold War*, Chapel Hill: University of North Carolina Press, 1982, pp. 137–66.

opinion. In January 1946, on the advice of the OSS officer who had
followed Rhee back to Korea, he replaced the KPG with a Representative Democratic Council. This was to include Kim Ku and be
chaired by Rhee. As Leonard Bertsch, another of Hodge's political
advisers, said, it 'was neither representative, nor democratic, nor did
it ever counsel'.[25] What it did do was protest at the Moscow
agreement. It also prompted a new grouping on the left. Yŏ Joined
his new People's Party to Pak Hŏn-yŏng's south Korean Communist
Party in a Democratic National Front. This called for the return of
power to the people's committees (The agents of the American CIC
who went to its meetings said that the Front was 'directed by a
competent group of Russian-trained communists'. This no doubt
fitted their preconceptions, but seems to have been mistaken. The
DNF did celebrate the inauguration of the Interim People's Committee in Pyongyang in February; but Pak and Yŏ and their associ-
ates – who had been together at the start of the KPR the previous
September – were all from the south; the few amongst them who had
had any foreign 'training' were those who had been with Mao in
Yenan before 1945, not with Russians.)[26]

The situation deteriorated still further. Hodge now offered to
resign, but was refused. The War Department, sensible of the over-
extension of American forces overseas, and aware that nothing was
being achieved in Korea, again pressed for withdrawal. But the State
Department persisted. Arguing that trusteeship was still the United
States' best hope, and seeing that Hodge was supporting political
interests which the Soviet Union could not accept, it asked him to

[25] Quoted by Cumings, *Origins*, p. 235.
[26] Cumings, *Origins*, p. 237. The southern communists, like all other Koreans,
had opposed trusteeship. They changed their mind in January 1946, in the
middle of a demonstration, crossing out the character for 'down' and substituting
one for 'up . . . with the Moscow agreement'. Who or what prompted them to do
so is not known but is not difficult to guess. Pak had sustained resistance to the
Japanese until 1933, when he was imprisoned, and again from 1939 to 1941. In
1941, he went underground as a brick worker in Kwangju, and once the new
Republic of Korea had been inaugurated in Seoul in August 1948, went to
Pyongyang. In September 1948, he was made vice-premier and foreign minister
of the Democratic People's Republic. In 1953, Kim Il Sung accused him of
having misled the DPRK on the support there would be in the south for the
invasion from the north three years earlier. There is no record of his having been
tried, but he is known to have been executed in Pyongyang in 1955.

disband the RDC for a more suitable grouping. Hodge again obeyed, and set Bertsch to work to form a new Coalition Committee. Bertsch decided that he had to separate Kim Ku and Rhee from the more moderate right and Pak from the more moderate left. He therefore chose to form the committee around Kim Kyu-sik, the one clearly honest and liberal ex-member of the old KPG, and Yŏ Un-hyŏng, 'the authentic voice', Bertsch thought, 'of the Korean peasantry'. At the same time, Hodge's military governor in Seoul announced that a half-elected and half-appointed interim assembly, a prelude to an interim government for the south, would be insti-tuted in the autumn.

The Coalition Committee was a promising move. But it failed. Rhee and Pak, now both isolated by the military government, opposed it. In September, Pak organised strikes in the cities. At the beginning of October, there were also uprisings in the countryside. These were prompted in part by a rice requisition policy that hurt many rural Koreans, but were most intense in those areas in which the people's committees had been strong (in the far south, they still were) and in and out of which there had also been considerable movements of population.[27] The Americans assumed that the pro-tests were being fomented by the north; they put paid to the Coalition Committee. But the protests did not prevent the military governor from pressing ahead with the elections to the interim assembly. But he only gave five days' notice. The local administra-tion in most parts of the country was still staffed by those who opposed the left. Other parts were disrupted by the uprisings. The constabulary and the often violent National Youth Movement were given a fairly free hand. Moreover, many rural Koreans had little idea of what they were voting for, and were happy to support their

---

[27] The rural uprisings are described by Cumings, *Origins*, pp. 351–81. The economic situation in the south had deteriorated badly. Information is sparse, but in addition to the problems with food grains, industrial employment had perhaps more than halved between 1944 and 1947, only about half the labour force had a job of any kind in 1947, and retail prices had risen between ten and twenty times in two years. The departing Japanese had printed a large amount of money, causing inflation; communists had done the same after 1945; Japanese administrative and technical staff had left; and neither the Americans, re-organising Japanese holdings in a New Korea Company, nor south Koreans did much to restore production.

local notable's request to vote for the conservatives. The results accordingly favoured the right. Even Washington agreed that they were worthless. Hodge tried to recover by appointing moderates to the non-elected places and making Kim Kyu-sik chairman of the new assembly. But the assembly and the interim government did little, and both were abandoned in the following July with the adjournment of the Joint Commission.[28] In that month also, in broad daylight and in sight of a police station in Seoul, Yŏ was shot.

The State Department itself was now losing hope in an agreed solution for the whole of Korea. The United States had two options remaining. It could withdraw at once from the south, as the War Department wanted. Or it could try to strengthen its position there with increased economic support, make one last attempt to persuade the Soviet Union to accept its conditions on who should be consulted in the formation of a provisional government for the whole country, and in the event of these conditions being rejected, make plans for a separate government for the south. It chose the second. In March 1947, having heard that the British could no longer support the anti-communist administrations in either place, Truman had asked Congress to vote for economic aid for Greece and Turkey. The administration agreed a similar policy for southern Korea; what it saw as the Soviet subversion there could, it believed, be countered by providing more resources. In April, the Joint Chiefs of Staff confirmed the importance of such a move, which would maintain the American presence, but without large numbers of troops. 'From the security standpoint', the joint chiefs argued, 'the primary reason for assistance to Korea would be that . . . this is the one country within which we alone have for almost two years carried on ideological warfare in direct contact with our opponents, so that to lose this battle would be gravely detrimental to US prestige, and therefore security, throughout the world. To abandon this struggle', they concluded, 'would tend to confirm the suspicion that the US is

---

[28] The interim government included a preponderant proportion of people who had served the Japanese administration or who had been owners or managers of enterprises before 1945, which usually meant that they had had Japanese support. The police still included a majority of men who had served under the Japanese (Cumings, *Origins*, p. 263).

not really determined to accept the responsibilities and obligations of world leadership.'[29]

At a meeting of foreign ministers in Moscow a week or two before, the Soviet Union had agreed to try once more for agreement. (The Americans interpreted this as a response to their new toughness.) Parties in both parts of the country which wished to be consulted in the formation of a provisional government had to endorse the Joint Commission's brief. When the Commission met again in July, three parties from the north offered their endorsement, and more than 400 from the south; these claimed a total membership or more than sixty million, three times larger than the total population of the zone; two-thirds, however, were on the right. The Soviet negotiators agreed with the Americans that their exclusion would mean a left-wing majority, and refused to accept them. The Americans broke off the talks. It was now clear that there was indeed going to be a separate government in the south.

But such a government had at least to appear to be legitimate. The United States accordingly took a proposal to the United Nations. This was for supervised elections in the whole of Korea by the end of March 1948, and the withdrawal of Soviet and American forces after the formation of a provisional government. Washington knew that Soviet Union would oppose the proposal, and hoped that in doing so, it would lose international respect. There was a need now for haste. In February, the Interim People's Committee in Pyongyang had said that it would 'in a few months' form a government for the whole of Korea. The Soviet Union had already proposed withdrawing its forces from the north. Chiang's collapse in China also seemed imminent, and was beginning to cause recriminations in Washington. Despite further protest and violence in the south, therefore, including protest from Rhee, who was now resisting international supervision, the United States proceeded. The Soviet Union and its allies in the General Assembly opposed the motion. But this did not prevent a general election in the south.

[29] Quoted by Barton J. Bernstein, 'The Truman administration and the Cold War', in Lacey ed., *The Truman Presidency*, p. 414. None the less, of the countries in the world whose security mattered most at that moment, the Joint Chiefs believed, to the security of United States, they ranked Korea fifteenth, and of 'secondary' importance.

This was eventually held in May 1948. A United Nations' Commission, which was initially divided on the advisability of holding it at all, reluctantly validated it; the left ignored it, the right won; Rhee was elected president by the new assembly; a Republic of Korea came into being in August; and despite objections from Rhee, which amounted almost to panic, the United States withdrew its combat troops (although not its military materials) at the end of June 1949, six months after the Soviet Union – now that there was also an independent regime in the north – had withdrawn its troops there. (The plan for a complete military withdrawal had been made in 1948, originally for the December of that year, but the State Department successfully pressed for a postponement to allow the new South Korea to stabilise. Notwithstanding Chiang's now virtually certain defeat in China and the revised policy for Japan, which in the State Department's view, required a supporting periphery of non-communist states, the military opinion prevailed in March 1949.)

Truman was relieved by the solution, and felt able more confidently to face his critics in Washington. In June 1949, asking Congress for further economic assistance, he argued that 'Korea has become a testing ground in which the validity and practical value of the ideals and principles of democracy which the Republic is putting into practice are being matched against the practices of communism which have been imposed upon the people of north Korea. The survival and progress of the Republic' in Seoul, he continued, 'toward a self-supporting, stable economy will have an immense and far-reaching influence on the people of Asia. Such progress . . . will encourage [them] to resist and reject the Communist propaganda by which they are besieged. Moreover', he added, alluding to China and the accusations that were increasingly being made of America's inadequate support for Chiang and its refusal to try to stem the communist advance into the south of China, 'the Korean Republic, by demonstrating the success and tenacity of democracy in resisting communism, will stand as a beacon for the people of northern Asia in resisting the control of the communist forces which have overrun them'.[30] But despite the departure of American troops, Rhee con-

---

[30] Quoted by Matray, *Reluctant Crusade*, p. 198. Truman had already had considerable internal difficulties. Republicans in Congress, who were in the majority in both houses until 1948, and some Democrats too, were unwilling to

tinued openly to threaten the north with war, which he said could be won in three days. In June 1950, however, after months of border skirmishing, it was the north which invaded the south. Interpreting this as a Soviet move, Americans concluded that containment had failed.

IV

In considering what might have been possible, we enter the world at what we judge to be the point from which the actual outcome did result. In considering whether the United States could have succeeded in its policy for Korea, we could suppose that the Japanese had not occupied the peninsula; or that the Second World War had not taken place; or that the United States did not enter it; or that it did not emerge as one of the two predominant powers. But suppositions such as these would take us back to a point at which the questions for Korea in 1945 would cease to be questions for that Korea. These questions, as I have said, are whether the United States could have decided not to occupy the southern part of the country in 1945, and once it did, whether it could have acted in such a way as to avoid the eventual division.

A deterministic view, of course, or a view of a determined conspiracy, which amounts to much the same thing, would rule such questions out. Matray sees no conspiracy, but his world was predetermined. After 1945, the European powers were going to be weaker, the Soviet Union more powerful, and China, now free from Japan, would be a presence. The weakening of the European powers would mean the weakening, perhaps even the end, of their empires, and the weakening also of Europe itself. The larger part of the world would be economically vulnerable, politically uncertain, and open to new manipulations. It would have required a strong nerve, even in a now great power that had been inclined to isolation, to leave it so.

In any event, great powers, Matray's kind of argument assumes,

maintain expensive American military presences abroad; and the Administration, eager to get money for its new policy in Europe, postponed a request for Korea until the Republicans took the decision out of its hands by saying that they would not vote for any more foreign assistance in the 1947 session.

have an urge to expand. This is not always driven by imminent threat or economic need. After 1945, the United States was faced with neither. There was no likelihood of attack, and its needs for materials and trade were not as great as those of the imperial states in eighteenth- and nineteenth-century Europe or of Britain still. Moreover, great powers expand into a space, and the properties of that space are important. The most important of these is simply that it is a space. Nothing very alarming or demanding has actually to be happening in it. What matters is what might. Powers expand to pre-empt; and great powers expand greatly. In so doing, they give themselves reasons for continuing to do so. Where there is not just one great power in the world, one expanding power will eventually confront another. If the powers have not agreed to stop, each will be made insecure. If the insecurity is not negotiated, the reasons for continuing to expand are given. And then, the issue will not just be one of confrontation at the edge. 'If you don't pay attention to the periphery', said Secretary of State Rusk in 1961 – the man who as a colonel in the Operations Division in the Pentagon on the night of 10 August 1945, was one of the two who decisively drew the line to divide Korea at the 38th parallel – 'the periphery changes. And the first thing you know the periphery is the centre.'[31]

The other argument for predetermination, which is an argument

---

[31] A recent restatement of this 'vacuum' thesis is Michael Mandelbaum, *The Fate of Nations: The Search for National Security in the Nineteenth and Twentieth Centuries*, Cambridge: Cambridge University Press, 1988, e.g. p. 137; Dean Rusk quoted from a press conference in May 1961 at p. 138. This thesis is a special case of that more general argument, usually called 'realist', which regards the pursuit of power under 'systemic' constraints as a sufficient explanation of the international actions of states (e.g. Kenneth Waltz, *Theory of International Politics*, Reading MA: Addison-Wesley, 1983); a more complex view, which comes down from Thucydides and Clausewitz, is that the nature of the poten-tially contending regimes is also important (e.g. Raymond Aron, *Peace and War: A Theory of International Relations*, New York: Doubleday, 1966), a view that perhaps has support in the fact that no two liberal regimes have ever gone to war with each other (Michael Doyle, 'Kant, liberal legacies and foreign affairs', *Philosophy and Public Affairs* 12 (1984), 205–35, 323–53). On Roosevelt's developing sense of the relation between the international balance and Ameri-can domestic politics, Robert Dallek, *Franklin D. Roosevelt and American Foreign Policy: 1932–1945*, New York: Oxford University Press, 1980. By the spring of 1945, perhaps the most pressing domestic pressure in the United States was against the prolonged use and further loss of military manpower.

from conspiracy, is from the left. The policy of the United States for the post-war world was in its essentials set, Cumings claims, and set by its imperial interests, before the end of the war. Roosevelt's internationalism, like the 'nationalism' which succeeded it, was in Cumings' characterisation a device for ' accommodating American security concerns', opening 'the colonies to American commerce and tutelage', and corralling 'communist and anticolonial revolution'. The decisions for Korea followed from that.

From neither the right nor the left, therefore, was there anything remarkable about American actions towards Korea in or after 1945. They were dictated by the logic of power or by the logic of a conspiracy of interest. Yet as I have already suggested, the detail in the explanations that Matray and Cumings and other historians have produced hints at alternatives. The United States might not have occupied south Korea; or once it did, it might not have undermined a joint trusteeship and eventual independence for the whole country. Power, after all, also enables restraint. The United States' actions were not perhaps predetermined after all.

V

Truman said that on the question of Soviet intentions, Averell Harriman was the decisive influence at the decisive moment. Harriman's diplomatic experience and his frequent meetings with Stalin after going as ambassador to Moscow in October 1943 gave him an air of authority, as Truman recalled in his memoirs, that no official in Washington could command. On his return to consult there after Roosevelt's death, Harriman explained that the Soviet Union was pursuing two distinct policies. One was to co-operate with the United States; the other, now evident in Poland, was to extend Soviet control by independent action. He had a receptive audience in Truman's new advisers. Roosevelt, and what the new advisers were calling Roosevelt's 'palace guard', had thought that the agreement on Poland did allow the interpretation that the Soviet Union had put on it. The advisers, however, disputed this, and agreed with Harriman that there should now be a review of Roosevelt's policy. There was a need for an American show of strength. Truman accepted this. Stalin had not unreasonably cited Britain's insistence on establishing friendly governments in Belgium and Greece in support of his own action in Poland. But Truman protested about this action to Foreign Minister Molotov just before the San Francisco conference in April. Their exchange was angry, and the president became even more determined to take a tough stance.[32]

Truman and his advisers began to extrapolate from Poland to Korea. They had seen that the agreement which had been made in Moscow in October 1943 for the Soviet Union to enter the war in Asia once Germany was defeated would give Stalin an advantage there. The State Department and the Office of Strategic Services had long been saying that the prospects for a strong and stable government in a liberated Korea were poor. They also knew that Chiang had ambitions for the peninsula, and that Mao's resistance to Chiang, which included Korean guerillas, was strongest near the Korean border. If Stalin himself extrapolated from Europe to Asia, it was likely that he would do all he could to establish a sympathetic regime in Korea, and that he would be able to.

In itself, this reasoning was sound.[33] The mistake was to believe that the United States had an overriding interest in resisting such a regime and the capacity to do so. By the spring of 1945, the United States was beginning to cease to try to find an accommodation with the Soviet Union. In the last week of July and the first week of August, it thought that it could pre-empt a Soviet advance into Korea by extracting a quick surrender from the Japanese. The Soviet army, however, started to move a week earlier than the Americans had expected. And in the absence of good intelligence, the SWNCC believed that it was moving more quickly than it was. Hence this committee's decision to rescue what it could on the night of the 10 August.

If the SWNCC really believed that despite his repeated

[32] Harry S. Truman, *Memoirs I: Year of Decisions*, Garden City NY: Doubleday, 1955, pp. 79–82.

[33] But Acting Secretary of State Grew's further inference (quoted by Matray, *Reluctant Crusade*, p. 34) that 'Mongolia, Manchuria, and Korea will gradually slip into Russia's orbit, to be followed in due course by China and eventually Japan', might be thought to have been a little wild; it nevertheless recalled the argument that Benninghoff and others had made in 1943.

agreement to trusteeship at Potsdam, Stalin's intention was to occupy the whole of the peninsula, it was not wise to indicate by an occupation of its own that the United States would resist him. The United States had long known that it did not have sufficient military capacity to do so, at least on land, and resistance from the air would be too inflammatory. If the SWNCC believed that Stalin would honour the agreement to a trusteeship, then its own convinced interpretation of his motives at his borders, to establish friendly regimes of the kind that he had already made a move to establish in Poland, could have made it clear that a Korean government which would be equally friendly to the United States would not be a likely outcome. And if the SWNCC believed that a Korea that was friendly to the Soviet Union would be a threat to Japan, they could have reflected that in a world in which there were to be two expanding great powers, there would have to be lines of confrontation somewhere; and that with American superiority in the sea and the air – its fast aircraft carriers and long-range bombers matched against the Soviet Union's technically backward airpower and its one warm-water port at Dairen – a line which ran between Japan and Korea would be more defensible than a line which ran through Korea itself. This is to say that even if one accepts the pessimistic view that almost all those in Washington were by August 1945 talking of Soviet intentions, and accepts also that the United States had some sort of interest, call it an interest in 'security', in the western Pacific – 'to be specific', a popular song of the time had it, 'it's our Pacific' – reflection could have revealed that this interest could not effectively be pressed by occupying just half of Korea.

These are not merely the considerations of hindsight. They are reflections that those men at that time, with the interests they had come to form and the information they had to hand, could have made. Indeed, some in the War Department were making them.[34] It

---

[34] The policy did have its internal critics, even among those who had long been suspicious of Soviet intentions. In the late 1940s, ex-Admiral James Forrestal remarked in his diary that 'our diplomatic planning of the peace . . . was far below the quality of planning that went into the conduct of the war'; 'we regarded the war, broadly speaking, as a ball game which we had to finish as quickly as possible, but in so doing there was comparatively little thought as to the relations between nations which would exist after Germany and Japan were

could of course be said that this underrates the haste in Washington between the early hours of 9 August, when Truman heard from Harriman about the Soviet army's advance into Manchuria, and the morning of the 15, when he signed the general order for surrender. The members of the SWNCC, the Joint War Plans Committee, and the Joint Staff Planners – to whom both committees were responsible – had many different things on their minds. (And there was in those days a cumbersome and to some also confusing division of responsibilities between the various groups in Washington.) Even after the SWNCC agreed on the division at the 38th parallel on the night of 10-11 August, there was anxiety about it, and argument; although this was mainly from naval men who believed not that the line should not have been drawn at all, but that it had been drawn one degree too far south. Decisions taken in haste are decisions taken in haste. But this does not explain why on the morning of the 9, on an Operations Division briefing paper for the SWNCC, a question-mark still had to be put after 'Objectives of US forces in Korea'. The fact remains that the decision to occupy southern Korea could consistently and coherently have been different. The men who took it, in the circumstances in which they did with the information that they had to hand and the interests they had come to formulate to themselves, could have decided otherwise, and little else would have had to be different for them to have done so.

VI

My argument suggests that in August 1945, the United States could have tried to pre-empt an excessive Soviet intrusion into the space between itself and the Soviet Union after 1945; that consistently with this, it could have acknowledged that Korea stood to the Soviet Union as Greece, Italy, France and Japan stood to Britain and the United States; that it could have accepted the advice of its chiefs of staff and the commanders in the Pacific; and that it could

destroyed'. Forrestal also thought that the insistence on the unconditional surrender of Germany and Japan 'would seriously unbalance the international system in the face of Soviet power' (quoted by Sandusky, *America's Parallel*, pp. 106–7).

have decided not to occupy southern Korea. The president and the Departments of State and War could have arrived at a less anxious interpretation of Soviet intentions, accepted their military limitations, and concentrated on the exclusive occupation of Japan. But the United States did enter Korea. Having done so, could it then have acted in such a way as to maintain its interests and not divide the peninsula?

Matray argues that 'Truman's policy before the north Korean attack was sensible because it recognised the superior strength of nationalism over communism as a force in international affairs.' What he must mean is that it recognised the superior force of nationalism over communism in ex-colonial territories. One can question the judgement. No one with a sense of the strength of nationalist sentiment could easily have supposed that a proposal to put a liberated colony under a new external administration, having first divided it in order to do so, would be gladly accepted. But there is little evidence to suggest that apart from Lattimore, who did not advise Truman, any influential American was sensitive to nationalist feelings. When the documents do discuss political ends, they do so only with the usual liberal abstractions. Apart from Langdon and Bertsch, who were junior officers and without much influence, the United States did confuse nationalism and communism in Korea.

It is true that there were a number of declared communists in the KPR in the south after September 1945, and Benninghoff described them as such. But although many of these people would no doubt have said, if asked, that the Soviet Union was their model, there then being no other (unless by chance they had taken to heart Mao's strictures in 1938 against 'eight-legged essays on foreign models');[35] and although some were members of Pak's new Communist Party; many were not, and even many of those who were had but a slight grasp of Marxism-Leninism. As in France, Italy and Greece after 1945, so in southern Korea: the 'communists' there included many who were simply in favour of the poor and against those who had

---

[35] Which Mao concluded by saying that 'there must be less repeating of empty and abstract refrains; we must discard our dogmatism and replace it by a new and vital Chinese style and manner, pleasing to the eye and to the ear of the Chinese common people' (Stuart Schram, *The Thought of Mao Tse-Tung*, Cambridge: Cambridge University Press, 1989, p. 70).

been in power, especially if these could be described as both 'fascists' and 'colonialists'.[36] But as in Europe, the Americans did not fully grasp that in Korea, 'communism' was the most convenient label for the radical nationalists who were hostile to foreign occupation (one indeed that had been put upon resisting Koreans by the Japanese); did not grasp that even convinced Marxist-Leninists may have adopted the doctrine *faute de mieux*, there being no other readily available rhetoric for radicals; assumed that self-described communists were the victims of Soviet subversion; and then supposed that American interests were served in supporting the professed anti-communists. As in Europe (including their zone of occupation in Germany itself), they thereby argued themselves into supporting those who had collaborated with the previous regime, and who to the rest of the population, were the least acceptable. It is easy to see how they aroused so much hostility; easy by contrast to see how easy it was for General Chistiakov, Hodge's counterpart in the north, to go with the grain of local aspirations and use the KPR's committees; and easy to see how it was that those on the right who had not collaborated, despite the distaste which most Americans felt for them – Rhee never ceased to infuriate Hodge, Kim Ku was a known assassin who continued to arrange murders in Korea, only Kim Kyu-sik seems to have been a decent man – came so repeatedly to the fore.

It might be said that regrettable though this was, it was the only likely state of affairs. None of the American soldiers or political officers in Korea were familiar with post-colonial politics; none, certainly, had any familiarity with Korea itself. Few had either the experience or the training with which to counter their prejudices.[37]

---

[36] Cumings makes a similar point, *Origins*, p. 477 n52. Also details in Dae-sook Su, *The Korean Communist Movement, 1918–48*, Princeton: Princeton University Press, 1967 and *Documents of Korean Communism, 1918–48*, Princeton: Princeton University Press, 1970.

[37] Lattimore was a rare exception. Hodge did overhear one of his officers speaking Korean, and at once made him an adviser. But this man was the son of missionaries, and his friends, Korean Christians of the middle class, became influential: Henderson, *Korea*, p. 126. Koreans described the American military administration in the early months as 'the government of interpreters'. More ordinary prejudices were pervasive. Soon after he arrived in Seoul, Hodge described Koreans in public as 'the same kind of cats as the Japanese'. An army lieutenant, when asked by an arriving journalist why fighter aeroplanes were

But Langdon's perception in the autumn of 1945 and Bertsch's negotiations the following summer, in which he tried to prise the moderates away from the right-wing RDC and its opposing DNF to form a new Coalition Committee, suggest that the prejudices were neither universal nor fixed. Bertsch's only previous political experience had been as a civil service commissioner in Akron, Ohio, and he had been in Korea for just five months; yet he had learnt the language and acquired a remarkably sensitive grasp of the local political actors and their positions.

Cumings and Matray suspect that if a coalition of this kind had been attempted earlier, it might 'have contributed', as Matray puts it, 'to the emergence of a united, democratic, and independent Korea'. This is highly unlikely. In the first place, the timing was crucial. In his first report to Washington on 15 September, Benninghoff had suggested that the KPG be asked to return. Another American adviser who arrived from Chungking a few weeks later endorsed the suggestion; what he referred to as the 'revolutionary Godhead' of the KPG was firmly 'anti-communist'; its members insisted on an independent Korea, but they would be friendly to the United States. Even Yŏ, who had included the absent members of the KPG in his KPR 'cabinet' on 6 September, urged Hodge to allow them back as individuals. Hodge eventually agreed, in early November, but insisted that Kim Ku's right-wing faction return before the moderates. Kim Ku eventually arrived on the 23, and Kim Kyu-sik on 3 December. A coalition of the kind that Bertsch was to put together the next summer could not therefore have been assembled before mid December. By then, Kim Kyu-sik was back, and Yŏ had been given the chance to distance himself from the KPR in his new People's Party. (The fact that Hodge created this party suggests that he was not so wholly committed to the right as to be opposed to the idea of a wider coalition.) But Hodge did not make the move. Instead, in January, in reaction to the Moscow agreement on trusteeship the previous month, he went in the opposite direction and included Kim Ku and Rhee in his new RDC.

swooping over fields near the airport at Seoul, replied 'psychological warfare: that's the only way to show these gooks we won't stand for any monkey business'. American sports events and other such functions were out of bounds to Koreans.

None the less, this is a point at which the military government could have acted otherwise. It could have brought the KPG back earlier than it did; and it could have avoided creating a 'representative' council so obviously inclined to the right and against trusteeship. But even if it had done each of these things, it does not follow that 'a united, democratic, and independent Korea' could then have emerged. It does not follow, as the optimists in the State Department had come by 1949 to suppose, that the United States could have achieved in Korea what it had already achieved in France and Italy. That would have required the Soviet Union to withdraw entirely from the north. But Moscow had no reason to consider doing so. The standing proposal was for a joint trusteeship. The Moscow agreement on this was for the establishment of a provisional government before anything else, and at the subsequent meetings of the Joint Commission, the Soviet Union insisted that only those Koreans who accepted the Moscow agreement and the Commission's terms of reference could be considered as possible members of this government. But the Americans disputed each condition. They knew that although two-thirds of the electorate was in their zone, any election in which those who rejected trusteeship were barred from standing would be won by the left. The Soviet Union would have its 'independent friendly' regime.[38] Only if the United States had been willing to accept this, could Korea have been reunified. But neither after the Moscow agreement nor before, was it willing to do so. To have accepted it in the autumn of 1945 would have meant abandoning its policy of trusteeship and conceding completely to the Soviet Union; it would also have made a nonsense of the occupation itself. To have accepted it after the

---

[38] Richard Robinson was an information officer for the military government in Korea who wrote a long account of the events of the late 1940s, the most critical of any account left by any of the participants – he was required to burn part of it before he left Seoul. He described the American insistence on 'freedom of expression' for all Koreans in the establishment of a provisional government as 'a false issue manufactured for the occasion to cloud the real issues and discredit the Russians' (quoted by Cumings, *Origins*, p. 246). What remains of Robinson's manuscript, which was an important source also for Henderson's *Korea* (Henderson served in Seoul at the same time as Robinson, but was less sympathetic to the Korean left than Cumings), is in the library at the Massachusetts Institute of Technology.

beginning of 1946 would have meant losing its one foothold on the Asian mainland; as Washington soon came to see it, to lose its 'prestige' in the world and to signal that it was not prepared to maintain what it was coming to call its 'bulwarks' against Soviet expansion.

Throughout 1946, the United States acted as if it wanted an agreement. In the early summer, the State Department persuaded Truman that Hodge's RDC was an ill-considered body, and eventually gave the order that produced Bertsch's Coalition Committee in the summer. The department also pointed out that one reason for the Soviet success in the north was that the administration there had instituted a series of popular reforms, dispensing commandered land to previous tenants, for instance, and providing opportunities for women, and had allowed these to be administered through local people's committees. In July, Truman accordingly announced a land reform for the south. He seems to have thought that measures like this, together with what Secretary Byrnes was calling an attitude of 'patience with firmness' towards the Soviet Union, would win the day. The Soviet Union would be faced down, and meanwhile, economic and social conditions which were conducive to what the Americans supposed was its subversion in the south would be alleviated.[39] But little was done, and the Soviet negotiators remained adamant. By the end of October, the military government had succeeded in mismanaging both the rice requisition programme and the elections to the interim legislative assembly, and it had strikes in the cities and rebellion in the countryside. It was not, as Henderson said, that the Americans had no policy at all. It was rather that the policies that they did have, as a group of Congressmen remarked after they returned from a visit to Korea at the beginning of September, were 'uncertain, fumbling' and 'confused'.[40]

Once again, the United States' attitude to the Soviet Union was inconsistent. Whether it believed that the Soviet Union was a defensive power with limited aims, or a revolutionary power with

[39] Neither Robinson nor Cumings find evidence that north Koreans were involved in any of the uprisings in the south in the autumn of 1946 (Cumings, *Origins*, p. 372).

[40] Quoted by Matray, *Reluctant Crusade*, p. 95.

unlimited aims – Kennan did not decide between these two interpretations in his long telegram in the spring of 1946–it had no
reason to believe that it would not stand firm on its intention to
secure a friendly regime in Korea.[41] Yet the United States continued
to press the issue of trusteeship, while at the same time making it
clear that it would not accept the Soviet conditions for it. It is of
course possible to see reason in this: a plan to put the Soviet Union
in a position which would draw attention to its intransigence and
thus justify a separate regime, friendly to the United States, in the
south. But this is very much the construction of hindsight. There is
no evidence from any of the documents or from any other source
that there had been any such intention. The United States only
began to form it at its point of desperation in the summer of 1947 at
which it realised that it did indeed either have to withdraw from
Korea or take the issue to the United Nations.

But despite the arguments of the War Department in Washington, which were for military withdrawal, and Hodge's intermittent
desperation in Seoul itself, the Truman administration never
contemplated politically abandoning southern Korea. The compromise for military withdrawal that was proposed by the National
Security Council and agreed by War, State and the president in
March 1949, NSC 8/2, insisted that the decision should be presented as 'in no way . . . lessening . . . US support of the Government of the Republic of Korea'.[42] Having got itself into Korea, it
believed that it had to stay there. This was not because it saw the
area south of the 38th parallel itself as essential to its 'security'; that
argument faded as it became apparent that there was no threat to
Japan. Indeed in January 1950, Secretary of State Acheson made it
clear in an address to the National Press Club in Washington that
Korea, like Taiwan, fell outside what the United States regarded as

[41] It is now all but certain that under Stalin, the Soviet Union was defensive,
and concerned only with securing its frontiers. (Stalin had been chastened by
the Kuomintang's murder of thousands of Chinese communists in 1927.) It was
only after his death that Moscow renewed its support for liberation movements
among what Lenin had called 'the peoples of the east', a support which *Foreign
Affairs*, the quasi-official journal of the foreign ministry there, conceded in
January 1989 had not been to its advantage.

[42] Quoted by Bernstein, 'The Truman administration and the Korean War',
p. 416.

its 'defence perimeter'. America would not automatically defend it in case of attack. It would expect it to do so itself, and if it failed, then to draw 'upon the commitments of the entire civilised world under the Charter of the United Nations'.[43] Nor was it because Kennan and others were beginning to think, as they were, that the Japanese economy should be revived, and that to be revived successfully, would need to be able to command materials and markets in this part of its old 'co-prosperity sphere'. The part of the old sphere of influence that Kennan and others had in mind was the south-east, not Manchuria or Korea.[44] It was, rather, that having got itself into Korea, the United States could not get itself out without indicating to others that it would not 'stand firm' against 'communism'. If there was a developing thread in American thinking after 1945, it was that the United States was going to be not just one great power amongst two or three, but the predominant one. And the predomi-

[43] This seems to have been Acheson's conclusion after considering (no doubt amongst many other things) a National Security Council paper on 'The position of the US with regard to Asia' (NSC 48) which was drafted, revised and approved in 1949, and perhaps also after reflecting on the criticisms which had been made of the apparently unlimited implications of containment, including the implication that it committed the United States to support all petty tyrants – of which Rhee, Acheson was clear, was an instance – as long as they were avowedly anti-communist. Cumings makes much of the first draft of NSC 48, which suggested the desirability of considering both defensive and offensive action against the Soviet Union in Asia. But the final version accorded exactly with Acheson's speech, the rationale of which Cumings seems to me to get right (*Child of Conflict*, pp. 32–49; also Bernstein, 'The Truman administration and the Korean War', p. 417).

[44] Bruce Cumings, 'The northeast Asian political economy', *International Organisation* 38 (1984), 1–40 at 16–22. At 16, Cumings retells the story of the American officer who walked into the Mitsui office in Tokyo in September 1945 and was shown a map of the Greater East Asia Co-Prosperity Sphere. 'There it is', a Japanese manager said. 'We tried. See what you can do with it.' In the event, and prompted by the Korean war, the United States came to help the Japanese to reconstruct it for themselves; this is summarised by Cumings and John W. Dower, 'Occupied Japan and the cold war in Asia', in Lacey ed., *The Truman Presidency*, pp. 388–9. 'The Greater East Asia Co-prosperity sphere – isn't it nice?', remarked a Japanese cabinet minister in 1969; 'we tried to construct it by military power in the past. This time we are going to create it by economic power' (quoted by Dal Joong Chang, *Economic Control and Political Authoritarianism: The Role of Japanese Corporations in Korean Politics, 1965–1979*, Seoul: Sogang University Press, 1985, p. 63).

nant power could not retreat in the face of another. Only if the United States had reverted to its wartime policy of accommodation with the Soviet Union, could it have accepted a regime for the whole of Korea which – as any freely elected regime would have been likely to do – would have favoured the left.

The Soviet Union itself pre-empted a free election in the north. Chistiakov removed Cho Man-sik from his leadership of the people's committee in Pyongyang in January 1946 when Cho refused – having been asked three times – to accept the Moscow agreement. He seems then to have supported Kim Il Sung. Kim's wartime career is much debated; but perhaps after fighting with other Koreans at Stalingrad, he led a small guerilla group on the Soviet–Korean border towards the end of the war, had received further Soviet training there, and arrived in Pyongyang at the end of September 1945. But Chistiakov may have decided to back him only after dismissing Cho, sensing that he was able and also sufficiently popular – Cho had himself given Kim a fulsome welcome at a rally in Pyongyang on 3 October – because he combined a commitment to communism with a nationalism.[45] Kim's coming to power was not preordained.

Yet even if Cho had not, as he appears to have done, misplayed his hand on trusteeship against Chistiakov, it does not seem likely that in the north, a more neutral Korean People's Republic, in its inclination perhaps like Bertsch's Coalition Committee, would have been allowed to prevail. After the Moscow agreement, the Soviet Union had every interest in trying to secure in Pyongyang a sympathetic provisional government for the whole of Korea. Even if a possibly united and independent Korea was not therefore bound to turn out to be exactly like the actual Democratic People's Republic in the north, because Kim Il Sung's domination there was not itself predetermined, it seems unlikely that it would have been anything other than some sort of 'people's republic'. In itself, and in the

---

[45] On Cho's dismissal, Cumings, *Origins*, p. 558. Cho had been named as minister of finance in the nominal cabinet of Yŏ's Korean People's Republic in September 1945. Chistiakov placed him under house arrest in January 1946, and visitors from the south found him still confined in the spring of 1948. His eventual fate is not known. On Kim Il Sung, Cumings, *Origins*, pp. 397 ff., especially p. 400.

hardening lines of the Cold War, which were being drawn by much more than events in east Asia, an independent and united Korea would almost certainly have been more sympathetic to the Soviet Union (and perhaps also to China) than to the United States.[46] This, of course, is what Americans in Washington and in Seoul itself almost immediately came to see. It is why the United States could neither have accepted the Soviet conditions for trusteeship nor simply abandoned south Korea without appearing plainly to have reneged on what it had come to define as its purpose there.

VIII

One impulse in the histories of the division of Korea, as in many histories of events of this kind, has been to blame or to excuse the protagonists for what they did and did not do. This has not been my own first concern. Even if it had been, I would have had first to ask whether any of the protagonists could have acted differently. This has been my question: could those men, at that time, in the circumstances in which they found themselves, with the information that was available to them, have acted other than they did? As I have said, my answer is that in August 1945, before the United States committed itself to southern Korea, the Americans could have done so; but that once in Korea, they could not. Or at least, they could not have done so unless they had been willing and able to revise their reasons for being in Korea in the first place; willing and able radically to revise their conception of what they were and why more generally they were doing what they were doing in the world. For by that time, they had created a set of circumstances from which they, as they had come to define themselves, could not retreat. Nevertheless, the question of what

---

[46] It is important to recall that from the start, Kim Il Sung pursued a fairly independent policy. In accord with the Soviet inclination, he advocated a Leninism from the top, in accord with Mao's a 'mass line'; and long before he developed his precept of *chuch'e*, or self-reliance, he annoyed both Moscow and Peking by purging Korean communists in Pyongyang who had been in the Soviet Union and China during the Japanese occupation.

the Americans could have done does lead naturally to the question of whether they were right in what they did. And this also is a matter of counterfactual analysis.

For it is only interesting to criticise someone for not being right if they could have been. That's to say, it is only interesting if, as the person he or she was in the situation in which he found himself, he could have reflected on the origins and likely consequences of his beliefs in such a way as himself to have been able to revise his ends, or to have been able to reconsider pursuing them in the ways that he was. And even if he could have reflected in this way, it does not follow that there is a determinate answer to the question of what he would have been right to decide.[47] What someone might have considered depends on his particular interests, his ability and his will; what advice he might have had in part depends on what advice he might have sought; what the circumstances dictated in part depends on interpretation, imagination and nerve; and none of these can be decided beyond all doubt. The kind of assessment that we have to make of them is the kind that is inherent also in trying to understand what it is that anyone actually did do and why, and why it had the consequences that it did. Understanding in this more usual sense, the sense that is usually captured – at least in discussions of method in the social sciences – in the German notion of *Sinnverstehen*, therefore turns on understanding in the sense that I explained in the previous chapter: on locating the actual in a space of possibles. But possibilities for politics, although they might become clearer in a discussion like this, can never in any strong sense be known. To understand more about any politics is thus to be less certain about it.

---

[47] Students of Critical Theory will recognise the similarity between these criteria and two of the three that the Critical Theorists have suggested. The third, the criterion of what has been described as 'epistemic validity', supposes that there is a fact of the matter about interests, and that reflection can therefore produce a true or false answer to the question of what they are. I do not see any way in which this can be defended. There is excellent discussion, to the same conclusion, in Raymond Geuss, *The Idea of a Critical Theory: Habermas and the Frankfurt School*, Cambridge: Cambridge University Press, 1981. See also Chapter 5, section VI, especially note 20.

— 4 —

Duccio's painting

I

Possibilities increase under explanation. To decide how plausible any such possibility, causal or practical, is, is not, I have argued, in any strong or simple sense a theoretical matter. None the less, explanations themselves may draw on theory, and to the extent that they do, the plausibility of the possibilities they suggest will bear back on the theory which informs them.

But this is ambiguous. The theory in question may be an account of how, causally or practically, the kind of thing we wanted to explain came about. Or it may be a theory in a more descriptive sense, in which what is first at issue is not how we might explain how something occurred, but how we should see it. If the possibilities that our explanations suggest bear back on a theory of the first kind, revisions to that theory will not necessarily affect our characterisation of what it was that had to be explained. The possibility that the incidence and effects of plague in some parts of early modern Europe could have been alleviated, or that rural fertility in seventeenth- or eighteenth-century France could have been lower, has a bearing on pre-existing explanations; but neither requires us to change our characterisation of what it is that we want to explain. Likewise, the possibility that the United States did not move to occupy southern Korea in 1945, or the possibility that once there, it worked to create a government for the whole country, do not require us to change our reports of what it actually did and did not do.

If the possibilities bear back on a theory of the second kind, however, they may. This is especially likely in the case of works of art. A work of art may well fall under one or another general characterisation, as an instance of a genre, for instance, or of a general mode.

But what of Monteverdi's *Orfeo*, or *West Side Story*, or the opinion of the old lady who is reported to have walked out of the first performance of the *St Matthew Passion*, complaining that the new opera had come to infect church music? What of Thomas Nashe's *The Unfortunate Traveller*, or *Don Quixote*, or *Ulysses*? What an opera or a novel is, unlike a case of plague, or a birth, can readily be contested. (How we might contest it will vary. We might perhaps draw the line between subject matters – to distinguish secular from sacred music dramas; or between modes – to distinguish narratives of the real from the picaresque, or all narratives from not-narratives; or between functions – to distinguish pictures for altars from those for church walls, or pictures for religious patrons from pictures for others.)

This degree of descriptive discretion – or as it used to be called, 'contestability' – is not, it is true, peculiar to art. It can also arise in the characterisation of political kinds. 'Absolutism', 'fascism', 'communism' or 'democracy' can be defined according to the content of the beliefs they embody, or the kinds of state and regime to which they give rise, or their effects in practice. And the lines that are drawn by one or other of these criteria may well be drawn in different places by different people. But in characterisations of works of art, the discretion goes all the way down. It is not difficult to imagine agreed reports of more particular procedures in politics, of what it is for only one group or party to have access to power, for instance, or of what it is formally to separate legislative, executive and judicial authority, to extend one or another right, to vote or even to have a choice in voting: reports which although by no means free of any descriptive presupposition at all, most people will in fact accept as at once reflecting and defining their experience. It is more difficult to imagine equally uncontested reports of the constituent elements of art. The difference may only be a difference of degree, but it is marked.[1] Of paintings, we will talk not only of the

---

[1] I take the distinction between reports and descriptions from W. G. Runciman, *A Treatise on Social Theory I: The Methodology of Social Theory*, Cambridge: Cambridge University Press, 1983. For Runciman, however, it is between characterisations which any reasonable observer would accept and those which are given by the agents themselves and are in that respect 'authentic'. I return to the distinction in Chapter 5, section IV.

materials that were used, their size, their authorship and other fairly uncontentious matters. We will talk also of the subject, the design, the composition and the use of colour; of realism and illusionism; of the 'handling' and the brushwork. And these are elements on which there is likely to be less like-mindedness. They are ways of talking about paintings which turn on how the paintings strike us (or some other particular audience), or on what painters are doing in painting, or indeed on some prior view of what 'a painting' more generally is.

Indeed 'all art', Ernst Gombrich insists, 'remains conceptual, a manipulation of a vocabulary'. Seeing it certainly does. In looking at past paintings, as in reading past philosophies or listening to past music, 'the question about a work', as Bernard Williams has put it, 'what does it mean?' is centrally the question 'what did it mean?'; and if 'the pursuit of that question', he continues, 'moves horizontally in time from the work, as well as backwards, to establish the expectations, conventions, familiarities, in terms of which the author could have succeeded in creating a meaning', the answers and the understandings that these answers might give are not uncorrupted by hindsight. 'This is not just because the understanding we bring to the explanations is a later one, although that is true and important, much as playing seventeenth-century music on seventeenth-century instruments according to seventeenth-century practice, admirable enterprise though it may be otherwise, does not produce seventeenth-century music, since we have necessarily twentieth-century ears.' It is also 'that our selection of the works we take to reward this inquiry is governed by their subsequent history and our present situation'; and that within the works themselves, what strikes us and strikes our historical curiosity is also governed in that way. Our sense of what we are reading or seeing or hearing is governed by our sense of what, we believe, happened in consequence of it, and where we stand in relation to that.[2]

[2] I have been helped in thinking about how we see paintings by Michael Baxandall's *Patterns of Intention: On the Historical Explanation of Pictures*, New Haven: Yale University Press, 1985, e.g. pp. 6–7; in his *Giotto and the Orators* (Oxford: Clarendon Press, 1971) Baxandall explains how much of our present language for talking about painting developed after Cimabue, Giotto and Duccio were dead. E. H. Gombrich, *The Image and the Eye*, London: Phaidon, 1982, pp. 70,

We may call this sense 'theoretical'. But it is clearly different from what we have in mind when we talk of a 'theoretical' grasp of vital events; different, if only in degree, from what we have in mind when we talk of a 'theory' of democracy. A theory of painting, a theory of any particular work or of a set of works, more than is even usually the case in a theory of political disputes, is a set of suggestions about how to grasp it, about how to frame and shape our discussions of it; and this theory will both affect and itself be affected by how we think it can be explained. Of course, our explanations may – in the loose sense of the word that I suggested in chapter 1 – be 'causal'. We may want to know about the external conditions, for instance; the available materials, the apprenticeship of the painter and his fellows, the pattern of patronage, and if we regard it as an external fact, the culture, painterly and other, in which he worked. Unless we believe that conceptually, the pre-post-modern 'painter' has died with the pre-post-modern 'author', our explanations may also be intentional. We may want to know why the painter in question responded to all this in the way that he did. And the better our explanations are, the better sense we shall have, as I have been saying, of what was possible. But because so much turns for our explanation of a work of this kind on how we shape and frame our initial characterisations of it, both the relation between our initial grasp of the works and the way in which we explain them, and the relation between our explanations, the possibilities they suggest, and our re-considered grasp are more internal than they are in explaining things like vital events and much of politics.

172. Bernard Williams, *Descartes: The Project of Pure Enquiry*, Harmondsworth: Penguin, 1978, p. 9. (Also Nelson Goodman, *Ways of Worldmaking*, Indianapolis: Hackett, 1978, pp. 38–9). Historians of art have tended to confuse what Rorty distinguishes for the history of philosophy as the three projects of 'doxography', 'the attempt to impose a problematic on a canon drawn up without reference to that problematic, or conversely, to impose a canon on a problematic without reference to that canon'; of rational reconstruction; and of *Geistesgeschichte*, 'the sort of history which has a moral', which attempts to decide whether A or B was 'on the right track' (Richard Rorty, 'The historiography of philosophy: four genres', in Rorty, J. B. Schneewind, Quentin Skinner, eds., *Philosophy in History: Essays on the Historiography of Philosophy*, Cambridge: Cambridge University Press, 1984, pp. 49–75).

II

On 9 October 1308, one Jacopo di Mariscotti signed a commission for a new altarpiece on behalf of the office of works, the Opera, of the new cathedral of Santa Maria in Siena. Nothing in this commission, which was to Duccio di Buoninsegna, a painter in the town, said what the piece was to be like. Duccio was merely instructed to do it 'as well as ever he was able and knew how to', to do it himself and not sub-contract it, and not to accept any other commission until it was done. He had already painted a number of triptychs and more permanent altarpieces, most recently, for Siena, one for the chapel of the Nove, the city's governing council, in the Palazzo Pubblico. This, for which he was paid in 1302, is long since lost, and there is no description of it. But from the work being done by others, and from what he presumes to have been Duccio's own development in the preceding twenty years or so, James Stubblebine has attempted imaginatively to reconstruct it. It was, he claims, adventurous for its time in having a predella of perhaps seven scenes; but it was otherwise ordinary, restricted, and painted only on the front. It did not approach the size and ambition in the altarpiece for the cathedral.[3]

This, which is usually known as Duccio's *Maestà*, was made of poplar, was a fraction under five metres high and five metres across, about twenty-three centimetres thick at its base. It consisted of one main scene, of the Virgin and Child with saints and angels, perhaps fifty-eight separate narratives, on the front of Christ's birth, on the back of his life, death and resurrection, and a further thirty separate figures. Duccio finished it in the summer of 1311. On 9 July, it was carried – presumably in parts – in elaborate procession to the cathedral from the Muciattis' house just beyond the Porta a Stalloreggi, where he had his workshop, and placed on the high

---

[3] James H. Stubblebine's reconstruction of the altarpiece for the Nove is in *Art Quarterly* 35 (1972), 239–68. The contract for the altarpiece for the cathedral is reproduced in Stubblebine, *Duccio di Buoninsegna and his School*, Princeton: Princeton University Press, 1979 I pp. 33–4 (all subsequent references are to the first volume) and by John White, *Duccio: Tuscan Art and the Medieval Workshop*, London: Thames and Hudson, 1979, pp. 192–3. There are valuable details also in Henk van Os, *Sienese Altarpieces 1215–1460 I: Form, Content, Function, 1215–1344*, Groningen: Bouma's Boekhuis, 1984, pp. 39–40.

altar. It stayed there until a new high altar was constructed in 1375. At the beginning of the sixteenth century Pandolfo Petrucci, the ruler of Siena, had it removed to the left transept and replaced with a bronze tabernacle. It was removed again two hundred years later. Having by then outlived its purpose, it was sawn into separate sections; the front was separated from the back, in the course of which a saw slipped and damaged the Madonna's face. It was then returned to the cathedral in a reconstructed but now incomplete state. In 1878, what remained of it in Siena was finally removed to the Museo dell'Opera, which is housed still in the unfinished fourteenth-century extension to the cathedral next door. It was restored between 1953 and 1958, and in the course of this, the Madonna's face was re-painted in a more sentimental manner than – to judge from the other Madonnas that he is known to have done – Duccio could have intended. At least fifteen scenes or figures, it is thought, are now lost, a further eight are scattered from Fort Worth to Washington, New York, London and Lugano, and four, all angels, although all of still disputed provenance, are also outside Italy.[4]

The idea of an altarpiece was relatively new. By the end of the thirteenth century, the debate within the Church over transubstantiation and the point and importance of the mass had been resolved. In 1215, setting the seal on what Giles Constable has called the twelfth-century reformation, the Fourth Lateran Council had decreed that Christ was physically present in the Eucharist as flesh and blood. (And all Christians had to take the sacrament, the council decreed, at least once a year.) In the consecration of the host, priests were from now on to make the person of the Redeemer immanent.[5] But they would begin to do so with their backs to the congregation, in a ceremony which thus ironically served at that point to separate them from the congregation. It was only after the

---

[4] The reconstruction is White's, *Duccio*: it is largely the same as Stubblebine's. But also van Os, *Sienese Altarpieces*, p. 44. The history of the *Maestà* is Stubblebine's, *Duccio*, pp. 34–8. Stubblebine includes Agnolo di Tura's vivid account, not written perhaps until 1350, of the procession of the *Maestà* from Duccio's shop to the Duomo.

[5] Giles Constable, 'The reformation of the twelfth century', Trevelyan Lectures, University of Cambridge, 1985. van Os, *Sienese Altarpieces*, p. 13.

consecration that the faithful below would have been able to see the symbols of their redemption. In the interval, the congregation's attention had cause to wander, and in the authorities' new enthusiasm for the consecration, the various bits and pieces which had previously adorned the tops of altars came increasingly to be thought insufficient to prevent this. These objects, caskets, ciboria, pyxes, reliquaries, eucharistic doves, small statues and other such items, were too small and together too distracting. There was a need for something more distinct to demarcate the altar from the space around it; something more definite to draw the eye and concentrate the mind. The elaborated altarpiece was the answer. From the front at least, since before the re-organisation of the space around the high altar in 1375, only canons in the ambulatory or the choir would have been able to see its back, the *Maestà* would like other such pieces have been expected to recall the mystery of the incarnation and excite feelings of devotion; such ends being the more effectively achieved, it was agreed, 'by things seen than by things heard'.[6]

The new altarpieces were extensions and elaborations of pre-existing statues and simpler paintings. Yet it was the Virgin rather than her son who was prominent on them all. Theologians, Anthony of Padua, Albertus Magnus, Bonaventure and Aquinas, and also the new mendicant orders, who were the most important patrons of religious painting in the thirteenth century (although not, as I have mentioned, of the *Maestà* itself), had come to insist on the importance of the Virgin as the mediator through which men could reach

---

[6] This phrase was John of Genoa's, quoted by Baxandall, *Painting and Experience in Fifteenth-century Italy*, Oxford: Oxford University Press, 1972, p. 41. It was not a new view (Judith Herrin quotes a remark of Gregory's to the same effect in the sixth century [*The Foundation of Christendom*, Oxford: Blackwell, 1987, p. 177], but it received a new impetus after 1215. The more self-consciously theoretical defence of the place of the visual senses in understanding, like John of Genoa's, postdates Duccio [David Summers, *The Judgement of Sense: Renaissance Naturalism and the Rise of Aesthetics*, Cambridge: Cambridge University Press, 1987]). There are two pictures of the *Maestà* in the place it came to occupy after 1375, reproduced by Kees van der Ploeg, 'Architectural and liturgical aspects of Siena cathedral in the middle ages' in van Os, *Sienese Altarpieces*, 1984, p. 145 and by White, *Duccio*, p. 92. The altar on which the *Maestà* stood was itself later encumbered with boxes, candlesticks and other items, and two ostrich eggs (common symbols of the Virgin birth) were suspended above it (van Os, *Sienese Altarpieces*, p. 55).

salvation in the grace of the Eucharist. Also, the relation between the holy mother and her child had separately become an object of popular devotion. (It was no doubt when this cult was thought to have become too divertingly intense that the images were removed in order to concentrate attention once more on the liturgy itself. This could be one reason why Petrucci ordered the *Maestà* to be removed from the high altar in 1506.) The later thirteenth-century altarpieces expressed this new emphasis on the humanity of John the Baptist and Mary and Martha and other such figures, of Christ himself and above all of his mother.

But there is a sense in which the *Maestà* was not commissioned by the Opera alone and only for the cathedral, but also by Siena. In September 1260, the city had formally submitted itself to the sovereignty of the Virgin. A Florentine army was at the gates, and in a moment of inspired panic, a prominent citizen, Buonaguida, had taken off everything except his shirt, put a leather strap around his neck, led a shouting crowd to the cathedral, and there, with the bishop and priests before the Madonna on the high altar, offered the city to the Virgin in return for her help in despatching 'the arrant curs' from Florence. In his account of the installation of Duccio's later altarpiece, Agnolo di Tura referred to the Virgin as 'advocate and protectress of the city' who defends it 'from all danger and evil'. The Sienese themselves had become convinced that she was. Since at least the early 1220s, the Madonna on the high altar had been the affectionately known *Madonna degli occhi grossi*, the 'Madonna with the bulging eyes'.[7] The day after Buonaguida's performance, and much to their surprise, the Sienese beat the Florentine forces in an engagement at Montaperti, just outside the city. The Opera immediately commissioned a new altarpiece, this time a wide gabled dossal, from the local painter Guido. In 1269, it is true, they were themselves beaten at Colle Val d'Elsa. And after that, Siena slipped into political subordination. But Montaperti reinforced the city's devotion to the Virgin, and Colle Val d'Elsa seems to have done little to reduce it.

---

[7] This powerful Madonna, with her large, compelling black eyes, looking directly out at the observer, and a very un-child-like Christ child seemingly suspended in front of her, is now in the Museo dell'Opera del Duomo in Siena.

The battles between Siena and Florence had in part been battles between Ghibelines and Guelphs. By 1287, this dispute was over, the Sienese had lost, and a Guelph oligarchy of the mercantile middle classes with its governing council, the Nove, was in control. For more than fifty years, the city was at peace and prosperous. The new cathedral had already been started. The first phase was completed in 1264 and formally dedicated in 1267. (Plans to extend the building were drawn up in 1316, and work was started in 1339, but as the visitor now sees, it was not to be finished. In the intervening period, the Opera, which functioned as a sort of public works department for the city as well as the cathedral, concentrated its energies and its monies on the Palazzo Pubblico, which was built more quickly and finished in about 1300.) The Nove commissioned their own now lost *Maestà* for the Palazzo from Duccio in 1302. Wierusowski believes this to have been one of the first paintings in Italy to have been commissioned by a commune. Goffen takes a *Maestà*, any *Maestà*, to be 'almost by definition a political image'. In it, saints are made smaller than the Virgin, and subservient; the contrast is with the later *Sacra Conversazione*, in which they were painted on the same scale and plane. Siena had become the *Civitas Virginis* and the new cathedral was its celebration. The new cathedral *Maestà* from Duccio was also a part of that.[8]

But how should we see it? What theory, in the descriptive sense of the term, should we have of it? We know that we should regard it as an altarpiece. We understand why altarpieces came to be commissioned by the new religious patrons. And although we are not thirteenth-century Christians, we do have some grasp of what altarpieces were intended to convey to the new and more numerous and non-literate congregations. But how should we approach late Duecento and Trecento painting, of which the *Maestà* is an instance? What do we need to know about how this painting, including any altarpiece, was produced and by whom? What is thereby

---

[8] Wierusowski's claim about the *Maestà* for the Nove is in *Speculum* 19 (1944), 14–33, Goffen's in *Art Bulletin* 61 (1979), 198–221. A contemporary Sienese document insists that 'among the matters to which the men who undertake the city's government should turn their attention, its beauty is the most important' (Daniel Waley, *The Italian City Republics*, London: Weidenfeld and Nicolson, 1969, p. 147).

suggested for how the painters might have painted? And how do our answers to these questions affect our perception of the works themselves?

III

The popular conception of central Italian painting in the Duecento and early Trecento, and until recently, the more considered conception of it also, has tended to be governed by a pre-emptive hindsight. It is in essence Giorgio Vasari's. And Vasari's was Florence's. Already in the 1330s, the large *Rucellai Madonna*, which had been painted by Duccio in 1285 for the Dominican society of Santa Maria Vergine at Santa Maria Novella in Florence, was in Florence itself being said to be by Cimabue. The Dominicans' contract for it came to light at the end of the eighteenth century, but in several accounts the false attribution stood even into the twentieth. Vasari had all but sealed it. In the first edition of his *Lives* in 1550, he not only gave the painting to Cimabue, but misdated Duccio, put him after his successors, held him responsible for a pavement laid down by another Duccio after Duccio di Buoninsegna had died, knew only by hearsay of the *Maestà* itself, and altogether dismissed its master in three short paragraphs. For the second edition in 1568 he did, it is true, travel the forty miles from Florence to look for the altarpiece, of which he had by then heard. But although he walked all round the cathedral, in whose left transept it then hung, still complete if now embellished, he did not see it.

In Vasari's heroic progress from Cimabue and Giotto to Michelangelo Buonarroti, Duccio stayed to one side and behind. Both the Florentines' first formulation of this progress at the beginning of the Trecento, when they could scarcely have imagined what it would be a progress to, and Vasari's influential elaboration of it in the 1550s and 1560s, were both extreme. Yet even now, many historians of painting, although they may discount this view, or at least, say that they do, still presume that there was, in Berenson's phrase, a 'real issue', the issue of realism. This, it came to be argued after the later fourteenth century, was the issue of naturalism and its achievement in a full perspective; 'he draws the bow in vain', punned Alberti in the early 1430s, 'who has nowhere to point the arrow'. The historians tend accordingly to align each painter they discuss to the extent to which he perceived the issue and pursued it. And Duccio, as many of them have said, did neither. When Florence, the conventional view has had it, 'was on the verge of a break with the Byzantine style, Siena . . . witnessed such a brilliant performance in the old tradition that Sienese artists remained under its spell for the next century and longer'. If Duccio had been more inventive, the hint has been, or perhaps more skilled; certainly if he had been a Florentine; if he had seen 'the real issue', had been more 'advanced'; then he might.[9]

The contrary opinion, that the development of this 'real issue' through the Renaissance was, in Piet Mondrian's word, a grand 'detour'; that 'the old running perspective and trompe de l'oeil,' as Carlo Carrà derided it in his Futurist manifesto in 1913, is 'a game worthy at most of an academic mind such as Leonardo's, or of a designer of sets for realist melodramas'; the view, as Picasso once

[9] Giorgio Vasari, Luciano Bellosi and Aldo Rossi eds., *Le Vite de'piu Eccellenti Architetti, Pittori et Scultori Italiani, da Cimabue insino a'tempo nostri*, 1550 edition, Turin: Einaudi, (1986, pp. 180–1. White, *Duccio*, p. 11. The contract for the *Rucellai Madonna* is reproduced by Stubblebine, *Duccio*, pp. 192–4, and by White, *Duccio*, pp. 185–7. Stubblebine recapitulates the history of the attribution of this painting at pp. 22–4. Bernard Berenson, *The Italian Painters of the Renaissance*, London: Fontana, 1960, p. 121. Leon Battista Alberti, *On Painting*, J. R. Spencer ed., New Haven: Yale University Press, 1966, p. 59. The conventional view of Duccio and his influence on the later Sienese is from Fern Rusk Shapley, *Early Italian Painting in the National Gallery of Art*, Washington DC: National Gallery of Art, 1969, p. 2. (It was this remark of Shapley's – which, to avoid unpacking, I read on the night that I arrived in Princeton in 1979 to start thinking about possibility – that first aroused my curiosity about Duccio.) If we take Goodman's subtly post-empiricist point that 'realism is a matter of the familiarity in symbols used in the telling', whereas 'truth is a matter of what is told, literally or metaphorically, by means of symbols familiar or fantastic' (*Of Mind and Other Matters*, Cambridge MA: Harvard University Press, 1984, p. 125), then the sense of revelation that was produced by painterly 'realism' in the late thirteenth and early fourteenth centuries was presumably due to surprise and wonder at the revealed familiar in each of these respects; also chapter 5, section IV. The further question of whether the 'real issue' of pictorial realism is also a real issue in psychology – that for reasons of practical survival and success, of 'fitness', it is what we have evolved as a species into cognitively responding to – is a fascinating one; but beyond my competence.

dismissively insisted in his conversations with Kahnweiler, that 'the paintings in the Louvre' are 'just charm, decoration', 'the charm', he added, 'of a prostitute'; the view, in Sonia Delaunay's formulation of it, that in the history of western painting 'the more "advance" there was, the worse things were'; is not, in any of the conventional histories, acknowledged. These modernist 'enemies of the Renaissance' – the description is Delaunay's own; artists who regarded it as 'an uncreative epoch which merely established the academicism that has continued into the present'; seem still to be thought, or so the historians' silence suggests, a little mad.[10]

They are still ignored. And indeed, their view is every bit as unhistorical as Vasari's. But there has been some advance. Thanks largely to Stubblebine, John White and Henk van Os, we have a better sense of what in a general way was being communicated to whom and why at the end of the thirteenth century and the start of the fourteenth. I have already indicated something of what that was, and shall return to it. But we are still not quite so clear as we might be about who, more particularly, was communicating it, and what artistically (if we can use the anachronism) it was that they were distinctively doing in so doing.[11]

At first sight, it was the 'artist' Duccio who conceived the form and content of the *Maestà*, for beyond wanting something large, and panels of 'histories', the Opera almost certainly had no definite idea; and there is no known precedent that was so elaborate. This is what Stubblebine presumes. In what has been in many conventional histories of art that smooth and linear and curiously passive

[10] Carlo Carrà, *La Peinture des sons, bruits, et odeurs*, Manifeste Futuriste, 1913, in Yale University Library, translated and quoted by Michael Kubovy, *The Psychology of Perspective and Renaissance Art*, Cambridge: Cambridge University Press, 1986, p. 121. I am grateful to Sunil Khilnani for Picasso's remark. Sonia Delaunay, *Nous irons jusqu'au soleil*, Paris: Laffont, 1978, pp. 178, 138. Some modernists, however, taking a more intellectualist view of 'the real issues', have been fascinated by the innovations in perspective; hence their admiration for painters like Masaccio and Piero. Some cubists argued that they had re-defined the premises of realism. I have failed to turn up any modernist view of Duccio himself.

[11] White, *Duccio* and *The Birth and Rebirth of Pictorial Space*, Boston: Boston Book and Art Shop, 1967, pp. 78–83 (3rd edition, Cambridge MA: Harvard University Press, 1987). The more recent Stubblebine is *Assisi and the Rise of Vernacular Art*, New York: Harper and Row, 1985.

conception of causation, a conception in which, as van Os puts it, 'it seems almost axiomatic to attribute excellence to the influence of outstanding works of art created elsewhere', or by someone else, Stubblebine supposes that Duccio was born in Siena into a Byzantine tradition. He would have been aware of the work from Guido's shop in Siena; indeed, he might even have learnt his trade there. Stubblebine certainly believes that his style is to be traced back to Guido's. It was Guido's *Madonna del Voto* – of which only the Madonna herself now remains, but which van Os believes might have been part of a wide gabled dossal, stretching across the altar – that had replaced the early thirteenth-century *Madonna degli occhi grossi* soon after the victory at Montaperti in 1260. And Guido's work – or at least the work from Guido's shop, for he himself remains a shadowy figure – had begun to depart from the older conventions; in his *Madonna del Voto*, which was itself replaced by Duccio's *Maestà*, the child breaks the silhouette of the Virgin, and is sitting on her knee in a recognisably infantile way, raising his arm toward her breast in a gesture which might just be one of blessing but also, as van Os sees, of play.[12] Duccio, Stubblebine assumes, would also have been aware of Coppo di Marcovaldo, a painter captured by the Sienese while serving as a shield-bearer for the Florentine forces at Montaperti and at once put to painting a Madonna (sometimes referred to as the *Madonna del Bordone*) for the Servite church in the city. This Servi Madonna, which carries an inscription of 1261, is more substantial, and its details, the throne, the robe, and the way in which the robe falls, above all the Virgin's relation to the child, are all quite different from those in any Sienese painting; quite different, for instance, from the Madonna painted in 1262 by the Sienese Master of San Bernardino.[13] The composition is less unified, more abstract and geometrical, as White describes it, more 'reticent', than that of Guido's *Madonna del Voto*; Coppo's execution, his use for instance of colour, which was already

[12] van Os, *Sienese Altarpieces*, p. 18. Stubblebine wrote also on Guido himself (*Guido da Siena*, Princeton: Princeton University Press, 1964). Guido's *Madonna del voto* is now in the Museo dell'Opera del Duomo.

[13] This painting, until recently attributed to Guido (e.g. by Bruce Cole, *Sienese Painting: From its Origins to the Fifteenth Century*, New York: Harper and Row, 1980, p. 5), is in the Pinacoteca in Siena.

becoming noticeable in Sienese work, is also more restrained. The Servi Madonna, one might say, is altogether more 'old-fashioned', indeed more similar to contemporary paintings from the shops in Coppo's own city than to any painting from that moment which survives from Siena.[14]

By the early 1300s, Stubblebine infers from his work on the *Maestà*, Duccio would have been exposed to each of those all but Platonic items which Stubblebine, like some others, thinks of as 'the antique', 'the Byzantine', 'the Gothic', and 'the Florentine'. This is why he believes that Duccio may have been to Rome. It is also why he believes that Duccio may have seen Chartres in the 1270s, and may even have been the 'Duch de Siene' who is recorded as having paid a tax in Paris in 1297. By 1308 and the Opera's commission for the *Maestà*, if not already by 1301 or 1302, when working for the Nove, he would have had a shop in the Muciatti's house. Segna and Ugolino would have been in it, as most other authorities agree, but so also, thinks Stubblebine, would the Lorenzetti brothers, Simone Martini and the creators of those early fourteenth-century paintings which some see as having stylistic affinities with Duccio's own, the masters of Citta di Castello, Tabernacle 35 and the Carole fresco. Duccio was an artist, Stubblebine assumes, and the *Maestà* is his work and that of the other artists in his shop.[15]

But we know little about Duccio's life. He was of course a local artist. But artists were then artisans, from the ranks of the *sottoposti*, barbers and bakers, carders and combers and dyers, tanners and makers of shoes and harness; relatively poor and of indifferent social standing. (One can of course imagine the opposite, either from events like the popular procession of the finished parts of the *Maestà*, or from the assumption that in a world in which there were few if any other popular cultural heroes, as we would now think of them, painters, and especially local painters, might have excited some of the same attention and wonder as media people do now; think for instance of Dante's remark. But the procession has other explanations – recall Buonaguida in 1260; the communal celebra-

---

[14] There is a detailed comparison of the *Madonna del Bordone* and the Madonna by the Master of San Bernardino in White, *Duccio*, pp. 27–32.

[15] Stubblebine, *Duccio*, pp. 3–16. van Os, *Sienese Altarpieces*, pp. 46, 25. Baxandall has, one hopes, decisively put the unreflective notion of influence to rest (*Patterns of Intention*, pp. 58–62).

tion of works of art, in the ancient world as in the medieval, says nothing about the social standing of the artists; and the analogy with the present, its anachronism aside, is speculative.) Painters did not even enter guilds until the 1320s, when Giotto, Taddeo and Bernardo Gaddi, trying to rise above the *sottoposti*, set a precedent and joined the guild of doctors and pharmacists in Florence. (Even as late as the 1520s, Michelangelo, exceptionally vain, it is true, and rebarbative, could resent the hint in being called 'a painter' that he was nothing better.) Duccio was often in debt and died so; in agreeing to the contract for the *Maestà*, for which he was to be paid a salary, he was asked to swear on the holy book that he would not defraud the Opera. (His wife rejected his inheritance for herself and their eight children; there were too many mortgages.) He had a moment of prosperity at the beginning of the fourteenth century, just after he did his *Maestà* for the Nove, just before his commission from the cathedral; he bought some land near Siena then, and a stock of wine. But his frequent disputes with the legal authorities in Siena, like his will, suggest that he was an indifferent manager of his practical life, and it is not at all clear that he would have been able to travel twice to France or even to Rome, let alone, as Berenson fancied, to Constantinople, which was in any event still closed to visitors from the west. We know for certain only that he did work in Perugia, Pisa and Florence.

Even if he was literate, which he probably was, he may not, in Duechler's phrase, have been 'Duccio doctus', a learned man, at home with manuscripts. He would perhaps at best have been familiar with the increasing amount of popular apocryphal literature which was by then freely elaborating on the lives of the Virgin, Christ, John the Baptist and others, a literature which is thought to have inspired the iconography of many of the monumental cycles of the time. He did come to run a shop, like other masters, and Segna and Ugolino (who may have been his nephew) do seem to have been there. But Martini and the Lorenzetti brothers do not appear in any record until 1311, seven or eight years before Duccio died, and there is nothing in any document to connect them with Duccio himself. (Even Stubblebine, giving the lie to his model of descent, admits 'that the moment they left the shop', in which he can only suppose they were, 'they ceased to be Ducciesque painters'.)

Moreover, the division of labour within such shops was within rather than between the separate works. It may thus be a mistake to read Duccio's contracts as requiring his labour and his alone, as perhaps later ones did for other men. It would have been understood that he would at least, but perhaps also at most, conceive the whole, guide the designs, and himself complete the Virgin and Christ and perhaps some of the other more important figures.[16] His single surviving inscription, which is on the Virgin's footrest in the *Maestà*, 'Holy Mother of God, be thou the cause of peace for Siena, and because he painted thee thus, for Duccio', could be a conventional prayer. It may say something about the spirit of the commission; it is not at all certain that it marks 'a change', as White is tempted to think, 'in the hopes and aspirations of artists', the inception of the self-advertising *auteur*. Duccio was not – in the sense in which Italians two hundred years or so later would, like us, understand the term – an individual artist, and however independent he may himself have been (he certainly seems to have been an independent character) he may not have conceived of himself as such. Such conceptions were foisted by others, retrospectively (or so it seems) on Bencivieni di Pepo, whose nickname, 'Cimabue' – 'ox-head', the stubborn one – may have had something to do with the appellation; then on Giotto; and they were foisted first in Florence. (One of the earliest apparently genuine signatures is Coppo's in the Servi church: in Siena, it is true, but the signature of a possibly disgruntled captive from Florence who had no wish to be taken for a Sienese.) At most, one suspects, the *Maestà* was conceived and painted by Duccio where

---

[16] Infra-red reflectography has recently revealed Duccio's distinctive under-drawings with quill pen and brush on two of the panels in the National Gallery in London; has further revealed that he changed his mind both about the arrangement of the figures in the space and about the space itself in the *Annunciation*; and in *Jesus Opens the Eyes of the Man Born Blind*, but not in the *Annunciation*, has made it clear that a different hand sketched the architecture and that a different hand also – perhaps the same, perhaps not – finished the work and in so doing ignored or overrode some of these first sketches (David Bomford et al., *Art in the Making: Italian Painting before 1400*, London: National Gallery, 1989, 78–89). Ruth Wilkins Sullivan has recently shown that Duccio also changed his mind about the composition of another panel ('Duccio's *Raising of Lazarus* re-examined', *Art Bulletin* 70 (1988), 375–87), although she arguably mars her account by casting the change in terms of a shift from 'the Byzantine' to 'the Gothic'.

'Duccio' is the name for a shop, an eye, and a guiding hand.[17]

What Duccio or 'Duccio' distinctively did in doing what he did, moreover, is open to even wider dispute. On the one hand, there is nothing in his work, even in his earliest surviving piece, the so-called *Crevole Madonna* from about 1280, of the formal majesty of the Byzantine. On the contrary, there is from the very start a delicacy, softness and grace; in the scenes and figures in the *Maestà* itself, often almost an intimacy. There is also a skilled and intensive use, especially in the *Maestà*, of colour. This is evident even now; it is what so entranced Sonia Delaunay about what she called the Italian *primitifs*. But Duccio did not attempt the analytical simplicity and the solidity, the stark, even frozen, realism, as we might now see it, of Giotto. He did not put a natural perspective first. That is why, seen also from Florence at the beginning of the fourteenth century and again by Vasari and others in the sixteenth, he is, when he is seen at all, put to one side and at the back. He did not even approach the naive realism of the cycle of St Francis in the upper church at Assisi, a cycle which has sometimes been attributed to Giotto, but which to Stubblebine's eye, and convincingly, is quite different from Giotto's more abstracted, even idealised, as Stubblebine himself calls it 'lofty' (but also naturalistic) style, more vernacular.[18]

The commentators accordingly waver. In his extensive monograph on Duccio, Stubblebine insists that the *Rucellai Madonna*,

[17] All the relevant documents on Duccio's life are reproduced by Stubblebine, *Duccio*, pp. 191–208. Most are also reproduced by White, *Duccio*, pp. 184–200. Florens Duechler's argument is in 'Duccio *Doctus*: new readings for the *Maestà*', *Art Bulletin* 61 (1979), 541–9. The influence of the popular literature is suggested by among others Anita Fiderer Moskowitz (*The Sculpture of Andrea and Nino Pisano*, Cambridge: Cambridge University Press, 1986, p. 19). Stubblebine's remark about the Lorenzettis and Martini is at *Duccio*, p. 15. White's view of the contract for the *Maestà*, *Duccio*, p. 80, and of Guido's Coppo's and Duccio's other inscriptions at pp. 25–27, 100; by van Os in *Burlington Magazine* 123 (1981), 167. Stubblebine mentions an earlier inscription than Coppo's, in Pescia in 1235 (*Assisi*, p. 16). It seems reasonably certain that the carpentry was not done in the artists' shops (White, *Duccio*, p. 49).

[18] Duccio's *Maestà* cannot now be seen as a whole; as White says, here Giotto, on the walls of the Arena chapel still and in other frescoes, has long since – since before Vasari – had the edge. On Assisi, Stubblebine, *Assisi*, e.g. p. 113.

which Duccio finished in 1285 or 1286, is 'the only truly Gothic painting of the thirteenth century in Italy'. Sullivan has more recently echoed that judgement. Robert Oertel, who also saw something of this quality, agrees that it 'reveals faint traces of the Gothic'. But he also saw it as 'a first step towards overcoming the dependence of the Duecento on the archaic'. Indeed, Oertel suggests that it is 'modern and progressive' even when set beside the Madonna painted for Santa Trinita in Florence by Cimabue, the first hero in Vasari's triumphalist *Lives*. Yet in the end, Oertel thought, although the *Rucellai Madonna* has a distinctive and perhaps 'personal' style, it does belong to the *maniera greca*. When he comes to consider the *Maestà*, Stubblebine at one point says that the scenes from the Passion on the back are 'inspired by contemporary Byzantine painting', and at another suggests that they were influenced by Cimabue. If there is a conventional wisdom, it is that Duccio stands at a point of transition; a point that was already being passed forty short miles away in Florence. Indeed, it is only a slight exaggeration to say that for many, if not most historians, Duccio has almost vanished to a point at the intersection of coordinates which are set by other painters, each of whom is taken to be a more important marker by criteria that the historians have themselves defined. It has as a result not been easy, even for some of those who have spent much time looking, steadily to see Duccio at all.[19]

In short, the more general argument has had it that somewhere in the second half of the thirteenth century, the 'real issue' in painting was grasped. Artists were captured by it and grappled with it and given what to us is its power, what happened later, and the minor premise of a mechanical 'influence', they can all be presumed to have been trying to realise it. In this accelerating ambition, it accordingly seems natural to suppose that an older artist will have been less 'advanced' than a younger one, and that any one artist will have been less advanced in his earlier work than he will have been later.

Even White succumbs. He does see Duccio's *Maestà* as articulating 'a new and vital visual language which, despite the different

[19] Stubblebine, *Duccio*, pp. 7, 52, 6. Robert Oertel, *Early Italian Painting to 1400*, London: Thames and Hudson, 1968, pp. 195–200.

dialects in which they spoke, was common to all the central Italian artists of the period', a language intended to bring 'the sacred narratives and personages more vividly and immediately alive before the eyes of the faithful'. And he nowhere presumes that Duccio must always have been striving to 'advance' to 'real issues'. But even he cannot in the end resist the suggestion that the new and vital visual language of the *Maestà* is the one which reached its 'final flowering' on the Sistine ceiling and in Raphael's tapestries for the dado beneath. Indeed, White's Duccio is more heroic even than this: he is 'one of that small band of painters who have changed the course of history'. Millard Meiss might have been right, White concedes, to see Sienese developments cut short by the collapse of the 1340s; the Opera was never again in a position to commission anything as lavish as the *Maestà* for the high altar in 1308 or Simone Martini's *Annunciation*, Ambrogio Lorenzetti's *Presentation in the Temple* or Pietro Lorenzetti's *Birth of the Virgin*, three altarpieces painted in the 1330s and 1340s for side altars in the cathedral.[20] But the path that leads almost at once from the *Maestà* to Ambrogio's *Good* and *Bad Government* for the Palazzo Pubblico in 1339 – the three side altarpieces were all simpler in conception – is a path that in White's eyes leads directly 'not to man and nature or man in front of nature, but to man in nature, as a natural part of it. It leads to Pieter Breughel and, eventually, to Henry Moore and the modern concepts of the fundamental unity of the whole of nature.' Even White finds it in the end impossible not to see Duccio from this side of the Renaissance; and in so doing, inadvertently to give grounds for his own complaint that 'it is hard to think of any major painter who . . . is less appreciated for himself, and on his own terms, and who is more consistently considered in a framework of relativities and qualitative comparisons'.[21]

[20] Martini's and Ambrogio's altarpieces are now in the Uffizi in Florence, Pietro's in the Museo dell'Opera in Siena.
[21] White, *Duccio*, pp. 9, 171, 160, 163, 15. The reference to Meiss is to *Painting in Florence and Siena after the Black Death*. Princeton: Princeton University Press, 1951. (Meiss's argument is rejected by Bruce Cole, *Giotto and Florentine Painting, 1280–1375*, New York: Harper and Row, 1976 and van Os, 'The Black Death and Sienese painting: a problem of interpretation', *Art History* 4 (1981), 237–49.) It is revealing that those who think of themselves as true modernists dislike Moore's work; they regard it as a superficially modern gloss on

IV

Duccio has been seen at once too generally and too partially. He has been seen in the general sweep of Italian painting to at least the sixteenth century, if not indeed in the sweep of all painting to the late nineteenth. He has also been seen (except by the modernists) as though the only issue in painting between the thirteenth and the nineteenth was the issue of realism. The Maestà, however, was conceived by someone who could have had no idea of what sixteenth-century skills and sensibilities, let alone our own, would be. And like all thirteenth- and early fourteenth-century paintings in Italy, his Maestà was not just a painting. It was not done just to be seen in and for itself, in the way in which we would now see such a work, on a wall or some other plain plane surface, isolated in its frame and aesthetically self-standing. It was an altarpiece. As such, it had to be clear, moving, and memorable, sacramentally correct and credible; and it had to fit its intended place on the high altar itself and in the framing space of the whole cathedral.[22] Even if it is true that for the new realists, like Giotto – working on walls, or if on altarpieces, on altarpieces (as in the instances that have been attributed to Giotto and his shop) that were much simpler in conception – 'the concentrated study of the *actual* appearance of the individual object, as you look at it', is what was most important, as it could be said now to be for us, this is unlikely to have been so for Duccio.[23]

For in planning the Maestà, Duccio was planning what we could now think of as a highly complex sacred cartoon for a very partic-

older 'academicisms', and its popular reception, for them, makes the point. (One has to remember that even Mondrian was himself able to sell almost nothing of his work, and Sonia Delaunay repeatedly drew attention to her circle's lack of worldly success in Paris itself, let alone elsewhere, until the 1960s. White's perception of Moore, of course, is perfectly consistent with theirs; he merely draws a different conclusion from it.)

[22] The five criteria for altarpieces are Baxandall's, *Patterns of Intention*, p. 106. The setting for the altarpiece is discussed by van der Ploeg in van Os, *Sienese Altarpieces*. One so far unanswered question, incidental to what I am arguing here, is how the Maestà was made to stand up on the altar.

[23] White, *Duccio*, p. 167, my emphasis. No altarpiece can incontestably be attributed to Giotto himself, and those that can do not begin to approach the complexity of the Maestà (e.g. White, *Duccio*, pp. 69–70, 140–50).

ular place. It had to be sacramentally correct and credible; it had to have sufficient majesty to meet what van Os describes as the 'megalomania' in its commission; but it also had to convey a narrative of Christ's life, death and resurrection. To do this, Duccio (not the Opera) decided to include on the back (albeit originally, only for the canons) forty-three or so separate narratives, scenes which not only had each to convey its own sense but had also to be able to be intelligibly read in the way that we might now read a cartoon strip. The first task, therefore, is to reconstruct the now dismembered whole. Only then can we begin to see how to read the work.[24]

Once the reconstruction, which we owe to White, has been made, it becomes clear that Duccio was constrained. He was constrained not so much by the size of each of the panels (in contrast, for instance, to the fresco cycle that Giotto had painted on the walls of the Scrovegnis' Arena chapel in Padua in perhaps 1306 and 1307), as by the fact that they were to be read both as a whole and in a sequence which should together be arresting and yet make it easy for the eye to move. For this, we can suppose, he had to make the lighting consistent, so that different scenes would not seem unnaturally to the observer to be seen from different angles (even if a difference should be marked between those that we know took place at different times of day). He had to concentrate the eye with colour, his use of which, as almost everyone has noticed, was both intense and subtle. And he had to control the perspective.

It is this last which is the issue which has so confused the critical understanding and thus muddied the explanatory accounts. In his earlier work on the subject, White suggests that instead of supposing that Duccio was in some way 'backward', or at least, that he saw the 'real issue' of naturalistic perspective but could not himself realise it, it may be easier to suppose that he just lacked any 'interest in the fundamental realism which', by the time that he was working on the *Maestà*, 'was typical of Giotto'.[25] It was this realism which Christian painting in the Byzantine had suppressed. In pre-Christian work –

---

[24] White's reconstructions, *Duccio*, pp 84–5, 106–7, and diagrams of how the eye might have travelled at pp. 129 and 130. van Os presents alternative readings (*Sienese Altarpieces*, p. 49).

[25] *Birth and Rebirth*, p. 80.

this is evident for instance in many of the surviving paintings at Pompei – it had become conventional to convey the solidity of objects with a fierce and uncompromising perspective. Three-dimensional objects were represented in such a way that they came out at the observer. The Christians' rejection of this convention, their deliberate 'reassertion', as White describes it, 'of the plane surface of the picture', was at one with their determined spirituality. It signalled a rejection of the mundane and of the bounded time within which mundane events occurred. It explains why Christian painting until the early thirteenth century, when the move was made to make the mysteries more accessible and thus more alive, had an iconic quality.[26]

This older view was also pictorially convenient. In thrusting angles out at the observer, the perspective of the 'extreme oblique', as White calls it, can disturb the picture surface. The difficulties that this perspective creates for space – the space, for instance, both around and between objects like buildings and rooms – can severely disrupt the organisation of the entire picture. As White convinc-ingly shows, this must have been a problem for Giotto in doing the Arena frescoes, a problem that he seems only to have been able to solve by avoiding a representation of more than one building where angles threatened to be too obtrusive, or by obscuring the angles with a human figure. Eventually, indeed, in his last work, Giotto moved away altogether from 'emphatic, self-isolating solidity' to a softer and more restrained, as we would now see it, less realistic perspective.

White points out that amongst the hundred or so Italian panels painted before 1300 which now survive and in which architecture

---

[26] Yves Bonnefoy, 'Time and the timeless in Quattrocentro painting', in Norman Bryson ed., *Calligrams: Essays in the New Art History from France*, Cambridge: Cambridge University Press, 1988, pp. 8–26. In Jaroslav Pelikan's way of putting it, an icon 'is what it represents; nevertheless, it bids us look . . . through it and beyond it', to the ideals which it embodies (*The Vindication of Tradition*, New Haven: Yale University Press, 1984, p. 55). To Bonnefoy, Peiro managed to recover that through the new realist conventions. (Did Cimabue, Giotto, Duccio and the others?) In contrast to idols, which in Pelikan's characterisation of them make 'the preservation and the repetition of the past an end in itself' and imply submission, icons allow revisable interpre-tation; see note 30.

appears, there are no examples of a normally seen oblique construction. Such 'normality' first appears after some of the restorative repaintings of fifth-century frescoes that Cavallini did in Rome in the later 1280s and the 1290s, in Cavallini's own mosaics in Santa Maria in Trastevere in Rome in 1291, and then in Assisi – which causes White to agree against Stubblebine's later judgement with the earlier and more conventional dating of the cycle – in some of the frescoes on the life of St Francis. But even then, fully half of the scenes both in Cavallini's own original work in the 1290s and in the Assisi cycle 'advance' only to a 'foreshortened frontal' perspective – representing the front of a building parallel to the picture surface, and indicating its depth merely with a gesture at one side wall. It is not until Giotto's work in the Arena chapel that the extreme oblique prevails. There, indeed, all but four of all the buildings are obliquely set within the picture space, and of the four exceptions, two are special cases dictated by the architecture of the chapel itself. If a more conventionally representational, realist painting was one of the reactions in the thirteenth and early fourteenth century to the changes taking place in the Church in the west, it was by no means immediate and immediately widespread.[27]

Duccio never uses even a softened oblique. In all the panels in the *Maestà*, he either just represents the front of a building, making no attempt at perspective at all, or uses the foreshortened frontal. He also continues the convention, which, striving for what we take to be the eye's natural compass, Giotto had abandoned, of depicting receding space in the way in which some of the Byzantine painters had done. Duccio's ground, which none the less has great volume and depth, slopes steeply up and away from the observer. ('For Giotto', White sharply remarks, 'what could not be done with solid figures on level ground was not worth doing'.)[28] Also, Duccio's figures are noticeably less plastic and solid than those of Giotto or even Cimabue. Was he then innocent of the 'real issue' that was already exciting these people – Cavallini from his encounter with ancient paintings in Rome, Cimabue and Giotto in Florence, and (if we were to accept White's more conventional early dating for them

[27] White, *Birth and Rebirth*, pp. 28–75.
[28] *Duccio*, p. 126.

rather than Stubblebine's) the fresco painters of the St Francis cycle
at Assisi? Was he just not interested, as White implies? Was he,
even, moderately incompetent?

In Duccio's painting, 'a more natural articulation and a limited
solidity', as White summarises it, 'were combined with a dominant,
linear surface pattern strengthened by exquisite colour'. Thereby
avoiding what were always for Giotto the 'the uncontrollable internal conflicts' in designs that were 'not yet sufficiently resolved to
contain such [an] intense realism', Duccio was 'accordingly free to
try for more daring representational effects'. His 'genius', White
concludes, lay in the fact that in his painting, there is none of the
'inherent dualism' of the supposedly more advanced men. It was not,
as White himself had earlier put it, that Duccio was not interested
in realism. The emotional intensity of his figures – it is tempting to
list endless examples, but for those who have access to it, or at least
to a good reproduction, the figures at the foot of the his crucifixion
on the *Maestà* are indicative – quite belies that.[29] It appears rather
that he modified a realism to realise his wider aim.

Indeed, if the point of religious painting was to excite devotion by
conveying spirituality, by conveying, that's to say, the delicate
distinction (which Aquinas secured) between adoring a picture for
itself, hated *idolatria*, and worshipping it as a symbol of what was to
be adored, *latria*; if the point of an altarpiece was to be clear,
moving, memorable, correct and credible; and if it was not until the
sixteenth century that any painter managed to deploy a fierce
perspective to do this – by deliberately inducing what Michael

---

[29] Further examples of Duccio's qualities are the panels depicting the An-
nunciation and Jesus opening the eyes of the man born blind (two of three
panels in the National Gallery in London); and indicating the volume he was
able to achieve with the perspective he did use, the panel from the back of the
Maestà depicting Christ's entry into Jerusalem (in the Museo dell'Opera in
Siena) and that depicting Christ's temptation on the mountain (in the Frick
Collection in New York). One composition of a crowd beneath a crucified
Christ, voluminous yet delicate, revealing a wonderful sense of the connecting
contrasts and compatibilities of form and colour, and dramatically powerful, is
on a triptych in the Museum of Fine Arts in Boston, which, although its
attribution has been disputed, is to my eye certainly Duccio's: compare the
comparable scene on the back of the *Maestà*.

Kubovy describes as 'a discrepancy between the spectator's *actual* point of view and the point of view from which the scene is *felt* to be viewed' (the discrepancy which the cubists carried to an extreme); then in the fine balance that he found between the purpose of the paintings he was commissioned to do and what was, at the end of the Duecento and the beginning of Trecento, the new fashion and the prevailing knowledge of painterly technique, Duccio himself, we might equally say, was at that time the more sophisticated and so 'advanced'. In brisker idiom, if we were to agree with Jon Elster that the way in which to see a work of art is as a 'maximisation under constraints'; that 'the practice of artists can only be understood on the assumption that there is something they are trying to maximise'; then Duccio, we might then say, was trying to maximise both immediacy and spirituality in an unprecedentedly complex and ambitious structure. And he did.[30]

V

The pressures in the thirteenth-century Church to make the mysteries of the faith more immediate to more people, together with the absence of any other means of doing so, explain why religious painting revived and became more vivid.[31] It was part of what

[30] On the fine but crucial distinction between *latria* and *idolatria*, Michael Camille, *The Gothic Idol: Ideology and Image-making in Medieval Art*, Cambridge: Cambridge University Press, 1989, pp. 203–20. Aquinas quoted at p. 207. Kubovy, *Psychology of Perspective*, pp. 16, 160–1, *passim*. White, *Birth and Rebirth*, pp. 78–83. Elster does not say what it is that artists may be trying to maximise, except not very plausibly to suggest that 'artistic or aesthetic value is timeless' (*Sour Grapes: Studies in the Subversion of Rationality*, Cambridge and Paris: Cambridge University Press and Editions de la Maison des sciences de l'Homme, 1983, p. 78).

[31] These factors were perhaps sufficient, but not necessary. Similar changes had also appeared in religious art in the east in the course of the 'Comnenian Renaissance' in the twelfth century, and were continued in the period of Latin rule in Constantinople in the next (a brief account in Irmgard Hutter, Alistair Lang trans., *Early Christian and Byzantine Art*, London: Weidenfeld and Nicolson, 1971, pp. 142 ff. On the ways in which Constantinople had earlier distanced itself from Rome, Herrin, *Christendom*, e.g. pp. 52–3, 307–53, and Camille, *Gothic Idol*, p. 205.)

Michael Camille has called the 'image explosion' of the thirteenth
century in Europe. The new pressures also explain why the painters
allowed themselves to be excited at the re-discovery of late Roman
realism. But the spiritual brief that these men were given, together
with the difficulties which they saw that they could get into in
pursuing more extreme perspectives on the two-dimensional surfaces
of the new cartoons, explain why almost none of them went as far as
did Giotto on the walls of the Arena chapel, why Giotto himself, in
his later work, lowered his ambition, and why Duccio conceived and
painted his Maestà as he did. The changes in the Church and its
liturgy were general conditions and external, and affected all
contemporary painters. The interpretation that (largely following
White) I have suggested of Duccio's response to them, however, is
internal, and the response itself is very much his. The interpretation
is an interpretation of him as a painter, considering his complicated
piece of carpentry and facing his picture surface with a particular
project in mind. He considered the possibilities, and he
compromised. It is an interpretation arrived at partly from trying to
connect how the Maestà now strikes us to what Duccio would have
been trying to do; and partly from a comparison between Duccio's
work on the Maestà and what some other painters were doing at the
time. (If Duccio is indeed a more 'Gothic' painter, it is not so much
that he may have been 'influenced' by painters from the north as
that he was responding to the representational task set by the
changes in the Church in the same way as they.) We – that is to say,
the thinking scholars, White, van Os and others – have perhaps
solved the Duccio question. The explanation seems complete,
perhaps even irresistible.

But possibilities, I have been saying, increase under explanation
as they also decrease. Do either the more general and external facts
of change in the Church in the thirteenth century, or the more
internal interpretation of why Duccio painted as he did, his view of
what was open to him and of what others were doing, suggest further
possible accounts of why he did what he did in the way that he did?
And if they do, how do these further accounts bear back on the
explanations which suggest them?

The question of Duccio, it is now clear, is best asked from the end
of the thirteenth century rather than from the ceiling of the Sistine

chapel in the sixteenth or the conventions of framed paintings in the twentieth. Why, unlike his contemporaries and near-contemporaries in Rome and Florence, did Duccio compromise? White has offered two distinct answers. Either Duccio was simply not interested in the issue of realism; or – White's later suggestion – he was, but came to see that the difficulties of trying to realise the extreme oblique on a two-dimensional surface were too great, and required sacrifices that he did not wish to make. But consider a third, which is also suggested by his style: a wish actually to distance himself from Cimabue and Giotto.

Duccio may have been in competition with Cimabue in 1285 for the commission for a Madonna from the Dominican society of Santa Maria Vergine in Florence. Cimabue, as he himself may have hoped, would have been the more obvious choice. Locals, especially Florentines, often favoured their own, and there is reason to think – not least from the work he had been doing at San Francesco in Assisi and from a commission I mention below that he might have received from Siena itself in 1287 – that Cimabue's reputation may have been rising. But the Dominicans did not choose him. There could be a simple explanation, that he had just been commissioned by the Franciscans to paint a *Crucifixion* for Santa Croce. The date of this painting (badly damaged in the flood in Florence in 1966 but now well restored and returned to the Museo dell'Opera at Santa Croce) is disputed. But if, which was not unusual, it was commissioned in the same year in which the plans for the church itself were drawn up, 1285, the Dominicans at Santa Maria Vergine, despite the fact that Cimabue had already done what the order may have thought was a satisfactory *Crucifixion* for San Domenico in Arezzo, might have preferred to ask someone else, or Cimabue himself may have let it be known that he was not available.

But if there was a delay in commissioning the *Crucifixion* for Santa Croce, there are two other possibilities. As Eugenio Battisti suggests, and despite the arresting qualities of the work which he had already done, Cimabue had acquired a reputation for having too sharp a tongue and for taking too long to complete. Dante retails the popular memory of him as 'arrogant' and 'disdainful', and remarked in the *Ottimo Commento* to the *Divine Comedy* that if anyone found fault with his work, or indeed if he found fault with it himself, he often abandoned it. There are certainly some tell-tale signs of haste, almost of clumsiness, consistent with rushing to finish, in the brushwork of his Santa Trinita *Madonna* – a work which may also have been painted in the 1280s – signs that are quite absent in anything that Duccio is known to have done. Second, as Battisti again and van Os, consistently with White, both hint, it is possible that Cimabue was unable or just possibly unwilling to reconcile his increasingly naturalistic impulse to the spiritual demands of the day; that to some influential contemporary eyes, and certainly in contrast to Duccio, he was simply too crude, or at least, came too danger-ously close to what might have been feared to be a pagan style.[32] This can suggest that far from being backward, Duccio was at that moment the best that money could buy. (This is White's own conclusion after comparing the *Rucellai Madonna* with other similar pieces.)[33] Moreover, patrons (then as now) were likely to have been less adventurous than the artists they patronised. And the Domi-nicans were famously fastidious. More than the other mendicant orders, the Augustinians, Carmelites, Franciscans and Servites, all of whom were more determinedly competing for a more popular allegiance, they took pride in being the intellectual defenders of the true faith, and may have been disinclined to too much naturalism in the paintings they commissioned. If this is so, Duccio would have realised that notwithstanding the size of the piece he was being asked to do, a size indicated by what, at the rate of the time, he was to be paid for it, moderation and restraint, delicacy rather than drama, were what was expected.

This possibility, moreover, can suggest two others. Each turns on each man's reaction to his success in this commission for Santa Maria Vergine. If Cimabue had received it, Duccio might have taken the point, tried to reestablish his competitiveness, and at-tempted a greater realism, so that his work after 1285 would not have been as it was. These painters were in a market, or at least, were competing with each other, and the Sienese workshops would have been especially sensitive to that, for even after the settlement

---

[32] Eugenio Battisti, *Cimabue*, University Park: Pennsylvania State University Press, 1967, pp. 63, 67. White, *Duccio*, p. 39.

[33] *Duccio*, p. 39.

with Florence in 1269 and the ensuing prosperity in Siena, there were too many for all of them always to be able to find work there. Financial security and artistic success, perhaps even survival – or at least, the ability to maintain a shop, which meant rent, apprentices, bills, and other enduring commitments, and for the all but perpetually indebted Duccio, no doubt just staying afloat – depended on acquiring and maintaining a reputation elsewhere; and in central Italy at that time, no reputation was more worth having than one in Florence itself. Alternatively, since Duccio did get the commission, and Cimabue, we are still supposing, did not, it is possible that he instead would have tried to change his style more nearly to meet what was wanted.

There are then at least five possibilities. First, Duccio was not interested in realism. Or he was, but decided that its demands conflicted with others, which took priority. Or he wished to distance himself from Cimabue and Giotto. Or he did not, and if Cimabue or someone else, painting in a more naturalistic manner, had received the Dominicans' commission in 1285, he would have tried to adapt his style. Or Cimabue himself, failing to get this commission, decided to adapt. There is no direct support for any of these. All but the first (and on one reading, the second) turn on the assumption that Duccio and Cimabue were in some sort of competition for the commission at Santa Maria Vergine. And we do not know that. Even if we did, we would need detailed records of how commissions were devised, negotiated and interpreted, the painters' own notes and memoirs (did they ever conceive of such things), and ideally, rough sketches and panels (always supposing that the cost of poplar in the already deforested countryside allowed this) that were tried and abandoned. If any of this existed, none – except the under-drawing and some changes that have been revealed by infra-red reflectography – now survives. The *sottoposti* left nothing but their finished work and a few legal traces which rarely bear on the nature of that work. But from the works that we do have, there are a few fragments of indirect, circumstantial evidence to say something about the third, fourth and fifth. (The date of Cimabue's Santa Croce *Crucifixion* is too uncertain to make it worth pursuing the simpler explanation that he could not have been a candidate for the Madonna at Santa Maria Vergine.)

First, consider the fifth, the possibility that Cimabue himself decided to adapt. In perhaps 1301, he did a Madonna for San Francesco at Pisa. (This was carried off by Napoleon's armies and is now in the Louvre.) What in this connection is interesting about this piece is that the throne is more similar to the one that Duccio designed for the *Rucellai Madonna* than to the throne that Cimabue himself designed for his Madonna at Santa Trinita in Florence in – it is thought by most – the 1280s. It is less massive, less solid and thrusting, more intriguingly and delicately angled. This could, it is true, have been a response to the gentler, less dramatic, taste of the Franciscans who commissioned it. But if this is correct, it does not explain why Duccio painted as he did, in a similar way, for the Dominicans. It could therefore be that having himself failed to secure the commission at Santa Maria Vergine, Cimabue had taken the point. On this argument, he and perhaps other contemporaries had between the 1280s and the turn of the century come to see Duccio as 'the more advanced', or at least, as better able than they to meet what was being expected in the commissions.

There is also the supporting evidence of two later pieces by Sienese painters, Ugolino's altarpiece for Santa Croce in Florence, which he is thought to have painted in 1324 or 1325, and Pietro Lorenzetti's for the Carmelite church in Siena itself in 1329. Ugolino – whose cross-hatching with the brush resembles that deployed by the second hand working on the panel from the *Maestà* which depicts Jesus opening the eyes of the man born blind – was painting for one of the richest churches in Florence, and yet, despite his unusually adventurous use of tone, which suggests an intuitive sense of the then unknown theory of complementary colours, he is intimate and intricate, quite unmonumental, in conception and style more like Duccio than either of the by then locally renowned realists. Likewise, although the Madonna herself and the child and the throne on Lorenzetti's piece for the Carmelite church in Siena are compositionally more similar to previous Florentine work – notwithstanding Cimabue's apparent reversion at the start of the century – than they are to anything that is known to have been produced by Duccio or any other shop in Siena, the predella, both in its illusionistic devices and in the use of colour, is more reminiscent of the scenes on the cathedral *Maestà*; and nowhere, for example in the architectural details, does Lorenzetti attempt anything of the kind that Giotto had tried to do in the Arena frescoes.[34] (But then, as I have already mentioned, Giotto himself departed from the stark solidity of these frescoes in his later work. Giotto also may have realised that he was having to pay too high a price, both artistically and financially, for pursuing naturalism.)[35]

Cimabue's change suggests that there may be something in the fifth possibility. The later painting in Siena suggests that there may be something in the third; the realists from Florence might have been thought to be too crude, and the Sienese, Duccio and others, wished to distance themselves from that. But there is also some circumstantial support in the other direction, which addresses the possibility – the fourth of the five – that if Cimabue had got the Dominicans' commission in 1285, Duccio would have changed his style. This support is in the stained-glass oculus in the cathedral at Siena, and it suggests that whatever might have prompted him to do so, in one respect at least, the respect which has dominated the critical discussions, he could not have changed.

This window was commissioned in 1287, and the records of the Opera indicate that it was finished a year or so later. There is no mention of who designed it or made it. Because the window is where it is, however, it was long attributed to Duccio. Yet as White argues, the attribution is unlikely to be right. The way in which the figures are related to the architecture, draping themselves or their hands over the edge of a throne for instance; the way in which, in the scene of the *Burial of the Virgin* in the lower window, the crowd is set four or five deep in a stunning but clear and wholly controlled perspective; and the very close similarities – so White reports, I have not been able myself closely to compare the originals – between the way in which some of the heads are modelled and painted and his

---

[34] On Ugolino's altarpiece, Bomford *et al.*, *Art in the Making*, pp. 98–123. On Lorenzetti's, van Os, *Sienese Altarpieces*, pp. 91 ff.

[35] There is admittedly the complication of the mysterious Stefano, whom Vasari describes as a pupil of Giotto's, and who, Vasari says, surpassed even his master – as another writer put it at the end of the fourteenth century – in 'aping nature'. But Vasari attributes the same work both to Giotto and to Stefano in his separate lives of each; he is once again not a reliable authority; and nothing that can reliably be attributed to Stefano survives (Vasari, *Le Vite*, pp. 130–3, White, *Duccio*, p. 150).

Crucifixion in the upper church at Assisi; all suggest Cimabue. No one else whose work has survived was achieving such effects at the end of the thirteenth century. And it makes one curious to know why, if we assume that he studied this window, Duccio did not attempt anywhere in any of the scenes on his altarpiece twenty years later to imitate what Cimabue – or whoever the designer of the window was – did.

If this line of thinking is correct, it seems unlikely that even if Duccio had failed to get the commission for the Dominicans in Florence, he would greatly have changed his style. This may slightly reduce the force of the more internal interpretation from the *Maestà* itself. On this interpretation, Duccio was simply balancing many considerations. Yet in the scenes in which he depicts people standing behind each other without the perspectival complication of an architectural setting, such as the *Apparition in Galilee*, in which Christ appears before a group of disciples, he could have striven for the effect that Cimabue achieved in the *Burial of the Virgin* in the oculus without disturbing the other effects. One would certainly like to know why he did not.

Nevertheless, the conventional view of the painterly Renaissance, which has affected how Duccio has been seen, remains disturbed. This view, it will be recalled, suggested that 'Cimabue thought to hold the field in painting, and now Giotto has the cry.' It suggested that there was a real issue, seen by the real genius of Cimabue in the 1280s and Giotto a few years later, the issue of realism; and that contemporaries who did not grasp it, or who could not realise it, were more backward. But a closer examination of who was trying to do what and how for whom, indeed of what, in the context of the new Christian patronage, painting then was, suggests that however talented Cimabue and Giotto were, and whatever they may now be seen to have begun, and however 'advanced' that may have come later to seem, they were not at the time unequivocally perceived, except perhaps by a few partisans in Florence itself (and even then the evidence from exact contemporaries is lacking), and cannot so readily be perceived by us either, to have been setting the pace. Only with hindsight, imputing the telos of realism, would that be so. And only on an heroic view of artistic activity, of the kind which comes down from Vasari and has been congenial to later romantics, a view in which innovation is prized over tradition, fashion over skill, and deviation over refinement, would compromise be a lesser virtue.

VI

It is impossible actually to decide whether any of the different interpretations of why Duccio painted as he did is correct, let alone at all precisely to weigh them against each other. For none, moreover, is there ever likely to be decisive independent evidence. But two more general points are clear.

In the first place, the more possibilities we entertain, the more judgements we can imagine Duccio making, the more fully do we see his painting itself. The more we do this, the better sense we have of what we are trying to explain; and the better sense we have of that, the more we are inclined to look at other work, and back again at Duccio's. It is a complicated business, and offends Michael Baxandall's belief that in appraising works of art, we should practice 'critical parsimony'.[36] Such restraint has its attractions, the attractions, we might say, although Baxandall does not, of analogous precepts in the sciences. Do not introduce complexity where simplicity and economy will do. Make a sharp distinction, as Baxandall does suggest, between the immediately active elements in a painter's intention and the more remote possibilities of what, more generally, he may have thought. And as a caution to the speculative preemption which has often run riot in the art-historical literature, this is no doubt wise.

Yet, the second – and from what I have been saying in previous chapters, perhaps now familiar – argument is that the wider the range of considerations that we think Duccio could have entertained, about what was required of him, about what other painters were doing, and about how both of these stood in relation to his sense of his own capacities and to his sense of his success and theirs, the more we understand. The more inclined we may accordingly be to revise our description of what that was, or if we already take the

---

[36] *Patterns of Intention*, pp. 120–1, 131.

revisionist view, suggested for Duccio himself by White and for later medieval images more generally by Camille, to refine it. This is not to say that we thereby become more certain about it; merely, that we might see it differently.

— 5 —

Explanation,
understanding and theory

I

Possibilities increase under explanation as they also decrease. The British Labour Party has depended on trade union support. It has also been constitutionally bound to take note of decisions taken at its conference and on its National Executive Committee. Could that constitution and the powers of the NEC have been modified? And whether they could have been or not, could the various elements in the Labour Party in the 1950s and 1960s have collaborated in a less mutually self-destructive manner? Some authorities in early modern Europe made effective moves to limit the spread and perhaps also the incidence of plague. Could they have acted earlier? And could other authorities have acted at all? The increasingly severe fiscal pressures on French agriculturalists in the seventeenth and early eighteenth centuries served to keep their fertility high. Could these pressures have been lower? And if they could, would other conditions have allowed fertility to fall? The new mood in Washington after Roosevelt's death, Harriman's advice to Truman, Stalin's decision to press his advantage in eastern Europe, and the seeming speed of the Soviet Army's advance into north Korea, all affected the State–War–Navy Coordinating Committee's view that the United States should occupy the south. Would that view have been different if Roosevelt had still been in power, or if Stalin had proceeded with more caution in Poland, or if his army had not moved so quickly into northern Korea, or if Washington had had a better sense of his general intentions? Duccio received the Dominicans' commission for a Madonna for their chapel of Santa Maria Vergine. But he did not conceive and execute it as we think Cimabue might have done. If he had not received the

157

commission, would his *Maestà* for the high altar in Siena have been different?

Also, what we first choose to explain, and the shape and direction of the explanations we suggest, are themselves informed by pictures of the possible. Some come from contrasting actualities. Several European social democratic parties have not been politically so dependent on trade unions. A few Italian authorities were controlling circulation in the sixteenth century in order to try to prevent the spread of plague; by the eighteenth, the authorities in France and on the eastern frontier of the Habsburg empire were managing to do so successfully. In the seventeenth and early eighteenth centuries, rural fertility in England was noticeably lower than in most parts of France. By the time that Duccio came to start work on his *Maestà*, Cimabue and Giotto were painting in a recognisably new way, which in Florence, may already have been the fashion. Other possibilities are not actual. Once its victory over Japan was assured, the United States was nowhere acting to conciliate rather than to contain the Soviet Union. Nor did the Americans or the Russians have any experience of dealing with post-colonial nationalism. And Cimabue did not receive the commission from the Dominicans in 1285.

All possibilities for a world, however, whether they are suggested by our explanations or by contrasts and comparisons with what we want to explain, should, I have been saying, start from a world as it otherwise was. They should not require us to unwind the past. And the consequences we draw from these alternatives should initially fit with the other undisturbed runnings-on in that world. Neither the alternative starting points nor the runnings-on we impute to them should be fantastic. Granada could not have defeated the Catholic kings in the 1490s. Al-Andalous was at its height as far back as the tenth century, and the Moors had been on the retreat since Toledo had been reconquered by the Christians in the late eleventh. Since the second half of the thirteenth century, indeed, Granada had been the only province not to be retaken, and even then, the Nasrid dynasty there had long been forced to pay tribute to Aragon. If it had nevertheless managed effectively to resist the combined forces of Aragon and Castile, it is difficult to believe (in contrast to what would have been the opportunities open to the Moors if they had been victorious both at the centre and on the western edge of their area in the eighth century) that with the resources that would have been available to it, it could have gone on to defeat armies that would have been deployed against it from elsewhere, and to create an alternative Europe. It is not so difficult, however, to imagine a more social democratic Britain in the 1970s, or a rather less democratic Confederate state in north America.

These distinctions between the more and less possible, however, may seem at once too sharp and too unsteady. Are the alternatives to any actual given only by the facts of that actual, or by possibilities that were canvassed at the time, or by very close comparisons? Are there not also theories to suggest possibilities that we would not otherwise have been able to see?

II

This is a distinctively modern expectation. The eighteenth century extended what Polybius had connected. For the pre-Polybians, like Aristotle, there was no connection between the typical, what generally is and might be, types, ideals and general possibilities, and the particular, including the particular in time. Historians, Aristotle argued in the *Poetics*, tellers of *storia*, had nothing to say to the poets and prophets and philosophers. It was Polybius who first argued that particulars could be seen as points in a cycle, and in virtue of this, that they had more general significance and connected to wider moral and political concerns. This Polybian 'philosophy teaching by examples', however, as a humanist described it at the beginning of the seventeenth century, was transformed in the eighteenth. An attraction to the new science, whose pictures suggested relations of a linear rather than a cyclical kind, connected to a new conviction of the place of reason in inquiry and of its workings in the world itself. It was strengthened by the sense that in Europe, irreversible changes were under way, changes which suggested that what we now think of as the 'economic' and the 'social', not the legal and political, were the prime movers, and that the futures they would produce would be quite different from any past. (The transformation is clear in the changing sense of 'natural

law'.) There were new truths to be had about the human world, and
they could be known in new ways.

In one respect, they were little different from the truths of
exemplar History. These also were general. Each particular was
classed in a set, and its attributes as a member of its set were sufficient to explain its connections to any other particular. But there
was a telling difference. Exemplar History allowed a space between
what theoretical reason suggested and what might practically be
done. Fortune's opportunities might be seized, and they might not.
In the new and more deliberately theoretical History, by contrast,
theoretical reason was thought to explain practice and to exist to
guide it. There was no room for reflective discretion. Indeed, in its
most extreme, sociological, form, in the nineteenth century, this
new History had no room for practical reasoning at all.

This may have its advocates still. But enthusiasm for it is fading.
This is in part due to the devastations, dislocations and disappoint-
ments of the twentieth century: the two world wars, 'fascisms', the
disruptions of decolonisation and attempted 'development', and –
the analogue for progressive intellectuals in the 1990s of the reservations about the effects of the revolution in France in the 1790s –
the failures of imposed state socialism. Intellectual changes also,
the decline of deterministic conceptions of non-human nature,
arguments against the older distinctions between science and philosophy, revised views of the sciences themselves, and the more
diffuse but nevertheless deep move through modernism to post-
modernism, have also played a part. The history of the retreat has
yet to be written. But we do not have to know it in order to see that
there are two good reasons for having made it.[1]

The first is that generalisable answers of what we conventionally
think of as a causal kind have ceased to be persuasive. The causal
connections or runnings-on that we have been able to detect in
human states of affairs have turned out either to have to be phrased
at a level that is so general as to be insufficiently informative and not
address our interests in explanation; or to be so conditional as not to

---

[1] This is not to say of course that much of the distinctively moral and
political, as distinct from the more purely analytical, ambition of the
Enlightenment – for various kinds of right, for example – does not remain.

be general; or, when they have generated testable predictions, to be false.[2] Because the answers to questions about social change, we now see, have to be hedged with so many conditions, any account of any particular change, if it is to respect the conditionality of the instance, has itself to be relatively particular and accordingly complex. And the more complex it becomes, as I have been saying, the more it suggests alternatives which reduce even such certainty as we can have about the particular itself.

The second reason for the retreat from the analytical programme of the Enlightenment is the increasing realisation, and not just in ethics, that a theory of practical reason has to connect to what Bernard Williams has called the 'subjective set' of the agents for whom it is intended. It has to give reasons that they could recognise as reasons for them from where they are.[3] Even where a theory of what some set of people have good reason to do is intended only to appeal to them in some single and abstract capacity, as citizens of a modern liberal republic, for instance, as a class, as women, or simply as 'rational actors', rather than as whole persons leading whole lives, it will fail unless it in some way connects to what, in the circumstances in which they find themselves, those people more particularly conceive themselves to be. If they claim that it does

---

[2] Some indicative false predictions: that nationalism would cease to be a potent force; that high-wage high-division-of-labour economies would do most to alleviate poverty; that the working class in capitalism would embrace socialism, that actually existing socialism would improve growth as well as provide more equitable distribution, indeed that socialism would always follow capitalism, and not sometimes precede it; that decolonised states would want to implement a competitive liberal politics; that there would be a progressive 'secularisation'; that an extending international trade would serve to make relations between states less belligerent; above all, perhaps, and guiding these more specific predictions, the general expectation that parochial allegiances would be transformed into an allegiance of a more 'universal' kind. (Sociologists will recall the models of 'modernisation' that persisted even into the 1970s.) Apparent counter-instances were the expectations of De Tocqueville and Max Weber, but it supports what I say, and does not qualify it, that their more successful prognostications were also the more paradoxical, and made with irony. Neither man was unequivocally attracted to the picture of an historical realisation of Enlightenment.

[3] Bernard Williams, 'Internal and external reasons', in *Moral Luck: Philosophical Papers, 1973–1980*, Cambridge: Cambridge University Press, 1981, pp. 101–13.

appeal to them solely as members of one or another category, they
will almost certainly be self-deceived; for there is the further question of why the appeal is to that category, and not others, and
the answer to that will be an answer about them as they are in the
circumstances in which they find themselves. Even where the point
of a theory of practical reason – the point, for instance, of so-called
Critical Theories which have extended the Kantian conception of
Kritik – is to transcend this fact, to encourage poeple to reflect on
their self-conceptions, to enlarge and extend them, perhaps even to
change them and to change the circumstances in which they have
formed them, or at the very least to be more consistent; it is still true
that any reflection they might make on what it proposes can begin
only from where they are, within their particular lives, and not from
without. Likewise with explanatory theories of the practical reasoning of actual agents. Even if we believe that a 'real interest' or some
general force of another kind is guiding people's reflections, we start
from what we take these reflections to be. If we do not, it is not clear
in what sense we are talking about the practical reflection which is
theirs. Social and political theorists have not often taken the force
of this. Indeed, they have usually resisted it. Theoretical reasoning,
they have believed, has been sufficient to explain why people do
what they do.

At the end of the twentieth century, the analytical retreat is
almost everywhere evident. Moral and political theorists now more
often make their answers conditional on particular circumstances.
Social theorists who remain committed to the eighteenth-century
project of a general history tacitly converge on the conclusion
that what they want to explain can only be accounted for in the
particular: if the question is about the early success of western
Europe, in the 'concatenation' in the medieval period, for instance,
of ancient and feudal modes of production, or in the coincidence
of the region's political geography and the opportunities in it for
agricultural growth and trade, or in the absence of obstacles to
economic growth that were elsewhere present. If there is a generalisation now to be had, it is that it is *un*predictability, what Roberto
Unger calls the 'plasticity' and adaptability of successful institutions
and ideologies, or as W. G. Runciman sees it, the advantages which
accrue to those who gain in the perpetual but never foreclosed
competition for economic, coercive or ideological power, which

explain. The Enlightenment project of a social theory has separated, and in each of its more distinct parts, normative and explanatory, assumed a new modesty.[4]

III

In reasserting the claims of particularity, however, I might seem merely to be restating old reaction. Already at the beginning of the

[4] Indicative instances of the tendency in modern moral and political theory are John Rawls' more recent papers ('Justice as fairness: political, not metaphysical', *Philosophy and Public Affairs* 14 (1985), 251–76; 'The Priority of Right and Ideas of the Good', *Philosophy and Public Affairs* 17 (1988), 251–76; 'The Domain of the Political and Overlapping Consensus', *New York University Law Review* 64 (1989), 233–55, and Charles Taylor's arguments (*Sources of the Self: The Making of the Modern Identity*, Cambridge MA: Harvard University Press, 1989, and more directly 'Cross-purposes: the liberal-communitarian debate', in Nancy L. Rosenblum ed., *Liberalism and the Moral Life*, Cambridge MA: Harvard University Press, 1989, pp. 159–82). The general historians I allude to are Perry Anderson, *Lineages of the Absolutist State*, London: New Left Books, 1974, e.g. at p. 422; Michael Mann, whose explanation is that western Europe just happened politically to be blocked to its east and to have an exceptional 'agricultural-cum-trading opportunity' to its west, *The Sources of Social Power I: A History of Power from the Beginning to A.D. 1760*, Cambridge: Cambridge University Press, 1986, e.g. at p. 510; E. L. Jones, *The European Miracle: Environments, Economies and Geopolitics in the History of Europe and Asia*, Cambridge: Cambridge University Press, 2nd edition, 1987, pp. 225–38, e.g. at p. 234, Ernest Gellner, *Plough, Sword and Book: The Structure of Human History*, London: Collins, 1988, pp. 171, 199, 273–8; and Roberto Mangabeira Unger, who picks out movements 'towards solutions that do not allow a rigid set of social roles and hierarchies to predefine the practical relations among people', *Plasticity into Power: Comparative-Historical Studies on the Institutional Conditions of Economic and Military Success*, Cambridge: Cambridge University Press, 1987, p. 207, also e.g. at pp. 7, 41, 56, 153 ff., 199–200. (Perry Anderson himself makes a similar point about an intersecting set of writers in 'A culture in contraflow: I', *New Left Review* 189 (1990), 72.) Even Runciman, who insists that his generalisation explains, agrees that 'nobody who has studied in any depth the evidence of the historical and ethnographic record, can fail to be struck by the way in which the most elaborate forms of culture and the most complex patterns of structure' constitute a sequence which 'is, no less than natural selection, both random in its origins and indeterminate in its outcome' (*A Treatise on Social Theory II: Substantive Social Theory*, Cambridge: Cambridge University Press, 1989, p. 449, also p. 285). My point here is not about the generality of the questions – the question, for instance, of the past success of western Europe – but about the generalisability of the answers.

nineteenth century, some were insisting that understanding could be perverted and practical projects subverted by the application of general principles. One such reaction produced a programme for another new History. In this, the historians were in Ranke's phrase to recover the past 'as it peculiarly was', in itself. They were to abstain from all abstraction and generality, immerse themselves in primary sources, and trace lines of unique descent. (In Ranke's own view, the historians in the German lands were to go to the German archives and trace the distinctively medieval origins of the distinctively German. The French claim that their theories and revolution had given a new 'universal' to history was to be contested.) In my suggestion that to grasp the actual is to understand it in the light of the particular possibilities which it suggests, or which closely comparable instances suggest for it, and not to subsume it in a generality, I might seem to be saying much the same thing.

Certainly, the conditions for inserting alternative possibilities into the world and then drawing consequences from them do not appeal directly to theory. For the starting points, where causal connections are at issue, there are two such conditions. The first, to which I have already alluded, is that the departure from the actual present should not require us to unwind the past or appropriate the future. We might agree that if Richelieu had not pressed his dispute with Spain and raised royal taxes, the fiscal burden on the poorer French agriculturalists would not have been so great. Their fertility might as a result have been lower. But it would still not have been as low as it was in England. In seventeenth-century France, nothing and no one could have compensated for the economic and social problems that had been accumulating in the countryside for at least three hundred years. Not to see this would be to consider an alternative for a France then not as in other respects it was, but for a France that branched from the actual somewhere before 1400. We might suggest that if Giotto had not got into the difficulties he seems to have got into in representing the perspective of the extreme oblique, perhaps Duccio and other early fourteenth-century painters, including Giotto himself at the end of his career, might have painted other than they did. But to secure this suggestion, we would have had not to have unwound the thirteenth century, but to have speeded it up, so that technical problems that were not finally to be solved until the end of the fifteenth were resolved much earlier.

The second condition for alternative starting points where causal connections are at issue, closely related to the first, is that the departure from the actual present should not require us to alter so much else in the present itself as to make it a quite different place. Public authorities outside Italy and southern Germany may in principle have been able to do more than they did to limit circulation and thereby control the spread and perhaps also the incidence of plague. But not only would that have required them, as some saw at the time, to alter too many of their established priorities; it would also have required many to assume powers which they could not assume. The United States, I have suggested, could have decided in the summer of 1945 not to occupy the southern part of Korea. Not much else would have had then to be different for it to do so. But once it was there, it was more difficult for it to withdraw. That would have required it to concede to the Soviet Union, but by the beginning of 1946, its commitment to containment was already too deep. In the 1950s, the British Labour Party could have paid more attention than it did to the social and economic changes that its own 'revisionists' were then describing. Had the left reflected on these changes more seriously than it did, and had the right been politically less direct in its opposition, then, like some of the social democratic parties elsewhere in Europe, Labour might have been adapted to them. By the later 1970s and early 1980s, however, when as a result of continuing low investment in British industry, poor management, over-manning, rising inflation and governments acting always to support sterling, the earlier hopes of high growth had faded, it was clear that the party had either to insist on a defensive socialism which, however sensible it may have been as a policy for the longer term, was electorally disastrous, or, as Mitterand's party was to do in France after 1981, quietly to abandon its commitment to the employment and welfare of a large number of its own supporters. It chose electorally disastrous socialism. For by then, its activists had been allowed to gain too much control. What was possible in the 1950s had all but ceased to be so by the end of the 1970s.

For those alternative starting points where considerations of agency rather than cause are at issue, what is more and less admissible is less easy to judge. This is because the line which divides the two lies at that point at which the agents in question would cease to recognise or to acknowledge themselves as the agents they were. Richelieu might have decided to have put the interest of France's cultivators above those of his dispute with Spain. Cho Man-sik might not have been so insistently nationalistic and accordingly so resistant to Chistiakov's request that he co-operate in the Soviet plan for a joint trusteeship. Aneurin Bevan might have been more pragmatic, Hugh Gaitskell less principled, Harold Wilson more far-sighted and courageous, and James Callaghan less fearful of the trade unions. And although here, the dispositions of the agents in question are more obscure, Cimabue might not have been so intransigent or Giotto so experimental. Each is imaginable. But none is a readily plausible possibility for the man as he was. Actual agents have dispositions and abilities, kinds of knowledge and states of mind which, so we judge, preclude their considering some alternatives for themselves, and thereby preclude us from considering those alternatives as alternatives for them.

None of these conditions for alternative starting points turns on what could be described as 'theory'. They turn on facts of the actual, on causal constraints and character. But the constraints on the consequences we can draw from the starting points are not so tight. Causal conditions can change, and even characters, before they die, can alter, or at least alter their beliefs. And occasionally, there will be a theory to hand to suggest how. In a labour-intensive economy, for example, fiscal pressures will increase the need for production and reduce security, and since in an early modern state, families are the best assurance of both security and labour, it is likely that the pressures will cause fertility to rise. Even then, the predicted effect can be offset, as in seventeenth-century England it arguably was, by the existence of effective institutions for relief.

More usually, however, there will be no such theory. At most, there will be mere precepts, even the most general conditions of which are unclear. Great powers are said by self-described realists about international relations to move into a vacuum. But in 1945, the United States and the Soviet Union were each unusual great powers. Each had been precipitated into its status from a previous isolation, and both were markedly more ideological than the powers they replaced. The ideology of each, moreover, was the antithesis of the other. Likewise painters, or so many art historians have presumed, are influenced by those who precede them; almost all, certainly, have teachers. Cimabue, Duccio and Giotto will all have had their masters, although in no case is there a record of who these men were. But all three were painting at a moment when their patrons were making new demands, were inventing, and were also, we can suppose, competing. The demands that were being made on them, together with their talent, make it highly unlikely that we can adequately explain what they did and infer what they might have done from where and how and from whom they learnt their craft. In these and innumerable cases of a comparable kind, we use the precepts that pass for 'theory' at the most to start to think how, as the kind of item it was, in the circumstances in which it occurred, the alternative that interests us would then have 'run on'. We cannot use the precepts actually to secure any such thought.

If we were to ignore the conditions for inserting an alternative starting point into the actual world or those for judging how the alternative world would then have run on; if we were instead to impose a general theory; the possibilities we would be entertaining would be possibilities not for an actual, but for what would itself be merely a possible. And at that point, our History or social science would have dissolved into a literature of the imagination. There may be a demand in literature of this kind, as Thomas Pavel suggests, for a 'salience' to the actual. But if there is, it is a demand at most for recognisable *kind* of circumstance, character, feeling, thought, action or relation. It is not a demand for a salience that is necessarily – indeed in our conventions for literary genres, even desirably – attached to actually existing whole things. In this respect – if not in the richness of detail that may be asked of the items which supply it – it is, when met, a salience which is analogous to that of abstract and general concepts in the imaginary worlds of abstractly theoretical social science.[5]

[5] Pavel deploys the logicians' imagery of possible worlds to suggest that the imaginary worlds of literature have to be salient to the actual, although the distinction I draw here between the two kinds of salience is mine, not his (*Fictional Worlds*, Cambridge MA: Harvard University Press, 1986). Social scientists conventionally suppose that stable populations, economies in

The possibilities that we consider for the actual, by contrast, start from particular agents in particular sets of circumstances as those agents and sets of circumstances actually were. Models, theories, or precepts may guide our speculations about what might then follow. But these will at most be theories which are grounded in inductions from other instances, in which case – either in themselves, or because it will be difficult to distinguish the theories themselves from their conditions – they may not be relevant. At worst, they will be mere precepts, and not stably grounded at all.

This might indeed be said to be a restatement of old reaction. I am resisting the simplification of abstraction in social science, but could seem to have accepted the presumptions which inform it: to have accepted either – and against what I argued in chapter 1 – that explanations in History and the social sciences have formally to be identical to what in the old 'covering law' model were supposed to characterise explanations in the sciences of non-human nature or –

equilibrium, Marx's 'universal class', prisoners in a dilemma and other such concepts, refer, if abstractly, to existing entities. And indeed, if realism is 'a matter of the familiarity in symbols used in the telling', and truth 'a matter of what is told, literally or metaphorically, by means of symbols familiar or fantastic' (Nelson Goodman, *Of Mind and Other Matters*, Cambridge MA: Harvard University Press, 1984, p. 125), theories which deploy such terms would appear to be offering true if simplified descriptions of the actual, and to be expressing them in a more or less realistic, that's to say familiar, way. The difference from the thick descriptions of history or ethnography would seem to be merely a matter of degree. But the thought is misleading. The terms and relations proposed in abstract models of this kind are not just more sparse than those in richer accounts; they stand in for their complexity. The terms and the suggested relations between them – or if, like a population which is stable or an economy in equilibrium, they are synthetic concepts, between the elements that they embody within them – cross the line between literal description and metaphor. Of course, their parsimony and the precision of the models in which they are deployed are conventions in what we call 'science'. But the truths they tell are 'salient' to the actual in the ways in which persuasive fictions are. At their best, abstract models in these inquiries are more akin to works of art. If they are 'scientific', they are so only in the sense in which mathematics is. They have attractions, but these are internal to the art, and stand apart. Some aspects of the dispute about the distinction between (social) science and literature in the eighteenth, nineteenth and early twentieth centuries in England, France and Germany are recovered by Wolf Lepenies, R. J. Hollingdale trans., *Between Literature and Science: The Rise of Sociology*, Cambridge: Cambridge University Press, 1988.

the one alternative which the theorists of the Enlightenment have left us – universally applicable theories of what all agents have good reason to do; and that if our explanations cannot conform to one or other of these types, we have no option but always to resort to the *ad hoc*. I might seem not, at least explicitly, to have allowed for what, in contrast to these old Enlightenment models of theory, of causal explanation and practical reason, often indeed in reaction to them, others have pressed as 'interpretation'.

IV

The first of the three distinguishable arguments for the privilege to be given to interpretation in History and the social sciences is also the least problematic. It turns on a suggested difference between reports and descriptions. Reports are in Runciman's view uncontested characterisations of what presents itself for explanation. They raise no issues of initial description, or at least presume that such issues have been resolved. They are neutral between theories and preclude none. They are what the recording angel, Runciman fancies, writes in her notebook. Descriptions, by contrast, do suggest one line of explanation rather than another, and do preclude others.[6]

'Richelieu raised taxes', 'The United States occupied south Korea' and 'Duccio never attempted the extreme oblique' are each reports. That we choose to select these facts rather than others as the ones we want to explain indicates only that these are the facts that we want to explain. None of these reports of them inclines us to one explanation rather than another, nor does any of them preclude

---

[6] See chapter 4, note 1. Runciman supposes that the requirements for explanation (which starts from reports) are the same in all the sciences: they require theories, sets of general laws. I have criticised that idea in chapter 1, section IV. Good descriptions, he thinks, must be 'authentic' and in order to override mere idiosyncrasy, also 'representative'; good reports have merely to be clear and uncontentious (*A Treatise on Social Theory I: The Methodology of Social Theory*, Cambridge: Cambridge University Press, 1983, pp. 145–222, 143–4, 236–44). As I explain below, I use 'description' more widely to refer to accounts, by agents or by others, which are not neutral; see also my comment on Rorty on agents' own accounts, note 16 below.

any. 'Richelieu overrode the interests of poorer cultivators', 'the United States confused international communism and Korean nationalism' and 'Duccio was conservative' lie somewhere between reports and descriptions. Each serves to suggest a more definite question. Each also does incline us more to one line of explanation rather than another: to an examination of Richelieu's political choices in the light of what we take the interests of the poorer cultivators to have been; to what gave rise to what we now see to have been a political muddle in the post-war, post-colonial world; and to what led Duccio to paint in what we now regard as a more orthodox manner than Giotto. But again, none actually prejudges the explanation we might offer. Richelieu may or may not have thought that he had any choice, or at least, a choice of this kind; indeed, the effects of his actions on agricultural livelihoods may have been quite unintended. The Americans may or may not have been affected by the Soviet acceptance of the Korean People's Republic and its committees in the north, or by what they were told by Korean conservatives and Christians, or by a more general presumption that to be 'anti-fascist' and 'anti-colonial' in 1945, and yet not to favour America's own particular kind of competitive liberalism, was to be inclined to some sort of more or less revolutionary socialism, or by some other factor. They may even have had an exact sense of the distinction between indigenous nationalism and international communism, and for their purposes, have chosen to elide it. Duccio may or may not have been able to experiment in the way that Cimabue and Giotto were doing, or have been sensible of the technical difficulties they encountered, or sensitive to what his patrons wanted, or affected by some other consideration. 'In pressing France's interests, Richelieu undermined them', however, 'the United States pursued its hegemonic interest in containing the Soviet Union in Korea', and 'Duccio's *Maestà* is at once an artistic compromise and a work of genius' are descriptions. Each all but directs the answer to the question it suggests.

The lines between reports and descriptions are far from sharp. But the issue is clear and in principle simple. It turns only on the interests we might have in explaining, on what in chapter 1 I called the 'context' of our explanation. (By extension, it can turn also on our interest in an evaluation of the relevant state of affairs. If we were to see 'containment' as a strategy for 'security', to see 'security' as a strategy for 'order', and to suppose that 'order' promises peace, we are likely to be commending it; most of us value peace. But the commendation is not entailed. We could easily introduce an undermining or over-riding argument in favour of mutual accommodation on the one hand – of what used to be called 'appeasement' – or of war on the other.)[7] These relatively innocuous distinctions between reports and descriptions, however, more usually disguise one or other and occasionally both of two deeper and more contentious differences.

The first of these is marked by the distinction, as the German post-Kantians who pressed it used to put it, between 'spirit' and 'nature', between those things which are distinctively human and those which are not. Kant himself had agreed that we can see ourselves and others from the outside, as objects ' affected through the senses', as appearance, or from the inside, 'in the use of reason', 'independent of sensuous impressions'. Others, without always endorsing his metaphysics of 'noumena', have reiterated his point. We can, they suggest, see double: see ourselves and others both from the outside and from within, 'objectively', as it has often been put,

---

[7] The relativity of explanations in the human sciences to our interests is neatly exposed by Hilary Putnam (*Meaning and the Moral Sciences*, London: Routledge and Kegan Paul, 1978, pp. 41–5). In Putnam's examples, the fact that the campus police saw the professor stark naked in the womens' hostel at midnight *can* be explained by invoking a law which says that as a human animal with the usual motor skills, the professor could neither put his clothes on nor leave the room faster than the speed of light; but this is obviously not what we want to know. Likewise, Willie Sutton's reply when asked why he robbed banks – 'because that's where the money is' – *can* be explained by a law-like generalisation to this effect for classes in which that particular, Willie Sutton, falls; but what the prison chaplain, who asked the question, no doubt wanted to know is why Willie robbed at all; and what (I imagine) the men in adjacent cells, overhearing the exchange, might have wondered is why Willie robbed banks, which have alarms and armed guards and are so very difficult to get away from, and not trains. (This is closely connected to Bas C. van Fraassen's point about what he calls the importance of 'contrast classes' and 'relevance' in our explanations; see chapter 1, section IV.) Charles Taylor makes the point about evaluation in 'Neutrality in political science', in *Philosophy and the Human Sciences: Philosophical Papers 2*, Cambridge: Cambridge University Press, 1985, pp. 58–90.

and 'subjectively'.[8] Many nineteenth- and twentieth-century post-Kantians, however, reacting to one or another kind of 'empiricism' or 'positivism', have all but devalued the natural and an objective stance. They have instead pressed the claims of the distinctively human. What exactly this is can be disputed, and endlessly is. But it could be said to include the capacity to know oneself, to grasp universals, to sustain relations to the inexistent, to use language, to act freely, and to form part of a social group; to include a non-spatial element; and not to be identified with any other object in the world. In whatever way they are is drawn, however, such differences from non-human nature are metaphysical. The argument has been that one or more of these qualities must make the case for an 'interpretive' explanation of human affairs rather than – or at the very least, as an essential addition to – a 'causal' one. Causal explanations, the argument is, are appropriate to the relations between events and states of affairs in the rest of nature, including the rest of human nature; to the relations between things which are in Kant's sense 'heteronomous', or 'phenomena'. Interpretive explanations, by contrast, are explanations of relations between qualities that are self-defining, perhaps even self-creating; of the relations between or within the 'autonomous', 'noumena'.[9]

---

[8] Kant, H. J. Paton trans., *The Groundwork of the Metaphysics of Morals*, New York: Harper, 1953, p. 125. Thomas Nagel argues for a double vision of ourselves in 'Subjective and objective', in *Mortal Questions*, Cambridge: Cambridge University Press, 1978, pp. 196–213; also Stuart Hampshire, *New York Review of Books*, 26/19, 6 December 1979, supplement d and *Innocence and Experience*, Cambridge MA: Harvard University Press, 1989, pp. 38 ff. In drawing the contrast between interpretive explanations and causal ones, I do not mean to suggest that causal explanations are the only non-interpretive explanations there are. There are functional explanations, for instance, in the mathematical sense, and others. The differences between these, however, do not bear on what I say here; and as I suggested in chapter 1, section IV, they are not differences that are themselves easy to sustain independently of any particular explanatory project.

[9] I take the inventory of the human from Richard Rorty, *Philosophy and the Mirror of Nature*, Princeton: Princeton University Press, 1979, p. 35; Rorty explains its connection with the related convictions at p. 353. Charles Taylor – Rorty's chosen antagonist in this matter – has offered influential defences of the importance of 'spirit' in e.g. 'Self-interpreting animals', in *Human Agency and Language: Philosophical papers 1*, Cambridge: Cambridge University Press, 1985,

The second of the two deeper and more contentious differences in the argument about explanation and interpretation in History and the social sciences is that between holists and anti-holists of content. The holists claim that the world is all of a piece. Our explanation of any one part of it accordingly requires us to locate that part in relation to all the others in what is presumed to be the internally connected and perhaps also indivisible whole. Anti-holists by contrast see no reason to believe in advance of any inquiry that the world has any one character rather than another, and certainly no reason in advance to believe that it is all of a piece. Our explanation of any part of it, they argue, is an open question, and can consist in making connections with any number of other things. In principle, a holism can apply to all the contents of the world; as a general argument, in Leibniz for instance, it has nothing to say to the alleged distinctiveness of explanations in History and the social sciences. None the less, a holism of content lingers still in those 'structuralisms' which suggest that structures or systems,

pp. 45–76, and 'Interpretation and the sciences of man', in *Philosophy and the Human Sciences*, pp. 15–57. He expands these thoughts and his criticism of what he now calls the opposing 'naturalism of disengaged reason' in *Sources of the Self*, e.g. pp. 495 ff. In its origin and development, however, the argument has more usually been German. Historians and social scientists from elsewhere have rarely been so preoccupied about it and have never had *Methodenstreiten* of such intensity about it. (There is an excellent account of its genesis in the German lands and of the arguments of one of its central advocates in Michael Ermath, *Wilhelm Dilthey: The Critique of Historical Reason*, Chicago: University of Chicago Press, 1978. An indicative sense of how causal explanation stood to interpretation for Dilthey himself can be gained from Rudolf A. Maakkreel and Frithjof Rodi eds., *Wilhelm Dilthey, Selected Works I: Introduction to the Human Sciences*, Princeton: Princeton University Press, 1989, pp. 87 ff.) Charles Maier wonders whether the force of the distinction in German thinking does not have its roots in what he identifies as a distinctive and long-standing disposition in that culture to what he calls 'structured decisionism': repeatedly to try practically to constrain outcomes by clear and firm procedure and when that proves impractical, as it often does, to call upon the contrary claims of pure subjectivity and to tip into (what is an often despairing) arbitrariness (*The Unmasterable Past: History, Holocaust and German National Identity*, Cambridge MA: Harvard University Press, 1988, pp. 156–9, where Maier mentions Jürgen Habermas's analogous worry about his countrymen, e.g. in 'Sovereignty and the Führerdemokratie', *Times Literary Supplement*, 26 September 1986, 1053–4; compare Habermas's penetrating criticisms of Max Weber in *Communicative Action I*, pp. 143–271, esp. pp. 269–71).

sets of elements related in such a way that a change in one causes a
change in all the others, actually exist. And there is a persistent line
of idealist thinking – Hegel may be its most influential modern
inspiration, and in chapter 1, I mentioned Oakeshott as an instance
of it – which has elided the alleged distinctiveness of 'spirit' with a
holist view to suggest that the one supports the other. The relations
between many if not all the items of consciousness, this claims, the
relations for example within a natural language, and many kinds
of relation between people and events, are neither external nor
contingent, but internal, and necessary.[10]

V

It is not surprising that the disputes about one or another model of
explanation and interpretation in History and the social sciences
should have been so heated and persistent. They have turned on
three issues which are frequently connected and often confused:
about what the world is like, about how humans stand in relation to
the rest of it, and about how all or any part of it is to be reported,
described and explained. Nor is it surprising that some of the
protagonists, like Runciman, have tried to ride above the *mêlée* to
suggest solutions to each of the issues that are sufficient to enable the
practising historian or social scientist to avoid the philosophical
mires and pursue his inquiries. Their intention is admirable. But
neither the questions which give rise to the disputes, nor the further
questions to which these in turn give rise, can be made so easily to
disappear. In order to resolve them, or at least, to come to a
conclusion which does not just avoid them, we have to stand back
and ask what it is that we want our theories, or theoretical attitudes,
to do.

When the fields of History and the social sciences were being

---

[10] Among sociologists, perhaps the most discussed internalism of an idealist
kind has been Peter Winch's reading of the later Wittgenstein (*The Idea of a
Social Science*, London: Routledge and Kegan Paul, 1958); my own remarks on
Wittgenstein in the next section. Charles Taylor offers an argument for what he
calls a 'holistic individualism' in *Sources of the Self* and for its extension to social
and political thinking in 'Cross-purposes'.

fought over only by one or another kind of 'idealist', 'realist' or 'empiricist', the answer was clear. Whatever divided the combatants, they all agreed about what they were fighting for. This was knowledge. The issues were what this knowledge was to be a knowledge of, how it was to be arrived at, and what authority could be claimed for it. Even where the driving interest was ideological, no one suggested that ideology alone could decide the issue. More recently, however, some pragmatists have wanted to change the rules. The issue is not, they say, about how to know, let alone about how to know that we know; nor is it about the authority to be given to claims to know. It is about how to cope. The very idea of a reality which we can come to know with our schemes but which is distinct from these schemes is, they argue, an idea given to us by yet another scheme. The distinctions between scheme and reality and cognition and non-cognition, perhaps even, in the way in which it was previously drawn, the distinction between philosophy and science, should go. What we say about the world is a function of the ways in which we connect with it and the interests that we have in so doing.[11]

This pragmatic rejection of a workable distinction between scheme and reality, versions and worlds, is not old idealism by another name, an anti-realism. Goodman mischievously thinks of it rather as an 'irrealism'.[12] It respects the world and our experience of it. But

---

[11] In what I say here about 'the pragmatists', I am of course running together a family of arguments from people like Quine, Davidson, Goodman and Putnam (and in this respect also Rorty) which differ considerably between themselves; see note 15. The argument is not, however, restricted to those who would think of themselves as 'pragmatists': van Fraassen, for example, calls his not dissimilar position 'constructive empiricism' (*The Scientific Image*, Oxford: Clarendon Press, 1980, pp. 11–13; *Laws and Symmetry*, Oxford: Clarendon Press, 1989, pp. 189–93).

[12] Nelson Goodman, *Ways of Worldmaking*, Indianapolis: Hackett, 1978. Putnam approvingly recalls William James' remark that the question of how much of our web of belief reflects the world 'in itself' and how much is our 'conceptual contribution' makes no more sense than the question of whether a man walks more essentially with his left leg or his right (*The Many Faces of Realism*, LaSalle: Open Court, 1987, p. 77). Putnam explains with an example: if one view is that there are three objects in the world and another is that there are seven (the original three and the four possible sums, $1 + 2$, $1 + 3$, $2 + 3$, and $1 + 2 + 3$), then there are two realities, each internal to what we can think

it does not regard our experience as naive. Our experience is guided by our schemes. And these are guided by our interests. Nor, as this might at first suggest, is irrealism an unacceptable relativism. To say that we see the world – in the sciences of nature, that we perhaps see the world better – from our own point of view, can be to suggest that there are or can be other points of view. If there are, however, these are either inaccessible to us, so that we cannot suggest where they are and what they deliver and compare them with our own; or they are accessible and intelligible, in which case they are a part of our own. Wittgenstein's remarks, for example, that 'the limits of my language are the limits of my world' and that 'what we call descriptions are instruments for particular uses', might seem to suggest that someone speaking another language would see the world differently, perhaps because he would want to do something different with it, as some pragmatists would say, would want to 'cope' with it in a different way.[13] But the limits of our world are the limits of all sense. We cannot see any possibility, including the possibility of this world seen differently, with any lights but our own. (This is the limit on *all* counterfactuals.) Indeed, in what we can read as his increasing curiosity about what philosophy could not say, Wittgenstein's apparent pragmatism was close to a transcendental idealism. At the end of the *Philosophical Investigations*, therefore, 'one finds oneself', as Williams suggests, 'with a "we" which is not one group rather than another in the world, but rather the plural descendant of that idealist "I" who also was not one item rather than another in the world'. And this is consistent with what Hilary Putnam has called the 'internal' or 'pragmatic' (as distinct from the Archimedean or 'metaphysical') realism which, if it is a realism at all, is all the realism that we can have.[14]

of as the intellectual practice of two observers. There are facts, in this case two sets of facts, but there is no fact of the matter independent of a scheme. Ontologies, as Quine puts it, are relative to a manual of translation (*The Pursuit of Truth*, Cambridge MA: Harvard University Press, 1990, p. 51).

[13] 'So I am trying to say something that sounds like pragmatism. Here I am being thwarted by a kind of *Weltanschauung*' (*On Certainty*, para. 422).

[14] Wittgenstein, *Tractatus*, 5.62; *Philosophical Investigations*, para. 291. On his later position, Bernard Williams, 'Wittgenstein and idealism', in *Moral Luck*, pp. 144–63, quotation at p. 160, and Jonathan Lear, 'Leaving the world alone', *Journal of Philosophy* 79 (1982), 382–403 at 382–392. As Lear observes (392n),

If this is right, however, and I think it is, then the pragmatist who insists that we are trying to cope rather than to know is forced back to the question of who we are, where we are trying to cope from, and what we are trying to cope with. There would seem only to be one or other of two answers. Either there is a usable distinction between scheme and reality, in which case it is only from some more or less transcendental or otherwise prior view of what we really are that we can see what our schemes are for. Or there is no such usable distinction, in which case we reach the limits in our general scheme of what we can say about the world and our particular schemes, and at any one moment – for future revisions can never be ruled out – have to accept the world as it appears to us, which in many important respects will be as it appears to us all. If we reject the first and more 'externally' sceptical answer, which presupposes a standpoint outside ourselves that we cannot reach, and accept the second, more 'internal', one, in which we are sceptical about the foundations of our beliefs, sceptical indeed about the very idea of foundations, but confident in the fact that they are ours, we have a reasonably clear position, and perhaps the only coherent one open to us, from which to decide what matters in the three arguments for interpretation and what does not.[15]

the conclusion – but not the argument to it – is similar to Donald Davidson's in 'The very idea of a conceptual scheme', *Proceedings and Addresses of the Aristotelian Society* 67 (1974), 5–20. (Davidson extends his argument to the issue of understanding others in 'Judging interpersonal interests', in Jon Elster and Aanund Hylland eds., *Foundations of Social Choice Theory*, Cambridge and Oslo: Cambridge University Press and Universitetsforlaget, 1986, pp. 195–210.) Hilary Putnam, *Reason, Truth and History*, Cambridge: Cambridge University Press, 1981, pp. 49–74. As Putnam there puts it, 'Quine and Davidson argue, in effect, that a consistent relativist should not treat others as speakers (or thinkers) at all (if their noises are *that* "incommensurable", then they are *just* noises), while Plato and Wittgenstein argue, in effect, that a consistent relativist cannot treat himself as a speaker or thinker' (p. 124); also *Many Faces of Realism*, pp. 3–40. (Rorty [*Philosophy and the Mirror*, also 'Method, social science and social hope', *Canadian Journal of Philosophy* 11 (1981), 569–88] inclines to the Quine – Davidson view, although unlike Quine, refuses to privilege descriptions in the manner of physics.)

[15] There is a difference (brought out by Alexander Rosenberg, 'Superseding explanation versus understanding: the view from Rorty', *Social Research* 56 (1989), 479–510) between those pragmatists (like Dewey – and perhaps, one might add, Putnam) who justify their claims by appealing to what they take to be

VI

First, we can agree that all descriptions, minimal or thick, are discretionary. We can also agree that any description will only be intelligible and defensible in relation to the set of descriptions of which it is a part. But this, which is as true of descriptions of practical reflection as it is of 'phenomena' – even though for the purposes of describing practical reasoning we may prefer the agents' own descriptions simply because they are theirs – does not diminish the possibility of a contingent convergence on how to see the world and explain it.[16] (Indeed, and against what many advocates of interpretation would lead one to expect, it is striking how convergent and mutually intelligible so many descriptions are. The interesting question is not so much whether this is so, but why.) My descriptions of a moment in the history of international relations in the Far East at the end of the war between the United States and Japan, and of the reasoning, in so far as we can recover it, of the protagonists in those relations; or my descriptions of painting in Italy in the late thirteenth- and early fourteenth-century and of what those commissioning it and those actually doing it may have reflected on; may differ from those offered by others. If I had thought

an agreed schedule of human needs and those (like Rorty himself) who insist on the contingency of all foundations and starting points, including any which appeals to needs. The distinction between 'external' and 'internal' scepticism is made by Ronald Dworkin in his reply to Stanley Fish in 'Interpretation and Objectivity', in *A Matter of Principle*, Cambridge MA: Harvard University Press, 1985, pp. 167–77. Fish was criticising Dworkin's 'Why law is like literature' (*Matter of Principle*, pp. 146–66) and has replied to Dworkin's reply to him in 'Wrong again', *Texas Law Review* 62 (1983), 299–316, reprinted in his *Doing What Comes Naturally*, Durham: Duke University Press, 1989.

[16] Rorty argues that 'the familiar claim that a speaker's description of himself [or, one might perhaps add, a description which he would acknowledge as his] usually needs to be taken into account in determining what action he is performing is sound enough. But that description may perfectly well be set aside. The privilege attached to it is moral, rather than epistemic. The difference between his description and ours may mean, for example, that he should not be tried under our laws. It does not mean that he cannot be explained by our science' (*Philosophy and the Mirror*, p. 349, also 'Method, social science and social hope'). To acknowledge someone's practical reasoning as the practical reasoning it is, however, is not, as Rorty fears, to have to acknowledge the reality of any inner essence; nor is it clear that it is a moral decision, unless practical reasoning itself is a moral category.

that it was decisive for what I was saying about these two cases, I would have expanded on the wider set of descriptions of which each was a part, on where each differed from the accessible alternatives, and why I preferred the one I did. But in general, I did not need to. I merely gave an indication of where these differences were, sufficient to make those points which I wished to make, and assumed that these would be intelligible.[17]

Second, 'spirit' may indeed be different in kind from the rest of 'nature'. But for what I have called understanding, we can remain agnostic about its properties. At most, it invites us (although it cannot be said to require us) to invoke 'reasons' in our explanations for actions as well as 'causes'. Similarly, I had no need to expand on the metaphysical qualities of the states of affairs and events – and in the case of the early Italian paintings, also the objects – I was describing in order to justify my talking about them as those things at all. By starting out from agreed reports or shared experience of what took place, by appealing to some historical evidence, and at least indirectly, to the eye, I took it for granted that my characterisations were initially accessible even to those who would rather characterise these things in a different way; and that even in an argument which, like my own about Duccio, suggests a different way of seeing them, a convergent conversation about them could be had. To the metaphysical idealist, we can therefore say that, apart from the question of the warrant for his beliefs, the burden is on him to show how his characterisation of mental states will disturb our more ordinary presumptions and invalidate the explanations we suggest. To the metaphysical realist, we can similarly say that it is he who has to show how our convergent conversation rests on error. (And to the eliminative materialist, who wants to excise any theory which alludes to mental entities or events because they cannot be nomologically linked to a science, we can more simply say that such a science will not do what we want it to do.)

---

[17] Compare Davidson's aggressive claim that 'the "basis" of interpersonal comparisons is . . . provided for each of us by his own central values, both his norms of consistency and what is valuable in itself. These norms we do not choose, at least in any ordinary sense; they are what direct and explain our choices. So no judgement is involved in having one basis or another, much less a normative judgement' (Davidson, 'Judging interpersonal interests', 209).

Third, the realist who is also a holist might be right. The world could be all of a piece, even perhaps set going by God, and connected in such a way that a change in any one element implies a change in all others; in the more secular, structuralist conception, connected in such a way that a change in any one relation implies a change in all others. But there is no way of knowing that this is so. As I tried to show about the talk of 'structures' in History and social science in chapter 2, the question is more fruitfully empirical, that's to say, a question for inquiry from within our presumptions, a question for experiment, where that is possible, for comparison, or for counterfactual analysis. Likewise with the claim that concepts connect in an internal rather than an external or contingent way, such that any one concept is inapplicable or even unintelligible apart from the others. This again, where true – and it will often be difficult, for instance with the concept of 'security' in international politics, or the concept of 'pulchrina' in early Italian religious painting, to decide whether it is – is a fact about actual sets of concepts in actual cultures. We may agree that trying to find out whether it is, to show how it is, and to elucidate the consequences of its being so, is an 'interpretive' matter; that it perhaps requires us to learn a set of rules; and that at bottom, there is no meta-rule to guide us; but on a post-Wittgensteinian, post-pragmatist view, that is not a truth in metaphysics or logic.

Indeed, once we abandon assumptions of a metaphysical or ontological kind, and take a more pragmatic attitude, none of the three arguments for the privilege of 'interpretation' in History or the social sciences has the force which its protagonists have claimed for it. None, certainly, has the force of the argument for what I have called 'understanding'. And if that itself requires that we 'interpret', it does so only in the commonplace sense of the word, in which to 'interpret' is always to leave room for dispute, and never certainly to 'know'.

VII

Yet those who defend one or another of the conventional arguments for 'interpretation' in History and the social sciences more or less explicitly resist this commonplace sense. Like those who have insisted that explanation in these kinds of inquiry is formally no different from explanation in any other, they take it that their task is a task in theoretical reason: to develop and defend a 'discourse which has to fit the world' that can eventually present us with 'a universe independent of our own selves and our own tastes and judgemental idiosyncrasies'.[18] They tend to assume that there is a fact of the matter to be had about which descriptions are authentic, what is distinctively human, what 'meanings' agents intend, or what the relations are within the 'whole'. They have a conventional interest, in short, in theory.

Many, it is true, are now questioning the usual expression of this interest in the human sciences. We aspire to abstraction and generality in science, Plato had suggested, for its painless beauty and the assurance it gives of stability. We aspire to the abstraction of pure value in ethics because it is absolute and true and beyond the contingency of our lives. The refinements of *techne* are the defence we need against *tuche*. Theory and method protect us from disorder and dismay. In the classical conception, as I have said, for Aristotle as for Plato, this had nothing to do with history. Imputing a meaning to events in time came later, in the moral stories of exemplar history and the Enlightenment narratives which succeeded them. It is these last which have shaped social theory, and in which many no longer find assurance. What once gave consolation now confines. There is a wish among many to escape from what Jürgen Habermas has dramatically described as 'the totalitarian characteristics of an instrumental reason that objectifies everything around it, itself included, and from the totalising characteristics of an inclusive reason that incorporates everything and as unity, ultimately triumphs over every distinction'.[19] Accordingly, post-structuralists have con-

[18] Bernard Williams, 'Consistency and realism', in *Problems of the Self: Philosophical Papers 1956–1972*, Cambridge: Cambridge University Press, 1973, p. 203; his contrast is with practical reasoning, which the world has to fit. The characterisation of the supposed end of theoretical reason is John Dunn's in 'Responsibility without power: states and the incoherence of the modern conception of the political good', in *Interpreting Political Responsibility: Essays 1981–1989*, Cambridge: Polity Press, 1990, p. 127.

[19] There is an extended account of the Platonic argument in Martha C. Nussbaum, *The Fragility of Goodness: Luck and Ethics in Greek Tragedy and*

tinued the (more conventionally theoretical) structuralist project of dethroning the human subject by rejecting the distinction between a subject and his objects which the idea of a subject and the extension of his reason implies. Post-modernists have attempted to reconstitute the subject in some new way, as neither singular nor rational, but committed only to deconstructive play. Habermas himself, opposed to these two moves, retains the Kantian aspiration to a firm model of practical reason, but has dispensed with Kant's own metaphysics and instead used speech-act theory and a psychology of cognitive development to suggest that in ideal circumstances, we can separately realise and together converge on a true view of the human world and of our inner experiences and thereby act with autonomy rationally to arrive at consensus.

It will by now be clear that I am driven by a similar wish to resist fixed pictures of the social world and make room again for practice. But I am sceptical of the ways in which these critics have done so. In the first place, they tend to substitute a new metaphysics for the old. In his post-structuralism, Foucault, who wanted to show how discourse has occluded possibilities which, once exposed, we can see to be possibilities for us, grounded his view of what these are in a conception of what he called our 'ontology'. In his post-modernism, Derrida, claiming that 'non-truth is truth', 'non-presence . . . presence', that '*différance*, the disappearance of originating presence, is at once the condition of possibility and the condition of the impossibility of truth', seems to suggest a first presence without a presence, an object before any subject. In his revised Kantianism, Habermas has replaced the metaphysics of noumena with a metaphysical picture of his own of what it is that we are always and everywhere doing in making claims in and about the world.[20]

Philosophy, Cambridge: Cambridge University Press, 1986. Habermas's remark in Frederick Lawrence trans., *The Philosophical Discourse of Modernity*, Cambridge MA: MIT Press, 1987, p. 341.

[20] Michel Foucault, Lawrence D. Kritzman ed. and intro., *Michel Foucault, Politics, Philosophy, Culture: Interviews and Other Writings 1977–1984*, New York and London: Routledge, 1988, e.g. pp. 86–95 at pp. 95, 30, 38–9. Gary Gutting rejects this and the claim often made by others that Foucault's arguments – at least in his earlier work – are self-refuting by suggesting that they should not be seen as ontological or epistemological arguments at all (*Michel Foucault's*

Second, and related to this, in rejecting what they often correctly take to be misplaced claims to theoretical authority on human affairs, the post-structuralist and post-modernist critics tend also to reject what is, for us, the authority of our experience: our experience of ourselves and others as particular agents of practical reason in what is, for any actual practice, an equally particular and often recalcitrant world. We can agree that the older theoretical pictures confine; that 'no institutional order and no imaginative vision of the varieties of possible and desirable human association', as Unger puts it, 'can fully exhaust the types of practical or passionate human connection that we may have good reason to desire and a good chance to establish'. But as Unger adds, and as Habermas insists also, it does not follow that we must be committed only to random anger or a passive resentment. Post-structuralism and post-modernism may be invigorating in their deconstructions, but they give no clear direction as to how we can continue to act reasonably in the world, or can describe and explain others who have thought that they were doing so. (And Habermas's own attempt to do so turns on

Archaeology of Scientific Reason, Cambridge: Cambridge University Press, 1989, pp. 272–87); and many of Foucault's other remarks are indeed consistent with Gutting's interpretation. Jacques Derrida, *La Dissémination*, Paris: Seuil, 1972, p. 194. I have been helped in my thoughts on post-structuralism and post-modernism by conversations with Kim Humphery. Habermas's early convictions were most succinctly set out in 'Knowledge and human interests' in Jeremy J. Shapiro trans., *Knowledge and Human Interests*, Boston: Beacon Press, 1973, at p. 314. His more recent convictions in *Communicative Action I*, e.g. pp. 272–338, and *II: Reason and the Critique of Functionalist Reason*, Boston: Beacon Press, 1987. His criticism of the post-structuralists and post-modernists in *Discourse of Modernity*. The best appraisal of his earlier views, in my opinion also relevant to his later ones, is Raymond Geuss, *The Idea of Critical Theory: Habermas and the Frankfurt School*, Cambridge: Cambridge University Press, 1981. If it is said that my characterisation of his argument underrates its ingenuity; that he is appealing to the way in which we do in practice try to communicate with each other, appealing, that is to say, to our 'internal' reasoning from our 'subjective set' and not merely to a set of 'external' reasons which, if we are rational, we should accept; it can be replied that his internality is too abstract and general to be able to guide, explain or allow us to criticise the practical actions of any actual agent. Pragmatists would also criticise Habermas's curiously naive assumption that the 'truth' to which all agents are appealing in speaking – in addition to aspiring to intelligibility, seeking justification and being sincere – is unproblematic.

a conception of a 'we' which is too distant from any actual agent.)[21]

Indeed, whether their concern has been to dethrone, divide, or once again to abstract the human subject, these critics of the conventional expression in History and the social sciences of the interest in theoretical reason share the assumption that humans are not to be trusted with saying what the human and the humanly possible is. In this, they fall under Stanley Cavell's charge of trying 'to get the world', or at least, something other than us, as we variously and particularly are, with our various and particular interests, 'to provide answers in a way which is independent of our responsibility for *claiming* something to be so (to get God to tell us what we must do in a way which is independent of our responsibility for choice)'; and to 'fix the world', or in the case of the new enemies of the subject, to unfix us, 'so that it can do this'.[22]

The 'pragmatic attitude', by contrast, cheerfully accepts this responsibility. Whatever we believe we know, we know in virtue of the ways in which our interests connect with the world. Knowledge which is to be 'unified and stable in the last instance', therefore, or absolute, would have to include knowledge also of this connection, and to transcend it. And this, even if imaginable, is too much to hope for. It is we who decide, with schemes which at once guide and are guided by our experience. At the same time, pragmatically to reject a sharp and workable demarcation between schemes and

---

[21] Roberto Mangaberira Unger, *Passion: An Essay on Personality*, New York: Free Press, 1984, p. 35. In his more general theoretical picture in *Politics* Unger distances himself both from the older conceptions and from the more radical post-modernists (*Social Theory: Its Situation and its Task, False Necessity: Anti-necessitarian Social Theory in the Service of Radical Democracy*, and *Plasticity into Power*, Cambridge: Cambridge University Press, 1987.) The attribution of resentment to many post-structuralists and post-modernists is made by Unger and also Harold Bloom (the latter quoted by Richard Rorty, 'Unger, Castoriadis and the romance of a national future', in Robin W. Lovin and Michael J. Perry eds., *Critique and Construction: A Symposium on Roberto Unger's 'Politics'*, Cambridge: Cambridge University Press, 1990, pp. 31–2).

[22] *The Claim of Reason: Wittgenstein, Scepticism, Morality and Tragedy*, New York: Oxford University Press, 1979, p. 216 (his emphasis). Cavell is not here though talking about the post-modernists. Notwithstanding their debt to Nietzsche and Nietzsche's own strictures against Christianity, one might wonder whether, despite themselves, some post-modern critics (Foucault though was an exception) do not share the Christians' fear and hatred of the human.

reality is not to cease to be concerned with our experience and how we think of it. It merely requires us to recast our ideas of the relations between the two, and to re-examine the interests in these relations. Indeed, were it not that 'commonsense' has acquired a bad name in what may loosely be thought of as theoretical argument, I would be tempted to say that against both the old defenders of theoretical reason in the human sciences and their modernist critics, I am merely insisting that we take our commonsensical experience of the human world seriously.

This is of states of affairs which have largely been set by the practice of others. And if this is so, then the idea that we might aspire to a cumulative and convergent understanding of these states which could also be said to be knowledge of them is mistaken. The standpoint of theoretical reason, the idea of a discourse which will fit the world, is not appropriate to such an understanding. It may be appropriate to explanation. What these states of affairs actually were or are is a function of what actual agents actually did in the actual circumstances in which they found themselves. There will be accounts which fit what we take to be the facts, and accounts which do not. But for understanding, we have to locate them in a space of possibilities, and these possibilities, as I have been saying, cannot be known. Theoretical reason may set their limits; but it is our practical judgement of the practical judgement of the relevant agents which defines them.

A 'demonstrative' model of theory, therefore, the mode which – whether we take a pragmatic attitude or not – works well for the sciences of nature, is not suitable to understanding in History or the social sciences. This would not be so, perhaps, if we had a psychology that was sufficiently general to be projected to all agents and yet sufficiently realistic to capture the practical deliberation of any. Our science could then proceed, as Aristotle agreed, 'from premises which are true and primary, or of such a kind that we have derived our original knowledge of them through premises which are primary and true'. But we do not have such a psychology, or the political science or sociology to support it, and the argument I have been pressing in this book casts doubt on our ever being likely to. We can at best agree that for any good, agents will have usually have wanted more of it rather than less. For anything less circular and more determinate, which, to be determinate, will have to answer to actual agents in actual predicaments, we are forced back to what Aristotle called 'dialectical' reasoning 'from generally accepted opinions' which, being opinions, are always revisable. For understanding, we are returned to persuasion, and debate.[23]

---

[23] Aristotle, *Topica*, 100a25–100b24. John M. Cooper argues that although Aristotle agreed that practical reasoning could be formalised after the event, he was clear that there was no formal method for guiding the deliberation involved in an action (*Reason and Human Good in Aristotle*, Cambridge MA: Harvard University Press, 1975, pp. 9–58). David Wiggins makes a similar argument and concludes with his own 'bare outline of a neo-Aristotelian theory of practical reason' ('Deliberation and practical reason', in *Needs, Values, Truth: Essays in the Philosophy of Value*, Aristotelian Society Series Volume 6, Oxford: Blackwell, 1987, pp. 215–38 at pp. 230–4), where he remarks that 'there is no reason to expect that it will be possible to construct an (however idealised) empirical theory of the rational agent to parallel the predictive power, empirical nonvacuity, and satisfactoriness for its purposes of an economic hypothesis . . . If prediction were essential', he continues, 'then a phenomenologist or someone with a strong interest in the value consciousness of his subject might do best. But what is needed here is not prediction, but the subject's own decision processes, constantly redeployed on new situations or on new understandings of old ones.' And if it is then objected that 'very little is said, because everything that is hard has been permitted to take refuge in the notion of aisthesis, or *situational appreciation*', then the objector has to ask himself whether his own 'harder' theory does indeed reflect what is involved in deliberation. The significance of not being able to arrive at an adequate psychology has recently been re-emphasised by Bernard Williams (*Ethics and the Limits of Philosophy*, London: Fontana/Collins, Cambridge MA: Harvard University Press, 1985, pp. 153–4). Even if we were to accept that as a species we had evolved 'innate social capacities', and to agree that these capacities gave the 'basis for a universalistic ethic of natural rights and a cognitive theory of truth' (as does Robin Fox, 'Darwin and the Donation of Durkheim II: Bradley and the Benison of Bergson', in *The Search for Society: Quest for a Biosocial Science and Morality*, New Brunswick: Rutgers University Press, 1989, p. 104), to know what these capacities were would not obviously help us decide what to do or in explaining what others have done in *particular* situations. Persuading others – themselves to act, or to read the actions of others in one way rather than another – requires the skills of what used to be thought of as rhetoric as much as it does those of what we have come to think of as science or demonstration. (The classical scope of rhetoric was reduced in the early modern enthusiasm for cognitive certainty and theoretical generality. Rhetoricians renounced their interests in the classical skills of invention, arrangement, and style, that is to say the skills of persuasion, and confined themselves to the more purely performative qualities of oratorical delivery and its twin aspects of voice and gesture [Paul Corcoran, *Political*

VIII

For these purposes, therefore, the most interesting distinction is not between 'science' and 'non-science', 'the human sciences' and 'the humanities', 'the social sciences' and 'History', or 'fact' and 'theory', but between the actual and the possible. But this is not yet another demarcation. This is because for understanding, each turns on the other. I have no new name for such an understanding. It respects the actual and its particularity and the experience we have of it, but it is not what is usually thought of, and practised, as History or the more discriminating kind of empirical social science. It allows for a degree of comparison, abstraction, and extrapolation, but it is not post-Enlightenment social theory. It returns our intellectual interests to us, but it is not just post-modern play. Names, however, although they dramatise, also obscure and confine. What matters always is the argument. Mine here has simply been that understanding human affairs starts and ends with our experience of the actual; but because it turns on what is causally and practically possible, it cannot produce knowledge, will rarely be general, and cannot simply consist in deploying a theory.

Language and Rhetoric, Austin: University of Texas Press, 1979, e.g. p. 124; also Walter J. Ong, *Ramus, Method and the Decay of Dialogue*, Cambridge M.A: Harvard University Press, 1983 and – of wider interest than its title may suggest – Wilbur S. Howell, *Logic and Rhetoric in England, 1000–1700*, Princeton: Princeton University Press, 1971]). It is interesting that post–modernists like Derrida continue to use 'rhetoric' in a deliberately disparaging sense.

Index

189